The Genesis
of Modern British Town Planning

INTERNATIONAL LIBRARY OF SOCIOLOGY
AND SOCIAL RECONSTRUCTION

Founded by Karl Mannheim

Editor W. J. H. Sprott

A catalogue of books available in the INTERNATIONAL LIBRARY OF
SOCIOLOGY AND SOCIAL RECONSTRUCTION and new books in
preparation for the Library will be found at the end of this volume

THE
GENESIS OF MODERN
BRITISH TOWN PLANNING

*A Study in Economic and Social History
of the Nineteenth and Twentieth
Centuries*

by

WILLIAM ASHWORTH

ROUTLEDGE & KEGAN PAUL LTD
Broadway House, 68–74 Carter Lane
London

First published in 1954
by Routledge & Kegan Paul Ltd
Broadway House, 68-74 Carter Lane
*London, E.C.*4

Reprinted 1965 *and* 1968

Printed in Great Britain
by Compton Printing Ltd
London and Aylesbury

SBN 7100 3320 6

'*Woe to her that is filthy and polluted, to the oppressing city.*'

ZEPHANIAH iii. 1.

Contents

ix

Preface

THIS book has been written in the belief that contemporary
efforts to improve the quality of urban living are more closely
linked to the experience of the last century and a half than is
sometimes realised and that they can be fully understood only when
set in the context of that experience. Not only our towns themselves
but also the methods of improving them that seem both practicable
and commendable are the legacy of the past. In surveying part of
this legacy and presenting it in relation to the growth of the modern
town-planning movement I have been to a considerable extent
generalizing from and contrasting the histories of many different
towns, as well as examining the ideas and influence of a wide variety
of investigators and reformers. I have tried to give the generalizations
and contrasts a firm basis of fact but it would, of course, be folly to
claim that they rest on a completely exhaustive examination of all
the possible sources. The materials of local history since 1800 are
so vast that no one could hope to deal exhaustively with more than
a very few districts, and though some important gaps have in recent
years been most admirably filled, the history of many of the chief
towns in this period has still to be made the subject of substantial
secondary works. When these histories have been written it may
well be that they will suggest changes in the emphasis of the present
book, though I have tried to make my selection of material as
representative as I could. In the meantime this study is offered as a
preliminary survey of the ground.

Its preparation has involved me in debts which it is a pleasure
to acknowledge. The book is a revised version of a thesis approved
for the award of the degree of Ph.D. in the University of London
in 1950. To the advice of my supervisor, Mr. H. L. Beales, and his
curious and profound knowledge of Victorian social history it owes

Preface

much. Professor David Glass read the whole work in manuscript, saved me from numerous errors, and gave me a great deal of encouragement. I have also been able to act on several hints from Professor G. D. H. Cole. Assistance of another kind came from the award of a Leverhulme Research Studentship which I held at the London School of Economics and Political Science during part of the time in which I was working on the book. Finally, I have to thank the editors of the *Economic History Review* for permission to reprint parts of Chapter V which appeared as an article in that journal.

W. A.

March 1953

INTRODUCTION

The Economic and Social Factors in Town Planning

THERE is no general agreement about the scope or content of town planning. In its narrowest sense, it has been regarded as primarily an aesthetic subject, as an extension of the art of architecture from the design of individual buildings to the arrangement of the relations of groups of buildings. To anyone so regarding it the test of its merit and its desirability was its success or failure in creating works of visual art. This attitude, usually with some modification, still persists in many people. One architect a few years ago expressed the view that 'town planning is, curiously enough, largely a matter of sky-line and sunlight'.[1]

Any formal history of town planning would be bound to give much attention to its aesthetic aspect. But this book is not a history of the planning of towns that has been proposed or accomplished in the last century and a half. Its aim is rather different. It is to try to discover why there has gradually arisen a widespread public demand that town planning should be adopted as one of the normal functions of public activity.

It is unlikely that this could be attributed merely to an increased sensitivity to visual beauty among many members of the community, to a wish that they themselves should promote its extension and a demand that they should be enabled to live in the midst of it. A powerful feeling of this kind has not manifested itself to any great extent in other activities. In fact, it is clear that, as the demand for town planning has increased, the proposals for specific schemes to implement it have sought to justify themselves mainly on other than aesthetic grounds, and it is natural to assume that there is an inter-relation between these two tendencies. A prominent exponent of town planning stated during the Second World War, 'The main

[1] L. Dale, *Towards a Plan for Oxford City*, note to plate III.

I

purpose of town planning today is to secure the health of the people in their homes and surroundings, and at their places of work'. He went on to point out that town design as a matter of lay-out or pattern had a long history but that the comprehensive study of town growth and development from the aspects of the health and convenience of the people was something comparatively new.[1] Others have sought to stress that town planning is a means of increasing not only social well-being but also economic prosperity and to associate this fact with its general acceptance. 'It has only to be admitted that Planning and Productivity are interlinked for it to become apparent that the necessity for planning is beyond doubt a basic essential in the evolution and maintenance of a well-regulated state.'[2] This also is something more recent than the traditional study of town patterns.

The fact that there has been this change of emphasis in the objects which town planning has sought to promote and in the nature of the results which have been claimed for it, at the same time as a strong public interest in and demand for it have developed, provides a clue to the origin of the latter phenomenon. There was no town planning movement worthy of the name until a sufficient body of people was convinced that town planning could make a unique and necessary contribution to the happiness, welfare and prosperity, particularly of townspeople, but ultimately of the whole nation. The principal origin of the movement must be sought in the slow creation of that belief. That process of development is the subject-matter of the following chapters.

But social ideas do not grow independently of their context. The idea of town planning was something that presented itself as an answer to a problem or group of problems which had arisen in contemporary urban life. Its formulation was a comparatively late stage in a gradual process which has to be traced out. There was first the emergence of the problem and the realization of its existence and then there were the attempts to find a solution of it. These were mainly empirical and followed a variety of methods, but they all contributed to a body of experience and thinking about fundamental questions of urban social life from which a recognizable town-planning movement emerged.

[1] J. H. Forshaw, *Town Planning and Health*, p. 1.

[2] J. F. Adburgham, 'Planning and Productivity', in *Journ. of the Town Planning Inst.*, vol. XXIV, p. 73.

The Economic and Social Factors in Town Planning

This sequence of events governs the design of the present book. Part I will deal with the rapid development of towns to their modern form and scale and with the way in which the characteristics of that development gave rise to problems which, partly by their nature and partly by their magnitude, demanded novel treatment. From the need to answer these problems has arisen the full range of contemporary social policy. To deal with that is, of course, beyond the scope of the present work. But in Part II an attempt will be made to describe the efforts made in one direction, viz. the reform of the physical environment of town life, which was acknowledged to be one of the basic needs and was expected to have an influence on all aspects of social life. The achievements resulting from three different approaches to the question will be discussed and it will then be possible in the last part of the book to consider town planning as a distinctive movement. The object of the concluding chapters is to show how somewhat disjointed elements in the experience of reforming the physical environment were, gradually and under the pressure of events, brought together and merged in an outlook and movement which were reasonably coherent (even though some of their spokesmen sometimes were not) and which received statutory recognition, and to show in general terms what was the content of the new town-planning movement.

This is essentially a study of the generation of a new social movement by the interaction of human thought with economic and social conditions. And economic considerations affect it in another respect by their influence on the practical achievements and prospects of town planning. The idea of town planning was not an end in itself but only a means to practical changes, and these involve a cost which someone has to bear. It is unfortunately very common for planners to try to avoid this issue by pointing to the profitable improvements which their plans will make possible. Very likely good planning does pay; so, no doubt, did earlier schemes of more piecemeal improvement. But there is a gap between the time of the initial outlay and the time when increased returns can be reaped and that gap must be bridged by finance, for which town plans must compete with other projects.

Thus it was not sufficient to create a belief that town planning was desirable; there was the further necessity of convincing people that it was sufficiently desirable to justify the spending of money on it. There was also a problem of meeting the cost of practical demon-

3

strations of the efficacy of town planning, which were essential before its exponents could carry a strong body of opinion with them.

As the progress of physical reform in towns is traced out there must also be developed incidentally this theme of the economic limitations on the practical achievement (which in turn affected the further course of ideas about reform). Thus this book is concerned not only with the direct influence of economic conditions on the growth of a social movement but also with the indirect influence which some economic factors exerted through their power over demonstrations of its immediate practicability.

PART ONE

THE PROBLEM

CHAPTER I

The Growth of Urban Population

THE most fundamental influence on the condition of towns and town life in the last century and a half has been the enormous and rapid increase in their population. A brief consideration of the bare facts of the scale and distribution of towns and the speed with which they were attained is an essential preliminary to the understanding of the creation of new conditions and problems within them. A recapitulation of the census figures of the total population shows the magnitude of the change:

Year	England and Wales	Scotland	Total
1801	8,893,000	1,608,000	10,501,000
1811	10,164,000	1,806,000	11,970,000
1821	12,000,000	2,092,000	14,092,000
1831	13,897,000	2,364,000	16,261,000
1841	15,914,000	2,620,000	18,534,000
1851	17,927,000	2,889,000	20,816,000
1861	20,066,000	3,063,000	23,129,000
1871	22,712,000	3,360,000	26,072,000
1881	25,974,000	3,736,000	29,710,000
1891	29,002,000	4,026,000	33,028,000
1901	32,528,000	4,472,000	37,000,000
1911	36,070,000	4,761,000	40,831,000
1921	37,887,000	4,882,000	42,769,000
1931	39,952,000	4,843,000	44,795,000
1939[1]	41,552,000	5,008,000	46,560,000
1951	43,745,000	5,096,000	48,841,000

A population which doubled itself in the first fifty years, doubled itself again in the next sixty, and thereafter still continued to increase, though much more slowly, was bound to be accompanied by a rapid expansion of the number and size of towns, however it was dis-

[1] *National Register. Statistics of Population*, p. ix. This is an estimate. The actual enumeration covered civilians only and the figures were England, 40,651,706; Scotland, 4,907,619; total, 45,559,325.

7

tributed. But in fact, throughout the nineteenth century, towns absorbed a growing proportion of the increasing population, as is shown by the following figures of the percentage of the population of England and Wales living in towns of various sizes:[1]

Year	London	Other towns over 100,000 *population*	Towns 20,000– 100,000 *population*
1801	9·73	0·00	7·21
1831	10·64	5·71	8·70
1861	13·97	11·02	13·22
1891	14·52	17·30	21·76

In the latter year the proportion of the population classed in the census as urban was 72·05 per cent and by 1911 it had reached 80·1 per cent, after which it was practically constant. A marked feature was the increasing concentration of population in the largest cities. In Scotland, Glasgow displayed even stronger magnetic qualities than London. In 1801 it contained 5·1 per cent of the population of the country, 11·5 per cent in 1851 and 19·4 per cent in 1891.[2] The growing dominance of the largest towns in the latter half of the century appears clearly in the table below in which figures relating to England and Wales are expressed as index numbers, with 1851 as the base year:[3]

Year	London	84 *Great Towns*	14 *Typical Rural Counties*	*Rest of England and Wales*
1851	100	100	100	100
1861	119	122	99·6	109
1871	138	148	99·7	121
1881	162	183	94·4	136
1891	179	217	95·7	150
1901	192	254	95·5	169

If later official statistics appear to cast doubt on the continuation of this trend in the twentieth century, the reason seems to be only that some of the great towns have spread beyond their boundaries into other local government areas which, though functionally part of them, are classified separately.

The outstanding characteristics were the development early in the nineteenth century of many more towns of substantial size, a steady increase in the size of what might be regarded as typical, and the emergence of a few towns to enormous size, so that a small number

[1] A. F. Weber, *The Growth of Cities in the Nineteenth Century*, p. 47.
[2] *Ibid.*, p. 59.
[3] Local Government Board, *Statistical Memoranda and Charts relating to Public Health and Social Conditions* (1909), p. 9.

of places contained a high proportion of the total population of the country. The course of this development can be presented in more detail.

In 1801, as for long before and ever since, London, which had a population of 864,845, was dominant. Manchester and Salford together, Liverpool, Birmingham, Bristol and Leeds were between 50,000 and 100,000 and there were in England and Wales eight other towns with populations between 25,000 and 50,000; these were, in order of magnitude, Plymouth-Devonport-Stonehouse (counted as one), Norwich, Portsmouth, Sheffield, Rochdale, Nottingham, Newcastle-on-Tyne, and Bath. In Scotland, Edinburgh and Glasgow were both between 50,000 and 100,000, and the only other towns over 25,000 were Paisley, Aberdeen and Dundee in that order. It is noteworthy that those towns which were the most important in 1801 have, on the whole, retained their leading position. Already in the early part of the nineteenth century it was the largest towns which were attracting the greatest absolute increase in the population and widening the disparity in size between themselves and the lesser towns. By 1841 the population of London had reached 1,873,676, Manchester (with Salford) and Liverpool had both passed 250,000, and Birmingham, Leeds, and Bristol were all over 100,000. The group between 50,000 and 100,000 consisted, in order of magnitude, of Plymouth-Devonport-Stonehouse, Sheffield, Rochdale, Norwich, Nottingham, Portsmouth, and Preston, and in England and Wales there were 28 other towns with populations over 25,000. In Scotland, Glasgow had topped 250,000 and Edinburgh 100,000 (despite a reduction in area); Aberdeen, Dundee, and Paisley were all over 50,000, and Greenock had entered the 25,000 to 50,000 group. The rate of increase of some of the largest towns was remarkably high. Manchester grew by 40·4 per cent between 1811 and 1821 and by 47·2 per cent in the next decade, during which Liverpool and Leeds also grew by 43·6 per cent and 47·2 per cent respectively. The population of Glasgow increased by more than 30 per cent in each of the first four intercensal periods. At the same time there was marked growth of many smaller towns which were either centres of mechanized industry or pleasure resorts. Apart from Glasgow, the only other towns with more than 25,000 inhabitants in 1841 which grew by over 30 per cent in each preceding intercensal period were Preston, Oldham, Cheltenham, and Huddersfield. Places which had fewer than 10,000 inhabitants in 1801 and more than 25,000 in 1841 were

The Problem

Brighton, Merthyr Tydfil, Bradford, Cheltenham, Southampton, West Bromwich, Woolwich, and Huddersfield.[1]

In the middle years of the century the main feature was the further expansion of towns which had already become prominent. In 1861, as compared with 1841, the only changes in grouping in Scotland were that the population of Paisley, owing to a change of area, had fallen below 50,000 and that Leith and Perth were added to the towns with over 25,000 inhabitants. The number of places in England with populations over 25,000 had risen from 41 to 62. Part of the increase arose because Salford and Devonport were counted separately and because the boundaries of some towns had been extended. London had gained 900,000 to reach 2,803,989 and Birmingham had passed 250,000; in the group over 100,000 there were, besides Leeds and Bristol, Sheffield, Wolverhampton, Newcastle-on-Tyne, Bradford, Salford, and Stoke-upon-Trent. Seventeen places had populations between 50,000 and 100,000, and another 33 had over 25,000 inhabitants. A few places had risen very rapidly to prominence: in the twenty years the population of Birkenhead had grown from 11,563 to 51,649, of Cardiff from 10,077 to 32,954; Merthyr Tydfil had almost doubled to reach 83,875, and there had been large rates of increase in towns on the north-east coast as well as in the established centres of large population such as Liverpool and Manchester.[2]

By 1881 so many towns had grown so much that those with fewer than 50,000 inhabitants seemed to have lost much of their significance, at any rate in England and Wales, where there were 47 towns above this limit. These were for the most part the same towns which had been the largest in the middle of the century and which had continued a steady process of expansion. Only two of the large self-contained centres of population were virtually the creations of this period: Middlesbrough, the population of which rose from 19,286 in 1861 to 55,934 in 1881, and the Rhondda Valley, where the area covered in 1881 by the Urban Sanitary District of Ystradyfodwg increased its population from 8,097 to 55,632 in the same twenty

---

[1] *Census of Great Britain*, 1841, *Enumeration Abstract Part I*, p. 10. It has been suggested that the rates of increase of population were exaggerated because of deficiencies in the enumeration at the earliest censuses. (*Vide* discussion on R. Price Williams, 'On the Increase of Population in England and Wales' in *Journ. of the Stat. Socy.*, vol. XLIII, 1880, pp. 497–508). It is very improbable that the error was large enough to have any significance in the present context.

[2] *Census of England and Wales*, 1861, vol. III (*General Report*), tables 43 and 46.

years. But there was also a significant growth on the fringes of old centres of population, testifying to a primitive suburban development which has now long lost many of its suburban characteristics. Near London, the population of Croydon rose from 30,240 to 78,953, of West Ham from 38,331 to 128,953; near Birmingham, Aston Manor's population increased from 16,337 to 53,842; the number of inhabitants in Manchester scarcely changed but 74,000 were added to Salford in the twenty years.[1] Scotland showed no startling new developments. By 1881 Glasgow had passed the half-million mark, Dundee and Aberdeen were over 100,000, and Greenock, Leith, and Paisley over 50,000, but no large new centres of population had risen, though a few smaller ones were growing quickly, notably Motherwell and Wishaw, which in 1861 had a combined population of 9,037 and in 1881 of 26,016.[2]

The census figures for town populations in 1881 display in general the characteristics which have distinguished them subsequently. The main centres of population were thoroughly established and what were the largest towns then have continued to be so, though not all of them by any means continued to attract much additional population. Very few places developed subsequently to be independent centres of substantial populations, though in Scotland, where the general scale of towns was smaller, there was still room for additions and in the thirty years before 1911 Kirkcaldy, Coatbridge, Clydebank, and Falkirk all grew rapidly to the 35,000–45,000 range. Above all, the tendency just beginning to appear in 1881, for population to settle more and more on the fringes of the existing largest centres, became increasingly prominent. It is true that new concentrations also began to appear on the coast, but the largest of these, too, had usually the 'dormitory' characteristics of suburbs. Between 1881 and 1891 the four towns with the largest rates of increase of population were all suburbs of London, viz. Leyton 133·3 per cent, Willesden 121·9 per cent, Tottenham 95·1 per cent, and West Ham 58·9 per cent, and of the four counties with the largest percentage increases in England and Wales, three were Home Counties, Middlesex 50·93 per cent, Essex 37·82 per cent, and Surrey 24·09 per cent (the other was Glamorgan 33·70 per cent).[3] In the next ten years the towns with the largest rates of increase were almost all on the edge of great

---

[1] *Ibid.*, 1881, vol. IV (*General Report*), table 9.
[2] Crown Agent for Scotland, *Return relating to the population of Scotland.* (1883)
[3] Weber, *op. cit.*, pp. 446–7.

cities. They included East Ham, Walthamstow, Leyton, West Ham, Willesden, Hornsey, Tottenham, Croydon, King's Norton, Handsworth, Smethwick, and Wallasey. The only place in a different kind of situation which was growing at a comparable rate was West Hartlepool.[1]

Some indication of the changing distribution of population can be obtained from a survey included in the 1921 census report which covered the growth in the previous sixty years of all the county boroughs, metropolitan boroughs and all other urban areas with over 50,000 inhabitants in England and Wales.[2] From this survey only those places have been extracted which had a period of very rapid growth, as indicated by an intercensal increase of over 30 per cent. When these are divided according to the decade in which their rate of increase was greatest the following results appear:

1861–71   Bradford, Croydon, Darlington, Dewsbury, Exeter, Gateshead, Grimsby, Leicester, Battersea, Hackney, Hammersmith, Hampstead, Islington, Kensington, Lewisham, Poplar, Middlesbrough, Rhondda, Rotherham, Southport, Stockton-on-Tees, West Hartlepool.

1871–81   Bournemouth, Burnley, Burton-upon-Trent, Eastbourne, Hastings, Hull, Leyton, Lincoln, Camberwell, Deptford, Stoke Newington, Luton, Nottingham, Oldham, Salford, Swansea, Swindon, Tottenham, Warrington, West Ham.

1881–91   Cardiff, East Ham, Enfield, Hornsey, Fulham, Wandsworth, Woolwich, Newcastle-upon-Tyne, Newport (Mon.), South Shields, Walthamstow, Willesden, Wimbledon (same rate as 1891–1901) Wood Green.

1891–1901   Acton, Blackpool, Edmonton, Gillingham, Ilford, Smethwick, Wallasey, Wimbledon (same rate as 1881–91).

1901–11   Ealing, Hendon, Southend-on-Sea.

1911–21   Nil.

In the last decade only three of the places showed an increase of over 30 per cent: Blackpool 64·0 per cent, Southend 50·0 per cent, and Hendon 44·3 per cent, and the figure for the first two was doubtless swollen by summer visitors as the 1921 census was taken in June.

[1] *Census of England and Wales*, 1901, *General Report*, p. 29.
[2] *Ibid.*, 1921, *General Tables*, table 11.

The only other towns which had over 20,000 inhabitants in 1911 and which increased by over 30 per cent between 1911 and 1921 were Bedwellty, Margate, Weston-super-Mare, and Dunfermline, and in the case of the last three of these also the figure was attributable to summer visitors.

After 1921 the settlement of population on the fringes of great cities went on apace and was by far the most prominent trend in the distribution of population. Of places with over 20,000 inhabitants in 1921 twenty-five increased by over 30 per cent by 1931 and nineteen of these were in the Home Counties. The others, with one exception, were seaside towns or city suburbs. They were Doncaster Rural District, Solihull Rural District, Blackpool, Worthing, Poole, and Bournemouth.[1] In the thirties the same trend continued unbroken, as is shown by the following table of the places showing the largest rate of increase from 1931–8:[2]

Area	Population Census (1931)	Population Reg.-Gen's Estimate (mid-1938)	Percentage increase 1931–38
Huyton with Roby U.D. ..	5,199	29,500	467·4
Ruislip-Northwood U.D.	16,035	40,820	154·6
Bexley M.B.	32,652	77,020	135·8
Chislehurst and Sidcup U.D.	27,156	61,750	127·4
Potters Bar U.D. ..	5,720	12,010	110·0
Carshalton U.D.	28,586	58,730	105.5
Hornchurch U.D.	39,389	76,000	92·9
Hayes and Harlington U.D.	22,969	43,930	91·3
Solihull U.D.	25,372	48,310	90·4
Harrow U.D.	96,656	183,500	89·8
Feltham U.D.	16,066	30,450	89·5
Orpington U.D.	25,858	46,320	79·1
Droylsden U.D.	13,340	23,710	77·7
East Barnet U.D. ..	18,549	32,830	77·0
Epsom and Ewell M.B. ..	35,231	59,930	70·1
Worthing R.D.	14,005	23,640	68·8
Haltemprice U.D.	16,757	28,230	68·5
Rickmansworth U.D. ..	11,529	18,700	62·2

Of these eighteen places, thirteen were suburbs or satellites of London and there was one suburb each of Liverpool, Birmingham, Manchester and Hull.

By contrast there were symptoms of decay in some of the smaller industrial towns which had been built up for the most part in the

[1] P.E.P., *Report on the Location of Industry in Great Britain*, pp. 294–8.
[2] *National Register, Statistics of Population*, p. xx. Places with populations under 10,000 in 1938 have been excluded from the table.

later years of the nineteenth century. Between 1921 and 1931 there were 11 towns with over 20,000 inhabitants at the earlier date which sustained a net loss of over 20 per cent by migration. Nine of them were in the industrial area of Glamorgan and Monmouth, the other two in County Durham. Nine of them also had populations of under 50,000.[1] It would appear that they had not the same tenacious hold on their inhabitants as older or larger towns.[2]

These numerical facts concerning the growth and distribution of population are bald, brief, selective. In themselves they answer no questions. But they do indicate something of the fundamental preliminaries from which urban problems sprang. They show first a sudden shooting-up of towns, which suggests the problem that must have lain behind it; to pack in multitudes of people somewhere, somehow, anyhow, as fast as possible, as many as possible. Then later they show signs that the problem was changing in kind, becoming less one of growth than of size; no longer was it a question of packing in the multitude but of spreading it out again, and in similar haste. Or if the growth had been later and shorter, there was that alternative problem of what should follow its cessation.

And these same figures indicate when the most characteristic features of town growth were most fully expressed in different places. In particular they draw attention to those towns which may be expected to exhibit continuously the development of the most pressing and typical urban problems and therefore of attempts to find answers to them. In the search for the origins of coherent and agreed views about the proper fashioning of towns, they thus point the way to the next stage of the enquiry: the observation in more detail of the processes of which they are the expression, the discovery of the more precise nature of the problems that emerged from those processes.

[1] P.E.P., *op. cit.*, p. 299.
[2] Between 1931 and 1951 somewhat similar signs of decline spread to a number of older and larger towns, e.g. Liverpool, Manchester, West Ham. This is probably to be attributed mainly to the greater diffusion of population over suburban areas, hastened by war-time evacuation and damage to buildings.

CHAPTER II

The Process of Town Growth

THE growth of towns has both a physical and a cultural aspect, but it is the former which is the more fundamental. In point of time, a town is a physical entity before it becomes, in any cultural sense, a community, and from its physical condition there is an influence on its social life and culture which is more immediate and more powerful than any link between the two which acts in the opposite direction, save only the economic function which in many cases calls the town into being. It was on the whole both natural and sound for the observers of urban life in the earlier stages of the industrial era to concentrate their attention primarily, though not exclusively, on the physical state of towns. A recapitulation of the outstanding features of town growth in that period must exhibit a similar preoccupation.

No set of generalizations can be applied universally to the growth of British towns in the nineteenth century. The idea that there was one typical Coketown, endlessly repeated, is a myth. But it does appear from an examination of the history and condition of a large number of towns that there were important features that were common to very many instances. The particular type of development was closely associated with the type of economic activity which the town was required to serve. Various functional classifications of towns have been attempted, some of them very elaborate. But, for a study of nineteenth-century growth, fairly broad distinctions appear adequate. Perhaps the most useful starting point is the classification adopted by the Select Committee on the Health of Towns in 1840, which divided them into the metropolis, manufacturing towns, populous seaport towns, great watering places, and 'county and other inland towns not the seat of any particular manufacture', while noting that some places, especially mining districts, would not fit conveniently into any classification.[1]

The fifth of these groups comprises what are commonly known as country towns. A study of these for most of the period has little to contribute to the subject in hand, for the simple reason that they did not undergo large expansion. As Mr. F. J. Osborn has pointed out,[2] country towns were classed with villages as part of a decaying fabric in the early literature of town planning, such as the writings of William Morris and Ebenezer Howard. These writers were only recording observable and long-standing experience. The importance of the country towns was eclipsed when the railway replaced the stage-coach; for some it never returned, and for few did it do so before the second quarter of the twentieth century, when various country towns took on a new form of existence as expanding residential satellites of large cities.

But throughout the nineteenth century there were many illustrations of the phenomena of rapid growth among towns of all the other types. These phenomena fall very broadly into two groups, according principally to the extent to which any person or authority tried to regulate the way in which the town grew. The evidence of forethought and regulation is mostly to be found in what were centres of conspicuous consumption, i.e. the great watering places, together with other holiday resorts and towns which were predominantly residential centres for the wealthier classes; while the more chaotic manifestations of blind growth were characteristic of those towns in whose lives the production or distribution of material goods in large quantities preponderated, i.e. the manufacturing towns and the great seaports. The varied character of the metropolis caused it to display in different districts phenomena of both kinds. These general remarks need more detailed illustration.

The physical nature of the growing manufacturing towns was the subject of testimony by a host of witnesses in the mid-nineteenth century and has left its own tangible evidence behind it. One thing was very easy to see: in the central districts of towns every scrap of available land was built on and none reserved for other purposes. A Parliamentary Committee reported in 1833 that 'with a rapidly increasing population, lodged for the most part in narrow courts and confined streets the means of occasional exercise and recreation in

[1] *Select Committee on the Health of Towns* (1840), *Report*, p. iv.
[2] S. Baron (ed.), *Country Towns in the Future England*, p. 21.

16

the fresh air are every day lessened, as inclosures take place and buildings spread themselves on every side'.[1] It found nearly all the textile and hardware towns which it examined (including Manchester, Salford, Bolton, Wigan, Blackburn, Bury, Birmingham, Sheffield, Wolverhampton, Leeds, Halifax, and Bradford), without any provision for public parks or open spaces.[2] A close arrangement of buildings was nothing new, but the vast increase in its unbroken area gave it a new significance.

The phrase of the Committee of 1833 about 'narrow courts and confined streets' referred to a condition in which not only was all the land in a district used for building but each building was confined to as small a space as possible and the very maximum density achieved. Thus buildings were erected back to back along narrow alleys or around tiny courts closed in on all four sides and entered by a small archway. Liverpool was a most striking example of this form of development. In 1840 it contained about 2,400 such courts, inhabited by 86,000 of the working class. Not only were the courts excessively close in design but they were also unsoundly constructed, unprovided with sewers, and uncleansed, so that their surface gutters were often choked with filth.[3] The same town contained over 7,800 cellar dwellings with a population of 39,000. A similar state of affairs on a rather smaller scale existed in Manchester; there were 12,000 people in Manchester and 3,200 in Salford who were living in cellars.[4] Such dwellings continued to be built in large numbers as long as there was no regulation to prevent them, and there was nothing temporary about them. In 1884 Liverpool still had 2,500 courts with 14,500 houses, built before 1846. Most of these courts were only ten or twelve feet wide and the commonest arrangement was to have five houses on either side, all back to back and usually comprising a cellar, two rooms and an attic.[5] Yet, despite this close building, there was a permanent shortage of housing and these courts continued year after year not merely in occupation but crammed with

---

[1] *Select Committee on Public Walks* (1833), *Report*, p. 5.

[2] *Ibid.*, p. 4. This deficiency was then apparently very recent. Up to about 1820 even so large and rapidly growing a place as Manchester still had a number of public open spaces. (A. Redford and I. S. Russell, *Local Government in Manchester*, vol. I, p. 152.) The massacre of Peterloo provides famous evidence of the public use of one open space in Manchester.

[3] *Select Committee on Health of Towns*, *Report*, p. viii.

[4] *Ibid.*, *loc. cit.*

[5] *Royal Commission on Housing of the Working Classes* (1884), *Report*, vol. II, p. 494.

people. There were parts of Liverpool where the density in 1884 was estimated to be 1,210 persons per acre.[1]

The excessive building densities were most common in the largest cities, but most of the new manufacturing towns, whatever their size, had some district of the same character. Even where, in the early days of their growth, there were still some survivals of a more rural character or less cramped development, the signs of neglect in the quality of building and the overcrowding of houses were soon evident. A typical example of a small industrial centre was Coatbridge, which began to develop as an iron town about 1830, when it consisted only of a few primitive one-story houses, roofed with tiles or straw-thatch and comprising but and ben, one of which was set aside for a four or six-loom weaving shop.[2] A description a few years later shows how it was changing.

'The population consists almost entirely of colliers and iron-workers . . . I visited many of the houses attached to some of the works, and usually found them in a most neglected state. . . . The garden ground usually lay a mere waste unenclosed and not a spade put into it: the children, in rags and filth, were allowed to corrupt each other, exempt from all restraints of school or domestic control. This domestic discomfort seemed attributable, amongst other causes, to the crowded state of the habitations, which, from the want of buildings to contain the rapidly increasing population, were filled with lodgers. I was assured that some houses, with a family and only two rooms, took in as many as fourteen single men as lodgers.'[3]

The overcrowding and neglect of certain areas in the manufacturing districts tended to be accentuated and prolonged by social changes in towns in the course of their growth. In most places members of various classes had lived in fairly close proximity, but as the rapid influx of population into any locality lowered its condition, so those of higher incomes moved into other districts as opportunity arose. A Dundee minister, writing in 1841 of the condition of his parish, which was quite comparable with the most crowded parts of Liverpool, noted the significance of this change for its future. He said that 'the newly-opened railways offer new

[1] *Ibid.*, vol. II, p. 498.
[2] A. Miller, *The Rise and Progress of Coatbridge and surrounding neighbourhood*, p. 12. The population of Old Monkland parish (of which Coatbridge was the centre) was 9,580 in 1831, and rose to 19,709 in 1841 and 27,332 in 1851.
[3] Quoted in S. Laing, jun., *National Distress, its causes and remedies*, p. 43.

facilities for uniting the business of the town with family residence in the country, and threaten, ere many years, to convert Dundee into one great workshop, with the families of its workmen wholly detached from the notice or sympathy of the families of any upper class'.[1]

Many other later writers noted similar developments elsewhere, and found that the exodus gradually involved people lower in the social scale. One of them, writing in 1871, stated that, besides other members of the middle classes, clerks and warehousemen were moving outwards, 'vacating their houses in town which are most frequently absorbed for shop or business purposes, or, where this is not the case, the houses are subdivided and sublet, until the dwelling which had served for one household contains as many families as it once did persons. What once was garden is built over with cottages, and what once was a healthy part of the town soon becomes an overcrowded pest place, spreading itself and its influence wider each year.'[2] Change in the use of buildings in central areas was an important feature of the later stages of the growth of towns, because it meant that although towns occupied more space in proportion to their population there was no relief of congestion at their heart, whether that was indicated by the proportion of land under buildings or by the density of population. It was observed in London in the seventies that despite the extension of the built-up area some of the older districts were becoming more closely packed than ever as a result of railway and warehouse construction.[3] In the next decade it was reported that in Newcastle-upon-Tyne, because houses had been replaced by offices and warehouses, there were no vacant dwellings to be had near the centre of the city and many old houses had been divided up and occupied as tenements, the working classes having to accept whatever accommodation they could find.[4]

There was in fact no very effective choice of locality of residence for large numbers of working people. Over and over again evidence was produced that they were forced to continue living in the centres of towns, because their employment was so frequently of a casual

[1] Rev. G. Lewis, *The State of St. David's Parish; with remarks on the moral and physical statistics of Dundee*, p. 6.

[2] G. T. Robinson, 'On Town Dwellings for the Working Classes', in *Transactions of the Manchester Statistical Society*, 1871–2, p. 68.

[3] G. Ross, 'The Artizans and Labourers' Dwellings Bill', in *Sessional Proceedings of the National Association for the Promotion of Social Science*, vol. VIII, p. 173.

[4] *Royal Commission on Housing of the Working Classes* (1884), *Report*, vol. II, pp. 239–40.

nature and they must be always on the spot or lose the opportunity of earning a few shillings, and because they must be in a district providing subsidiary employment for women and girls, whose earnings were required to make up an adequate family income.[1] The situation was succinctly, if a little too simply, described by the chairman of the Local Government Committee of the London County Council at the end of the century, when he said, 'A slum, in a word, represents the presence of a market for local, casual labour'.[2] Since masses of people were unable to move their residence very far and land was required for additional uses in the same district, further congestion was, for physical reasons, inevitable. Financial influences reinforced the same tendency, for the effect of the increased demand for business premises was to raise land values considerably and residential rents in central districts had to move up correspondingly. But, although in the later nineteenth century wages were generally rising slightly, it was impossible for working people to pay more than a small absolute increase in rent. Much residential property could maintain its profitability only by more intensive use. The evidence of such a situation gives added force to the opinion of the outstanding philanthropist of the time, Lord Shaftesbury, who said in 1884, as a result of nearly sixty years' experience, that however great the improvement in the condition of the poor in London had been in other respects, the overcrowding had become more serious than it ever was.[3] London was England's most serious example, but in some degree a similar condition characterized most of the larger towns.

The financial influences on overcrowding at the end of the century provide a clue to the reasons why from the beginning the new industrial and commercial towns developed as they did. The people responsible for building them varied enormously in character, resources, and interest. But, in general, working class districts were built purely as a commercial undertaking which had to compete for capital with the most remunerative alternative investments; they were supplying a demand at the level at which it was effective, and were not making allowance for desirable minima in quality. The Select Committee of 1840 observed that congested property, built back-to-back in confined areas, was constantly increasing simply

[1] *Ibid.*, vol. I, p. 18.
[2] B. F. C. Costelloe, 'The Housing Problem', in *Trans. Manchester Stat. Socy.*, 1898-9, p. 48.
[3] *Royal Commission on Housing of the Working Classes* (1884), *Report*, vol. I, p. 7.

because it was a profitable investment, although it imposed a heavy cost on the community and contributed little to the rates.[1] A description of part of Leeds in 1842 emphasized the significance of the financial influence:

'The courts and culs-de-sac exist everywhere. The building of houses back-to-back occasions this in a great measure. It is in fact part of the economy of buildings that are to pay a good percentage. In one cul-de-sac, in the town of Leeds, there are 34 houses, and in ordinary times, there dwell in these houses 340 persons, or 10 to every house; but as these houses are many of them receiving houses for itinerant labourers, during the periods of hay-time and harvest and the fairs, at least twice that number are then here congregated. The name of this place is the Boot and Shoe-yard, in Kirkgate, a location from whence the Commissioners removed, in the days of the cholera, 75 cart-loads of manure, which had been untouched for years, and where there now exists a surface of human excrement of very considerable extent, to which these impure and unventilated dwellings are additionally exposed. This property is said to pay the best annual interest of any cottage property in the borough.'[2]

Such property was generally owned by people who had neither the outlook nor, at any rate initially, the resources to make them add anything to their building beyond what was absolutely necessary in order to command a rental. Thomas Cubitt, who not only was one of the greatest building magnates of the first half of the nineteenth century but also took a very active interest in working class living conditions, declared in 1840 that 'poor people's houses seldom belong to any but those who are glad to get any money they can; they belong to a little shop-keeping class of persons, who have saved a little money in business; as they advance a little in life they possess themselves of that sort of house . . . I think very few persons of great capital have anything to do with them at all.'[3] But undoubtedly long periods of property ownership raised many of these people to the comparative affluence which repute attributed to them.[4]

---

[1] *Select Committee on Health of Towns, Report*, p. ix.

[2] Poor Law Commissioners, *Report on an inquiry into the Sanitary Condition of the Labouring Population of Great Britain*, p. 41.

[3] *Select Committee on Health of Towns, Report*, p. 205. Detailed local studies in statistical form might well modify this general impression of the preponderance of the small capitalist in the ownership of cottage property.

[4] e.g., *ibid.*, p. 145, evidence of Dr. Duncan of Liverpool.

The continued extension of congested, unsound property was also facilitated by the means and outlook of the occupants. As Edmund Ashworth put it, 'there are two inducements; the one, the fact of the small cottages being more lucrative to the builder, and the other, that they are cheaper to the occupant. I have known a man and his family, with a good income, go from a good cottage to a bad one to save a shilling a week.'[1] That was not an isolated experience.

Haphazard development by commercial investors was, of course, not a rule without exceptions. Sometimes manufacturers built not only their factories but also a residential area nearby, and some of them paid respect to quality and amenity. Edmund Ashworth, for instance, was able to claim for himself and his brother in 1840 that for twenty years they had continued to make every successive set of cottages more expensive and more convenient than its predecessors, and found that that was an appreciated policy, for the most expensive cottages were those most sought by their workpeople.[2] But they were operating in Lancashire villages, not in large towns. In many places the results of estate development by local employers were no better than those of speculative building. In Swindon, for instance, a town with an exceptionally high proportion of property of low value, the most closely built district was the original estate erected by the Great Western Railway Company.[3] In any case, employers built settlements only in the immediate vicinity of their own works and then usually only if they were located in not very densely populated districts. The iron-making district of South Wales provides an illustration. There the industrial settlements which actually contained iron-works, Nantyglo, Beaufort, Blaenavon, and to a less extent Clydach, were built by the large local employers, whereas a working-class dormitory town, Brynmawr, was not.[4] Its development was closer to the common pattern. At first, early in the nineteenth century, individual workmen built their own houses and then local tradesmen began to build as a speculation, but this small town differed from greater ones in that throughout the century

---

[1] *Ibid.*, p. 111.

[2] *Ibid., loc. cit.*

[3] W. R. Davidge, *Planning for Swindon*, p. 12. Although the layout was close the houses themselves were apparently well-designed and soundly built. (H. B. Wells, 'Swindon in the nineteenth and twentieth centuries', in L. V. Grinsell and others, *Studies in the History of Swindon*, pp. 126–7.) Compact layout continued after the cessation of house-building by the company in 1853–4. (*Ibid.*, pp. 104, 127, and 149.)

[4] H. Jennings, *Brynmawr. A Study of a Distressed Area*, p. 84.

private building kept pace with the growth of population so that a separate house for each family was always normal.[1]

Mention of the early building of houses by workmen for themselves draws attention to another contribution to the creation of towns. Very probably, so far as it went, it was a beneficial one. It was observed in 1840 that in Hyde the houses constructed by the men for themselves were generally larger and more substantial than those built by the employer,[2] and Hyde had the reputation of being one of the most benevolently conducted of the new manufacturing towns. But few working men had sufficient resources to be able to build a house for themselves and their contribution to town development was small, though in the later years of the century new building by working men with the aid of building societies was of some significance.[3] For the most part, however, and particularly in the case of the great cities, it was the private builders, operating piecemeal and without regulation, in whatever area had an immediate demand, who built the towns.

Naturally they needed to be able to make suitable arrangements with landowners, but most of these were not averse to developing their property as opportunity offered. If changing economic conditions or other external circumstances induced them to offer land on lease which previously they had withheld, there was usually no difficulty in finding a builder who would take it up. Such a change of attitude on the part of landowners, partly stimulated by the passing of a local Improvement Act, appears to have influenced the growth of Cardiff in the seventies. It received a strong response from builders, and it was estimated that in five years from 1875 about £1,025,000 was put into new building, almost all of it speculative development.[4] In some cases the influence of the ground landlord was exerted to secure a better layout of his estate. It was noted in the forties, for instance, that the streets in the newer part of Ashton-under-Lyne, unlike those of many contemporary industrial towns, were wide and regular,

---

[1] *Ibid.*, pp. 84–6.

[2] W. Cooke Taylor, *The Natural History of Society*, vol. II, p. 273.

[3] Examples of working class activity in this field are discussed in J. Hole, *The Homes of the Working Classes with Suggestions for their Improvement*, especially p. 85, which treats of the Freehold Land Societies in Birmingham; and in the evidence of T. Fatkin to the *Royal Commission on Housing of the Working Classes* (vol. II, pp. 371–7). Building through building societies was noted as an important feature at Brynmawr from *c.* 1880 onwards. (Jennings, *op. cit.*, p. 87.)

[4] Anon., *Growth of Cardiff from 1875 to 1880: with some particulars of Cardiff in the Last Century* (reprinted from *South Wales Daily News and Cardiff Times*), pp. 2–4.

chiefly because of the conditions which Lord Stamford, who owned most of the land, put into his leases.[1] Even where the landlord did little to regulate the layout he sometimes imposed conditions concerning the maintenance of buildings which prevented the very worst features of neglect, for a time at least. This was the case at Brynmawr. Although the early development there was very congested,[2] the agent of the landowner, the Duke of Beaufort, from the very beginning permitted land to be taken up for building on very reasonable terms and aided the town by the gift of land for tipping and other common needs. For a time the landowner also maintained certain roads. Whenever conditions warranted it, the Estate Office exerted pressure to ensure that buildings were kept in good repair, making this a condition of renewal of leases;[3] since, however, most leases were for 99 years this was not always a very effective lever.

Regulation of development, by landlords or anyone else, was exceptional before the general adoption of building by-laws under the provisions of the Public Health Act of 1875,[4] and where it existed its effectiveness was hampered by a very limited appreciation of what factors needed to be taken into account. It might be that an estate was deliberately laid out so as to avoid some particular evil while no attention was paid to other errors equally obvious and equally pernicious. A prominent figure in the building world, George Godwin, pointed out a glaring instance, the construction of Canning Town in the eighteen-fifties. This was a deliberately planned district, laid out as a whole and catering largely for those dependent on the docks. It avoided the degree of congestion of buildings which characterized some comparable districts and conformed to a fairly regular pattern; but no account was taken of the suitability of the site in Plaistow Marshes, much of which was below the level of Thames high water; the roads were not made up and there was no proper drainage: in one street the only drain was beneath a pump and passed into a well which was the only source of drinking water.[5]

The idea of town planning as something that might usefully be applied to the whole of any town was not dead even in the middle of the nineteenth century. Several witnesses before the Royal Com-

---

[1] *Royal Commission on State of Large Towns and Populous Districts* (1844-5), *2nd Report*, appendix, part II, p. 21.
[2] Jennings, *op. cit.*, p. 88.
[3] *Ibid.*, p. 91.
[4] 38 & 39 Vict. c. 55.
[5] G. Godwin, *Town Swamps and Social Bridges*, pp. 57-8.

mission on the State of Large Towns and Populous Districts (1844–5) discussed it. But the prevailing view of its content was rather narrow; the problems within its scope were almost entirely those of civil engineering. The best idea of what was intended was probably given by Butler Williams, Professor of Geodesy at the College for Civil Engineers, Putney. He emphasised the importance of public surveys for each town, which should be used to guide future improvements. Such surveys should show the ground plan of the objects in the town; contour levels; geological formation; materials, character, and use of public buildings and houses; the different construction of roads; the courses of existing sewer, gas, and water pipes; the average amount of traffic; and statistical details of internal structural improvements. Williams had demonstrated the feasibility of such surveys by guiding his students in the preparation of one covering the City of London.[1] His views on the application of a physical plan to a town were perhaps a little rigid, for he recommended that Wren's plan for London should be used as a guide in laying out new urban areas, without apparently paying much attention to major local variations. But he did insist that even in an existing city, some form of uniform plan could be applied to new building, as experience in Paris had demonstrated.[2]

A more flexible approach to the problem was shown in the suggestions submitted to Edwin Chadwick by Capt. James Vetch, who later, in the eighteen-fifties, took a prominent part in the supervision of the London main-drainage schemes. Vetch had noticed that most British towns expanded first along their radiating roads, the spaces between these ribbons being later filled by building laid out in the most haphazard fashion. He tried to show how this manner of growth could be improved by an adaptation of the geometrical forms found in the ground plan of towns in British and Spanish America. He proposed to enclose the existing built-up area of a town by an irregular polygon, each side of which would be treated as a normal line to which all new streets in the vicinity would be either parallel or perpendicular. The perimeter of the polygon itself was to be formed into a series of wide streets suitable for public buildings, especially schools, and perhaps planted with trees so that they might serve as public walks. He illustrated his ideas by drawing a plan for the future extension of Birmingham.

[1] *Royal Commission on State of Large Towns and Populous Districts, 1st Report*, p. 375.
[2] *Ibid., 1st Report*, p. 387.

Vetch readily admitted that no uniform plan of building was generally applicable, but he urged that it was nevertheless possible to follow certain general principles. He suggested that municipal authorities should offer prizes for the best designs for the extension of their town and leave the selection to a majority of the ratepayers.

He also had a number of suggestions for the improvement of existing built-up areas. They included the conversion of blind alleys into thoroughfares and the extension of the principal streets through the buildings on which they abutted, the opening of wide straight streets through the most crowded districts, the opening of squares or public walks or gardens by the removal of some buildings, the replacement of dead walls by iron railings, and the prohibition of burials within large towns.[1]

The breadth of Vetch's views on town development was somewhat exceptional. Perhaps more representative of the time was Professor Hosking of King's College, London, who in his work on the regulation of buildings in towns gave to the arrangement of streets the briefest of his chapters. He confined himself to pointing out that the first consideration in building or extending main thoroughfares should be the provision of adequate space for traffic (including vehicles parked in front of buildings), whereas cross streets should be designed with the first object of ensuring adequate ventilation.[2]

However narrow or comprehensive were the ideas of reformers about the things which ought to be considered as towns expanded, existing practice often fell short of them. But there were some favourable conditions. The Board of Ordnance was prepared, for a suitable fee, to carry out surveys of towns which covered many of the items suggested by Williams. Some local authorities took advantage of this facility and made use of the results in schemes of drainage and sewerage in the third and fourth quarters of the century. Others rejected the opportunity either from indifference or on the score of expense.[3]

---

[1] Poor Law Commissioners, *op. cit.*, pp. 382–94.

[2] W. Hosking, *A Guide to the proper Regulation of Buildings in Towns, as a means of promoting and securing the Health, Comfort and Safety of the Inhabitants*, pp. 71–3.

[3] Gateshead was one example. 'No general survey has been made either for facilitating drainage or for other purposes. The town council . . . applied to the Board of Ordnance on the subject, but on learning that the probable extra expense of a plan of the Ordnance Survey on a scale of 5 feet to a mile would exceed £300, it was deemed inexpedient to incur this expense, as . . . "the state of the borough fund would not justify it, however desirable the possession of such a plan might be".' (*Royal Commission on State of Large Towns and Populous Districts, 2nd Report*, appendix, part II, p. 176.)

Of planning in a fuller sense, to ensure that buildings for a variety of social and economic purposes were erected in suitable proximity and as nearly contemporaneously as possible, there was virtually none. Employers built factories in accordance with their own requirements and as population flooded into the district speculative builders erected housing on any land available close to the places of prospective employment. It was taken for granted that those interested in catering for the various incidental needs of the district would individually make suitable arrangements to do so, and that shops, public houses, churches, and schools would come almost automatically into existence; someone was interested in their provision, either on pecuniary grounds or from moral principle: therefore they would be created. Not all these things were strictly comparable. Premises intended for use as shops were sometimes erected as a speculation, the suitability of their location depending on the judgement and opportunity of the builder. But churches, schools, and hospitals were built only to order and usually in arrear of the need for them.

To the haphazard provision for the common needs of a town there were very occasional exceptions, usually where a town was entirely dependent on one person or firm. Such, for instance, were the new maintenance and constructional centres of the railways. A mid-Victorian description of Wolverton shows the extent of the provision which the company found it desirable to make:

'It is a little red-brick town composed of 242 little red-brick houses—all running either this way or that way at right-angles—3 or 4 tall red-brick engine chimneys, a number of very large red-brick workshops, 6 red houses for officers—one red beer-shop, two red public-houses, and, we are glad to add, a substantial red school-room and a neat stone church, the whole lately built by order of a Railway Board, at a railway station, by a railway contractor, for railway men, railway women and railway children; in short, the round cast-iron plate over the door of every house, bearing the letters L.N.W.R., is the generic symbol of the town.'[1]

The railway company also provided at the edge of the town 130 allotments of 324 sq. yd. each, which it let at trifling rents,[2] and a reading room and library of 700 volumes, for which no subscription was charged.[3]

---

[1] Anon. [Sir F. B. Head], *Stokers and Pokers* (new edn. 1861), p. 82.
[2] *Ibid.*, p. 89.   [3] *Ibid.*, pp. 89–90.

Wolverton was a very small place,[1] but Crewe, which was a more substantial undertaking taken over from its predecessor, the Grand Junction, by the London and North-Western Railway Company, exhibited similar characteristics. The same writer's account of it at the same period states that it then contained 514 houses, a church, three schools and a town hall, all belonging to the railway company. New houses had originally been built only for railway workers, but it soon became necessary to provide many more for shop-keepers and others who were attracted to the growing town.[2] The company made itself fairly fully responsible for the running of the town. It paid the salary of a clergyman who superintended the day schools,[3] and gave a house and surgery to a doctor who attended to all the railway workers' families in return for regular fixed weekly subscriptions.[4] The steam pump at the locomotive works was also used to provide an adequate water supply for the town.[5] The company had its own gasworks which supplied the town, and it used the coal-tar produced there, mixed with gravel and ashes from the railway workshops, to provide an asphalt surface for the footpaths of the town streets.[6]

For a manufacturing town to grow in this way, developing both physically and communally under a single control and under the binding influence of common interests, was an unusual experience; and if the growth went on for a long time, the town passed beyond the control of any single private body and became, like most others, more subject to the incidence of immediate chance influences. The emergence of a town into some sort of social unity was usually left to the operation of time and experience with little positive assistance apart from the manifold but diffused exertions of private philanthropy.

In the earlier stages of their growth many towns had little to bind them together. In the forties the rapidly expanding settlement of Merthyr Tydfil and Dowlais was not unrepresentative. There it was remarked that there was a constant immigration of workmen who

---

[1] At the time of this description, the population was only 1,405, of whom 638 were under 16 years old (*ibid.*, p. 82).

[2] *Ibid.*, p. 110. As the population was estimated at 8,000 at this time it would appear that there must already have been many more houses which were not owned by the railway company.

[3] *Ibid., loc. cit.*   [4] *Ibid.*, p. 109.   [5] *Ibid.*, p. 101.

[6] *Ibid.*, p. 112. A full account of Crewe at this stage of its history is contained in W. H. Chaloner, *The Social and Economic Development of Crewe, 1780–1923*, esp. chap. II.

lived together clannishly, the Pembrokeshire men in one quarter, the Carmarthenshire men in another, and so on.[1] But the general expectation that what was needed for social life would be forth-coming through the ordinary action of individual interest was not altogether unjustified. The buildings to be earliest supplied in abundance were shops and public-houses, especially the latter, which hastened to fill the vacuum caused by the absence of any other provision for relaxation or indoor meeting place. The description of Merthyr and Dowlais in 1847, for instance, declared that 'beer-houses abound to an extent wholly unnecessary for any good pur-pose. There are said to be more than 200 such houses in Dowlais alone.'[2] For forty years after 1830 there was not even general negative control by licensing, as it was permissible to retail beer and cider without a justice's licence.[3] The superabundance of public-houses that came into existence in these circumstances continued to char-acterize many towns for years afterwards. In Birmingham in 1848 there was a public-house to every 166 inhabitants. At the beginning of the twentieth century the older wards of the city were still heavily supplied in this respect: St. Mary's had one to every 177 inhabitants, St. George's one to every 239, St. Bartholomew's one to every 275, St. Thomas's one to every 287, St. Martin's one to every 285 and Deritend one to every 316; but by contrast, Saltley, an entirely working-class district, most of which was built after 1870, had only one to every 1,822 inhabitants.[4]

Social buildings with less commercial prospects were not so readily forthcoming. In contemporary upper and middle-class opinion nothing was more necessary to the welfare of a district than an adequate number of churches and chapels. But the supply of them fell steadily behind the growth of population in most places. Some temporary improvement was made as a result of the Parliamentary grant in 1818 of £1,000,000 (subsequently increased to £1,500,000) for the building of new churches as a thank-offering for the successful conclusion of the war. From this fund 520 churches were built and endowed in many parts of the country.[5] But new districts continued

[1] *Commissioners of Inquiry into the State of Education in Wales, Report*, Part I (*Carmar-then, Glamorgan, and Pembroke*) (1847), Appendix, p. 304.

[2] *Ibid., loc. cit.*

[3] F. Tillyard, 'English Town Development in the Nineteenth Century', in *Economic Journal*, vol. XXIII, p. 554.

[4] *Ibid.*, p. 555.

[5] C. B. P. Bosanquet, *London: some account of its growth, charitable agencies, and wants*, pp. 58–9.

to be built over and occupied by the working class without any religious edifices. The difficulties of providing for the religious needs of urban areas can be well illustrated even from a comparatively wealthy diocese like London. In some others they were still greater. Bishop Blomfield in 1836 established a Metropolis Churches Fund supported by public subscriptions, out of which 68 new churches were built before the fund was merged with the Diocesan Church Building Society in 1854.[1] During the twenty-eight years of his episcopate Bishop Blomfield consecrated 198 churches, of which 107 were in London. The effect of this was to increase the total number of churches in the diocese by about two-thirds.[2] Yet great deficiencies persisted. In 1851 the Report on the Census of Religious Worship pointed out that church and chapel accommodation was required for approximately 58 per cent of the population, if all who were free to attend at various times on Sunday were to do so. But all denominations in London could seat only 29 per cent and the Church of England only 18 per cent of the population there. Three districts in St. Pancras in 1858 had only one clergyman for 10,000 inhabitants, and one district, Somers Town, with a population of 12,000, had no clergyman at all.[3] In 1862 the Bishop of London could still point to 82 parishes in his diocese with populations ranging from 10,000 to 38,000 and only one church each. Next year he launched a new effort to raise £1,000,000 in ten years for church extension,[4] and in the sixties, as a result, not only were new churches built, but in many poor quarters where sites were not readily obtainable, penetration by the Church effectively began, often with only a converted dwelling-house or a temporary iron building as headquarters to serve as both school and place of worship.[5]

It was not only churches and chapels which were slow to appear in growing towns. The same was true of buildings and sites for social and recreational activities of all kinds, partly of course because the most suitable sites had been occupied for other purposes before the need was realized, and partly because the need itself and the response which any attempt to satisfy it would evoke, continued for long to be imperfectly realized. A writer in 1874 who was emphasizing the continuing need for further recreational facilities was able to point to an outstanding example of what was required and appreciated: the Crystal Palace, which then had been visited in twenty-two years

[1] *Ibid.*, pp. 60–1.   [2] *Ibid.*, pp. 61–2.   [3] *Ibid.*, p. 92.
[4] *Ibid.*, pp. 95–6.   [5] *Ibid.*, p. 100.

by over 30,000,000 people, of whom, he noted approvingly, less than one in 1,000,000 had been reported drunk and disorderly.[1]

But, however little consideration was given originally to anything other than houses and factories, every new town gradually became very much more than a collection of bricks and mortar. People living and working close together discovered or developed common interests, found means to express them and a place in which to carry them on. Two industrial towns, far apart, may serve as examples: Merthyr Tydfil and Coatbridge.

Among the constantly immigrating population of Merthyr new groupings gradually came into existence which cut across the old and made their mark on the town. Friendly Societies were an important influence: about 1830 the Oddfellows had 27 lodges with a membership of between 2,000 and 3,000.[2] Other bodies grew from small beginnings. Eight men in 1836 founded the Merthyr Welsh Temperance Society, which strengthened its position until in 1852 it was able to build a Temperance Hall.[3] Similarly a small group which used to meet for discussion established a subscription library in 1846, and by 1861 was able to move into larger premises.[4] The supply of schools also steadily increased. In the eighteen-forties there were one National School, a Roman Catholic School and separate schools for boys, girls, and infants in connexion with Dowlais works. In 1856 the first British Day School in the district was founded and three more National Schools came into existence before 1871.[5] All these developments, together with parallel attempts to promote physical improvement, especially after the creation of a local Board of Health in 1850,[6] did something to impose a measure of unity on the diverse elements that went to the making of the town, and to increase the individuality of the place and its attractiveness for its own inhabitants. Nothing perhaps better reflects the growth of that individuality than the rise of a public for a truly local press. The first newspaper to circulate in the district, at the end of the eighteenth century, was, surprisingly enough, the *Cambridge Intelligencer*, which was introduced by Guest, the founder of Dowlais works. Early in the nineteenth

---

[1] F. Fuller, 'On our Paramount Duty to provide Wholesome and Pure Recreation and Amusement for the People, and the Dire Results and Dangers which attend our neglect of it', in *Transactions of the National Association for the Promotion of Social Science*, 1874, p. 748.

[2] C. Wilkins, *The History of Merthyr Tydfil*, p. 531.

[3] *Ibid.*, p. 530.   [4] *Ibid.*, pp. 404-5.

[5] *Ibid.*, pp. 507-19.   [6] *Ibid.*, p. 433.

century its place was taken by *The Cambrian*, which was published in Swansea. It was not until the thirties that Merthyr had a newspaper of its own, the *Merthyr Guardian*. By that time there were important local issues to discuss. The *Guardian*, for instance, was strong in opposition to the local employer and M.P., Sir John Guest. But there was still not a sufficient unified and literate population to keep a local newspaper in existence. The *Guardian* migrated to Cardiff, and other Merthyr newspapers of this period, the *Merthyr and Cardiff Chronicle* and *Udgorn Cymru*, had only brief lives. In 1855 a more permanent local newspaper was at last established, the *Merthyr Telegraph*, which campaigned prominently for local sanitary improvement and against the truck system, some of the worst abuses of which existed in some of the ironworks of the district. The *Merthyr Telegraph* itself lasted for only twenty-five years, but after 1855 Merthyr always had a newspaper of some kind.[1]

Coatbridge was smaller and grew less quickly, but its experience was similar, especially in the fusion of diverse groups into one community. When the manufacture of malleable iron began there in 1839 most of the skilled workmen needed were brought from England and Wales, especially from Staffordshire. These men at first were paid very highly and set themselves apart from the rest of the population, with whom they were frequently brawling. But gradually the divisions disappeared as other people learned the work done by the English immigrants, wages were more equalized, and intermarriage took place.[2] Common activities began to loom larger: in 1849 a bowling club and a curling club were founded and in 1855 a cricket club; in 1863 a theatre was opened.[3] Workmen joined together in meeting the contingencies of their daily lives, running sick funds, funeral clubs and benefit societies.[4] As everywhere else, continuous proximity and sharing of experience exerted their own unifying influence, though at Coatbridge the process was delayed by the influx of more and more Irish, some of them deliberately introduced as strike-breakers, from whom the original coalminers of the district for long held aloof.[5] But, however grim was its physical embodiment, a community was by one means and another established in the course of time where none had existed before.

The fact that real communities gradually came into existence seems

---

[1] *Ibid.*, pp. 448–9.
[2] Miller, *op. cit.*, pp. 171–2.
[3] *Ibid.*, p. 100.
[4] *Ibid.*, pp. 82–3.
[5] *Ibid.*, p. 187.

to have exerted more influence on contemporary opinion than the delay in achieving that result, the difficulties and frictions that arose while the community was still in formation, and the great deficiencies in its equipment when it was complete. At any rate, the towns which grew up late in the nineteenth century were left to develop socially in much the same way as those which grew up earlier. Where newer residential areas were expected to attract people from old over-crowded districts this lack of communal facilities, together with the absence of the stimulus of familiar company, proved at first a great handicap. For instance, in 1884 the Vicar of St. Mary, Charterhouse, remarked that people were packed together in his parish because of low rents, security from police interference, and the sociability of life there. The attractions of the society were strong enough to out-weigh the physical discomforts, while the proximity of well-established markets, such as did not exist in the newer areas, meant a real saving of expense.[1] Consequently people declined to move out.

For most of the nineteenth century working class areas thus continued to develop both physically and socially in the most haphazard way. But where whole towns or quarters were given up to occupation by a wealthier class, or where, later on, they devoted themselves to catering for the upper strata of workers on holiday there was more deliberate foresight. Spaciousness, amenity, and recreational facilities had obvious attractions, and there was a public which was able and willing to pay for them. Sometimes members of that public took joint steps to provide these advantages for themselves. If they did not, then there were others who supplied them as a business venture.

There was an eighteenth century tradition of town improvement, but it operated only in a restricted sphere. It continued into the nineteenth century, but is alleged by most writers to have disappeared about 1830. This conclusion is derived from too exclusive a pre-occupation with architecture. The architectural expression of the tradition changed drastically and, as most now think, for the worse. And areas adjacent to those which had lately been laid out in an aristocratic manner were sometimes given up to quite different uses and marked by planlessness and squalor. Such a transition is plain enough in Edinburgh to any observer on Calton Hill, who lets his

---

[1] *Royal Commission on Housing of the Working Classes, Report*, vol. II, p. 130.

glance pass from the New Town towards Leith.[1] But in other places there was still evidence of town design (though a very different kind of design) and of continual efforts to promote amenity. Tastes changed and the newer rich settled and disported themselves in different places from the old, but for those who could afford it the tradition that there should be created a town or a quarter suited to their needs continued as it had done before.

Perhaps there was a difference in this respect: that in the late eighteenth and early nineteenth centuries properly constituted local bodies, corporations or more commonly Improvement Commissioners, took a more prominent place, relatively to private persons, landlords or speculators, than they did a little later. But the change was only a minor one of degree, and in the latter part of the nineteenth century the influence of public bodies was gradually reasserted.

Of the great schemes of town improvement or extension in the late eighteenth and early nineteenth centuries, none was more striking than that of Edinburgh, and there the town council was the initiator, a position it was well situated to assume as it was developing unoccupied land in its ownership. The scheme began in 1763 with the draining of the North Loch and the building of the North Bridge to connect the existing city with the council's vacant lands and with Leith.[2] Then in 1767, having obtained additional powers by Act of Parliament, the council threw open to competition the planning of buildings to be erected 'in a regular and handsome manner' and adopted the designs of James Craig. Thereafter the building of the New Town proceeded rapidly, beginning with Prince's Street. But much of the actual construction was carried out by private persons, building lots being readily bought or feued from the magistrates.[3] It was estimated that in thirty years after 1763 £3,000,000 was spent on buildings and public improvements while the value of rents of houses paying cess or land-tax trebled.[4] In the early nineteenth century the extension of the New Town continued as the owners of adjacent land decided to develop their property. About 1825 the Earl of Moray's 30 acre estate of Drumsheugh, running to the ravine of

[1] Sir P. Abercrombie notes that even in 1834 a map-maker showed the extension of Edinburgh north of Calton Hill and along Leith Walk as laid out in the tradition of Craig's New Town, whereas the actual building was subsequently carried out 'without design, grace or gardens'. (*Town and Country Planning*, p. 76.)

[2] J. Anderson, *A History of Edinburgh from the earliest period to the completion of the half century* 1850, pp. 231-3.

[3] *Ibid.*, p. 237.   [4] *Ibid.*, pp. 341-3.

the Water of Leith, was built up according to a plan prepared by Gillespie Graham, whereupon Sir Henry Raeburn laid out his estate on the other side of the Water of Leith.[1]

The creation of the New Town gave its proprietors an interest in the maintenance of its integrity and in its improvement. Many of them, in the period after the Napoleonic Wars, joined together to resist schemes for building between the Old and New Towns and finally in 1826 a group, guided by Lord Cockburn, succeeded in obtaining statutory guarantees of the preservation of Prince's Street and the Mound from further building.[2] City improvement and the layout of estates were ordinary topics of discussion among the leaders of society in Edinburgh for many years.[3] If what had been done was attacked it was not because it was characterized by forethought and a care for amenity but on the ground that the planning had been badly done or subordinated to self-interest, and counter-charges of indifference to the public interest were frequently exchanged. Even as late as 1838 an anonymous observer could write:

'If proper measures had been followed up, it might have been a perfect model of architectural beauty and design. Well would it have been for the city if the *improvers* had been in a sound sleep for these last 50 years, or that the management and superintendence of the projected changes had devolved on *one* individual of good taste, instead of being left to the collective wisdom of interested men, who knew nothing about it and cared as little for the result.'[4]

He went on to add a warning that 'the good citizens of Edinburgh hereafter should ponder well before they build a house or root up a tree. It is easier to commit a fault than to find a remedy for it.'[5] Undoubtedly the feeling that planning was necessary in the growth of a town was strong, though it was applied only to one quarter of the town and not to the remainder, which needed it most, since it was concerned with those functions and groups which were growing most rapidly.

While in Edinburgh the city council provided much of the impetus

[1] *Ibid.*, p. 383.

[2] *Ibid.*, p. 385, and Lord Cockburn, *Memorials of His Time* (1945 edn.), p. 245.

[3] Cockburn, *op. cit.*, pp. 172–8 and p. 245. Note, e.g., the keenness with which Lord Cockburn himself argued for the preservation of existing trees in estate planning (*ibid.*, pp. 176–8).

[4] 'Sebaldus Naseweis', *Edinburgh and its Society in* 1838, pp. 103–4.

[5] *Ibid.*, pp. 107–8.

for the creation of the New Town and exercised guidance over its development, the manner of growth of new wealthy quarters in some other cities depended more completely on private landlords. This was so, for example, in eighteenth-century London, in which large and carefully-planned additions to the West End were made at the instance of several great landowners, especially in the years just after the Hanoverian accession and again after the Peace of 1763. The Burlington, Grosvenor, Cavendish, Harley, Portman, and Bedford estates all underwent considerable development in one or both of these periods, the second of which lasted until the French Wars imposed a serious check on new building at the end of the century. Even then private estate development by wealthy landlords did not entirely cease and there was a rapid revival after 1815.[1]

An outstanding example of what was done was the development of the 112-acre Bedford estate in Bloomsbury. This was begun in 1774 by the Dowager Duchess, while the Duke was still a minor, and continued intermittently for more than half a century. Twenty acres were first laid out as gardens for the use of lessees, the intention being that the buildings should be grouped around greens scattered over the whole area. Considerable restrictions were imposed on lessees, although the landlord accepted no reciprocal limitations. No lessee was allowed to put up any sign or to use a house as a shop or restaurant; the entrances to the estate were closed by gates, and persons with no business in Bloomsbury were not admitted. Thus was the character of the quarter preserved, and all the more easily as only a small proportion of the leases expired at any one time, this being a deliberate precaution against the possibility of ever having to re-let a large part of the property at a time when the prevailing level of rents was low.[2]

By the early nineteenth century, however, the improvement of London was becoming, temporarily, a matter even more of public than private design. The Crown itself was an important landowner, especially after Marylebone Park reverted to it in 1811, and the desire to develop its property with suitable elegance and magnificence led to the formation of large-scale schemes which went beyond the confines of Crown land, schemes which were discussed in Parliament, and the execution of which was in part paid for by the Government.

[1] On the whole subject of private estate development in eighteenth-century London *vide* J. Summerson, *Georgian London*, esp. pp. 81–93 and 146–59.
[2] S. E. Rasmussen, *London. The Unique City*, pp. 189–94.

The creative spirit in all this was John Nash, who planned the most comprehensive improvement ever given to London. Not all his plans were carried out and he was not the architect of all the buildings, but the transformed West End that came into existence in the fifteen years after Waterloo was his monument. Regent's Park was laid out, its terraces and its two picturesque Park Villages built, and this new park was linked by the great new Regent Street to St. James's Park, which was replanted. Buckingham House was made into a palace and the site of the abandoned royal residence of Carlton House was used for the building of Carlton House Terrace and Carlton Gardens. Just to the north, another new line was created by the building of Pall Mall East and Trafalgar Square, and the rebuilding of the north side of West Strand. Nash had still larger schemes in view, but when both he and his patron, George IV, were dead, public improvement reverted to a subordinate position in a rapidly changing London. Nash's pupil, Pennethorne, carried out some of his master's own designs and himself executed, in 1832, a commission to prepare a plan of further improvements. But only a fragment of this plan was accomplished, the most important item being the cutting of New Oxford Street through St. Giles' under the Improvement Act of 1839. Henceforward it was once more private estate development that was predominantly responsible for such additions to planned improvement as took place in London.[1]

Planning of estates, whether by landlords or by public bodies, was, however, not sufficient in itself, since these promoters did not usually make themselves responsible for much of the actual building, but leased out sites to others. The activity of builders was equally important and where they were constructing in advance of orders imposing residential squares and terraces for the wealthy they had to be men of large resources. In London in the first half of the nineteenth century no one did more in this field than Thomas Cubitt who began in a small way and died a millionaire.[2] He it was who, after erecting solid middle-class residences in Highbury and Islington, actually built a considerable part of the Duke of Bedford's estate, including Upper Woburn Place, Woburn Walk, Endsleigh Street, Gordon Street, Endsleigh Place, and most of Gordon Square, in the middle eighteen-twenties. Then he turned to cater for still

[1] For a short account of public improvements in London after Waterloo *vide* Summerson, *op. cit.*, pp. 160–85.
[2] *Dictionary of National Biography.*

more expensive tastes and having in 1824 leased 140 acres on the western fringe of the town built thereon Belgrave Square, Lowndes Square, Chesham Place, Eaton Place, and Eaton Square, probably the most fashionable district of London. Subsequently he extended his estate southward towards the river and built most of Pimlico, and he also developed the 250-acre estate of Clapham Park.[1] All his work was characterized by broad and airy streets, spacious squares and formal design, with the use of a considerable number of trees, and contrasted markedly with much higgledy-piggledy development at the same time in other districts catering for less wealthy residents.

In some other places besides London it was often some large builder who was responsible for the development or redevelopment of a considerable estate in conformity with a unified plan of his own making. An outstanding example was the work of Robert Grainger at Newcastle-upon-Tyne, mainly between 1826 and 1836. He completely rebuilt part of the centre of the town, using waste land of irregular contours and the site of old property worth £145,937 which he demolished. His plan for this central area included nine new streets with a combined length of one and one-sixth miles, three large markets, a Central Exchange (which in fact was used as a news-room), a theatre, a dispensary, a music-hall, a lecture room, a company's hall, two chapels, two auction marts, ten inns, twelve public-houses, four banks, forty first-class private houses, and 325 houses with shops; in fact, a good deal of the equipment which a commercial city needed.[2] The quality of the work was such as to induce an enthusiastic and peripatetic visitor to declare that outside London, only Edinburgh and Bath could show anything comparable to it.[3] Grainger later turned his attention to other districts of the city and purchased 570 acres on the banks of the Tyne to develop as a new business and wealthy residential quarter,[4] but he was unable to carry out most of his later plan as his earlier building of large, expensive houses had outrun the demand for them.[5]

Grainger's activities were business ventures and owed little to the support of any public authority. Indeed, when in one of his plans he reserved a site for new court buildings, the corporation hesitated so long over the proposal that he finally withdrew his offer and used

---

[1] Sir S. Tallents, *Man and Boy*, pp. 32–4.
[2] A. B. Granville, *The Spas of England and Principal Sea-Bathing Places,* vol. I, pp. 271–6.
[3] *Ibid.*, vol. I, p. 272.
[4] *Ibid.*, vol. I, p. 281.
[5] J. C. Bruce, *A Hand-Book to Newcastle-on-Tyne,* p. 115.

the ground for other purposes, including the erection of bank build-ings.[1] Grainger was assisted, however, by the influence of his friend and legal adviser, John Clayton, who was Town Clerk of Newcastle,[2] as well as by the existence of ready-made plans for the improvement of the town, prepared by a distinguished architect, John Dobson. In the earlier eighteen-twenties Dobson had unsuccessfully tried to interest the Newcastle corporation in a number of his plans for new streets, squares, and markets.[3] When Grainger took up some of these plans on his own account, the support of Clayton was very valuable in overcoming the financial objections which Dobson had had to face, and the corporation was actually persuaded to employ Grainger to build the markets which Dobson had designed. Dobson continued to be active in the execution of Grainger's schemes. All the new streets were planned and levelled by him and he designed many of the elevations. He also planned several other streets which were subsequently made by other builders.[4]

When virtually new towns were created in the early or mid-nineteenth century to serve a fairly wealthy public their first develop-ment was usually the work of enterprising landowners and specu-lative builders, just as in the case of the amorphous new manufactur-ing towns. But it was a more thoroughly planned and less intensive development, just because it was intended to serve a public with a much higher level of income and expenditure. Leamington, which became fashionable after 1820, was the creation of speculators: builders, shopkeepers and hotel-keepers, among all of whom bank-ruptcy was common.[5] New Brighton, which dates from about 1835, was originally the speculation of one man, who bought the land for very little and began to let it for the building of villas, and soon attracted the cream of Lancashire society as holiday-makers.[6] The new town at Eastbourne had its character largely determined for it by its chief landowner, the Duke of Devonshire. He himself con-structed the Grand Parade which served as a defence against the sea and was lined with large houses and an hotel.[7] Before he ever let any land on lease he first made the roads (even to the erection of lamp-posts) and installed main drainage.[8]

[1] *Ibid.*, p. 113.
[2] M. J. Dobson, *Memoir of John Dobson of Newcastle-on-Tyne*, p. 64.
[3] *Ibid.*, pp. 59–61.   [4] *Ibid.*, pp. 66–8.
[5] Granville, *op. cit.*, vol. II, p. 225.   [6] *Ibid.*, vol. II, pp. 11–16.
[7] J. H. Powell, *Powell's Popular Eastbourne Guide* (1863), p. 10.
[8] F. Verinder, *The Great Problem of Our Great Towns*, p. 7.

The development of some of these prosperous residential and recreational centres, which in some cases was scarcely less rapid than that of contemporary manufacturing towns, deserves more attention. Birkenhead was once a prominent example. It came into existence after the Napoleonic Wars as a place of residence for the wealthy merchants of Liverpool, families being 'allured by pleasant country scenery, fine river views and the wonderful ease with which they were able to pass from the bustle of the town to the quietness of the country'.[1] For them was built Hamilton Square, which its inhabitants claimed to be one of the finest in Europe, and which with its private gardens, occupied 6½ acres of ground surrounded on each side by stone-fronted houses, four stories high.[2] But Birkenhead quickly showed signs of developing a dual character, and industrial features began to appear with the commencement of Laird's shipyard in 1824.[3] It was perhaps the threat of industrialization to residential amenity that stimulated the comparatively rapid introduction of joint action through the Improvement Commissioners. In 1843 these took the almost unprecedented step of promoting a private Act to enable them to purchase land for a public park. This park, which occupied 180 acres, cost £120,000 and was laid out by Paxton, who afterwards achieved immortality as the designer of the Crystal Palace.[4] Not only was it free to the public and therefore a valuable place of recreation, but it served another purpose, in acting as a barrier between the wealthier and the artisan quarter of the town. Birkenhead in its earlier years was in various ways far better regulated than most contemporary towns. A local doctor in the forties said that 'few towns in modern times have been built with such regard to sanatory regulations as Birkenhead; and in no instance has so much been done for the health, comfort, and enjoyment of a people, as by those energetic individuals with whose names the rise and progress of Birkenhead are so intimately connected.' Among other things, he claimed that it was the best sewered town in the kingdom[5] and the unusual range of its equipment extended even to the provision of a public slaughter-house under official superintendence.[6] But already signs of deterioration were evident and after the

---

[1] T. Baines, *Liverpool in 1859*, p. 136.
[2] Anon., *The Strangers' Guide through Birkenhead* (1847), pp. 12–13.
[3] *Ibid.*, p. 17.
[4] *Ibid.*, p. 34.
[5] J. H. Robertson, *The Present Sanatory Condition of Birkenhead*, quoted in *ibid.*, p. 64.
[6] *The Strangers' Guide through Birkenhead*, p. 60.

building of the docks, which were begun in 1844,[1] Birkenhead rapidly changed its character; the wealthy residential element ceased to be an important proportion of the population, the practice of carefully-ordered development came to an end and the town became one more industrial and commercial area spreading out haphazard.

A more continuous record of ordered development characterized some of the places which kept apart from industrial expansion, especially the new seaside residential towns and some inland watering-places. Southport did not exist until the end of the eighteenth century and then was gradually built up for fifty years by private landowners and speculators studying the demands of a fairly prosperous public. It was in the seventeen-nineties that the shore began to be used for bathing by a few people from the hinterland and neighbouring towns and one William Sutton built for their accommodation some temporary wooden huts, made partly from old shipwrecks, an unpromising enough beginning. But Sutton himself in 1799 built a permanent domicile for eating, drinking and lodgings, and others began steadily to build terraces of houses and hotels.[2] An increasing number of wealthy residents was attracted, especially from Liverpool and especially after the opening of the Liverpool, Crosby and Southport Railway in 1848, and the typical ancillary occupations of a wealthy residential town, such as the keeping of boarding schools, began to establish themselves.[3] The early development was quite unregulated and its quality controlled only by the nature of the public for which it was provided. Not until 1846, when a Local Improvement Act was obtained, was there any activity by a public body, but growth hitherto had been slow enough to prevent any unmanageable problems from arising and the Commissioners set to work rapidly on measures which facilitated both immediate improvement and future healthy growth. In the first three years of their existence they provided street lighting in winter, introduced a licensing system for all recreational animals and vehicles, placed couches for invalids along one side of the main street, erected public pumps, installed a good drainage and sewerage system, and flagged and repaired all the pavements of the town.[4]

[1] *Ibid.*, p. 28.
[2] J. S., *A Guide to Southport and the Surrounding Neighbourhood and Parish* (1849), pp. 22–3.
[3] The directory for 1849 lists 129 'resident gentry' and 14 'boarding schools or academies'. (*Ibid.*, pp. 37–41.)
[4] *Ibid.*, p. 24.

Bournemouth might be taken as a model of the manner and style of development of the middle-class residential area in the mid-nineteenth century. The initial impetus came almost entirely from local landowners. The first to realize the possibilities of the site was L. D. G. Tregonwell who, early in the nineteenth century, built there a mansion for himself, a roadside inn, and a few cottages to which invalids occasionally resorted.[1] But it was Sir George Tapps-Gervis, on his succession in 1835 to the property on the east side of the valley, the largest estate in the district, who really founded Bournemouth. He called in B. Ferry as architect to prepare a complete plan for the establishment of an extensive watering-place and, though the whole of the plan was never executed, parts of it were put in hand immediately. One of the conditions laid down in the plan was that only detached houses standing in their own grounds would be permitted.[2] The result was described in 1850: 'a number of detached villas, each marked by distinct and peculiar architectural features, have sprung into existence, affording accommodation of varying extent, so as to be suited to the convenience of either large or small families, and adapted, some for extended, others, for confined, establishments.'[3] Sir George himself took an active part in the development. He chose some of the furniture for the first hotel, which was completed in 1838; he arranged the purchase of bricks, lime and cement for some of the buildings, had Westover Gardens laid out, and arranged for the building of a church. After his death in 1842 the estate passed into the administration of trustees, who for a number of years employed Decimus Burton as their architect.[4] The owners of neighbouring estates also soon began to undertake development on similar lines.[5]

Much of the physical character of Bournemouth was determined by Sir George Tapps-Gervis, the trustees who succeeded him, and their architectural adviser. Burton presented a long series of reports on the estate, recommending avoidance of formality in the building plan, the preservation of an appearance of rusticity, the retention of the best-grown trees, the liberal provision of walks and drives, a wide cliff-top esplanade, and the laying-out of the Bourne Valley as

[1] Anon., *The Visitor's Guide to Bournemouth and its Neighbourhood* (3rd edn., 1850), p. 11.
[2] C. Mate and C. H. Riddle, *Bournemouth: 1810–1910*, p. 66.
[3] *The Visitor's Guide to Bournemouth and its Neighbourhood*, p. 13.
[4] Mate and Riddle, *op. cit.*, pp. 67–9.
[5] *The Visitor's Guide to Bournemouth and its Neighbourhood*, p. 14.

ornamental pleasure grounds. He also recorded the schemes that had been carried out, including, besides building, the construction of certain pleasure grounds, the provision of various paths, the installation of drainage, and the creation of a burial ground.[1]

Until 1856 the development of Bournemouth was governed entirely by its landowners, who acted in accordance with carefully prepared plans and paid much attention to amenity yet were still frequently neglectful in such matters as drainage and the making-up of roads. In 1856 Improvement Commissioners were constituted[2] and from that time onwards the development of the town was largely shared between the civic authorities and private business undertakings, with the former taking an increasing part, not only in arranging for the satisfaction of basic sanitary needs, but also in supplying the special attractions likely to appeal to both residents and visitors. In the sixties, for instance, the Commissioners built the first pier, improved the sea-front and laid out cliff-walks.[3] In 1903 the Corporation took over also the Boscombe pier which had been completed fourteen years earlier and operated, without financial success, by a company.[4] The Winter Garden which a company opened in 1875 was another financial failure and was taken over by the municipality as a concert hall.[5] The local authority made many new walks and drives, including an Undercliff Drive completed in 1907, laid out the Chines as pleasure grounds and did much to extend the area of parks and pleasure grounds generally, especially in the twentieth century.[6] From the later nineteenth century the plans of individual landowners were far less dominant in determining the appearance of the town.

That Bournemouth was not an example of deliberately and carefully ordered development, just as the aristocratic town extension and improvement schemes of the immediately preceding period were, is a statement less of fact than of the prejudices of those who do not care for the particular type of development which it embodied. The change in appearance was due not to the abandonment of town planning but to a change in the taste which the designers served. This was perhaps more obvious in a town which was not new but was accommodating an increasing number of the well-to-do in both the eighteenth and nineteenth centuries; in Tunbridge Wells, for

[1] Mate and Riddle, *op. cit.*, pp. 90–2.   [2] *Ibid.*, p. 105.
[3] *Ibid.*, p. 121.   [4] *Ibid.*, p. 152.
[5] *Ibid.*, pp. 142–4.   [6] *Ibid.*, pp. 163–6.

instance. As that town grew in the early nineteenth century it began
to abandon the formal patterns of the previous age. The artificial
informality which Decimus Burton applied to Bournemouth was
tried out by the same architect at Tunbridge Wells. He laid out most
of the Calverley estate there, beginning with Calverley Park, a 26-acre
site on which he left a lawn sloping down to an ornamental lake,
and on which he built nineteen detached villas behind a romantic
shrubbery with meandering paths. Burton did much other work at
Tunbridge Wells and not all his buildings were taken up for the use
which he had intended, but his general estate design proved very
popular and was a great factor in restoring to the town as a residential
centre the attractiveness which it had ceased to exercise as a holiday
resort.[1]

Other places serving a very similar public were shaped by much
the same influences as Bournemouth. At first everything depended
on the landlords and then, gradually, further improvement came to
be shared between the local authority and outside business enterprises. Torquay came into existence at the end of the eighteenth
century on a site divided between only two owners, who both participated in the early building. Much of this seems to have been badly
arranged and of poor quality, and a contemporary lamented that the
two landowners did not agree to work on a joint uniform plan which
would have made Torquay equal to any watering-place.[2] But the
larger landowner, Sir L. Palk, had at least some basic ideas on the
development of a town. Early in the nineteenth century he laid out a
number of new roads, declaring that he was spending money in anticipation of visitors;[3] in 1820 he built a public market, but after 1825 he
seems to have operated by letting out land for building, over which he
exercised little control, and to have done little building for himself.[4]

Further substantial improvements had to await the formation of
a stronger local authority than the Select Vestry which functioned
until 1835. For some years new building was probably such as to
diminish the amenity of the town. But after 1850, when a local Board
of Health was set up,[5] things improved. Torquay was one of the
places which had itself mapped by the Ordnance Survey and after
1852, when this was done, it kept a check on the subsequent extension
of streets, sewers, water mains and gas pipes.[6] The Local Board of

---

[1] M. Barton, *Tunbridge Wells*, pp. 323-4.
[2] J. T. White, *The History of Torquay*, p. 115.
[3] *Ibid.*, p. 159.   [4] *Ibid.*, pp. 151-2.
[5] *Ibid.*, p. 159.   [6] *Ibid.*, p. 182.

Health in the fifties acquired new public gardens and built a promenade for visitors[1] and in the sixties carried out extensive street improvements.[2] New companies began to add to the equipment of the town: baths, hotels and a new market were all supplied by them in this period.[3] The chief landowner still took an interest in the development of the town, letting further land for building and occasionally giving a site for some public purpose, but on the whole the landowning influence diminished. For instance, until 1856 the town was dependent on the local landowners for its water supply, but the local authority bought up their private water-works and built new works which were completed in 1858.[4]

Nineteenth-century Scarborough owed its attractions mainly to the activities of private enterprise. The manner of the extension of the residential area seems to have been left to whoever was interested in house-building, but the increase of amenities throughout the middle of the century was largely the work of the Cliff Bridge Company which was formed in 1826 by some of the most influential residents of Scarborough and York, and which took over the Spa from the corporation.[5] For many years it continued to increase its property, extending the promenades and building, among other things, shops, a theatre, Italian terraces and balconies, and a carriage road along the undercliff.[6] Only from the eighteen-seventies did the corporation resume a very active part in the development of the town. After that it built new roads, including a Marine Drive completed between 1897 and 1908, acquired and laid out more and more gardens and stretches of the undercliff, and eventually bought a considerable stretch of the cliffs themselves. The cliff property on the north side it developed as a new health resort.[7]

It would be wrong to maintain that the wealthier residential towns and holiday resorts of Great Britain in the nineteenth century grew altogether in accordance with conscious preconceptions. Much was left entirely to chance or to immediate individual interest or whim, and many important matters received no attention. But in many instances someone, whether it was an individual or a private or public corporate body, did think about what an estate would look like when it was completely developed, did realize that space has its

---

[1] *Ibid.*, p. 192.   [2] *Ibid.*, pp. 262–3.
[3] *Ibid.*, *passim.*   [4] *Ibid.*, pp. 204–5.
[5] A. Rowntree (ed.), *The History of Scarborough*, p. 273.
[6] *Ibid.*, p. 275.   [7] *Ibid.*, pp. 282–4.

profits no less than density, and acted accordingly. The results were decidedly favourable for quality. By 1875 a critical observer could claim that in its sea-bathing places, at least, Great Britain had gained pre-eminence: 'they are superior to all others in natural beauty, in ranges of magnificent houses, in piers and jetties, and very generally in bathing grounds.'[1]

Moreover, these towns had the inestimable advantage of being intended for something more than working and sleeping. Consequently more care was taken to provide for some of the social needs of the people. Sometimes social requirements were approached from a negative point of view. When the Cliff Bridge Company built its new bridge at Scarborough it provided a walk which was not only a place of recreation for the wealthy but one from which the 'improper classes' were excluded.[2] There was also the fact that much more attention was given to formal recreational facilities, such as parks, gardens, and bathing establishments, than to other common needs, and that even recreation was not always adequately catered for: among other deficiencies was remarked the decline in the provision of outdoor refreshment.[3] But these towns on the whole grew in such a way as to make it much easier for their inhabitants and visitors to live the kind of life they preferred than was the case in most of the other expanding towns. Imperfect they always were; doubtless, often insipid. They were in many ways exceptional, yet they arose in response largely to the same forces as other contemporary towns. They show that significant qualifications must be made to the account of Britain, in the process of urbanization, proceeding from squalor into deeper squalor, from which gradually and with very incomplete success it strove to shake itself free.

[1] J. Macpherson, 'Health of Watering Places' in *Transactions of the National Association for the Promotion of Social Science*, 1875, p. 495.
[2] Rowntree, *op. cit.*, p. 274.
[3] Macpherson, *op. cit.*, pp. 497–8.

CHAPTER III

Problems of Town Life and Their Public Recognition

THAT living in towns involved the whole of society in peculiar problems which were neither self-terminating nor removable merely by the process of reducing the legal privilege of corporate authorities was a truth which spread only slowly among the politically influential members of nineteenth-century society. Every prosperous citizen knew that it was desirable for his own neighbourhood to have certain services. The long succession of local Improvement Acts in the eighteenth and early nineteenth centuries makes clear that the most generally required of these services were 'paving, lighting and watching', and also that if a corporation was in existence these things would need to be put in the charge of some rival authority. Hence the great attack on the privileges of Municipal Corporations in 1835, so formidable in appearance, so insignificant in the amount of difference it made to the conduct of local government in England and Wales.

To supplement one authority by another was often the best means of effecting some improvement in the condition of a town or part of a town, but there were large and growing urban areas over which no authority, whatever its title, sought to exercise any active supervision. Their inhabitants were in no position to obtain the constitution of any additional body, and for a time no one from outside felt much interest in discovering what their problems were or, indeed, that they had any special problems of their own. But the societies of the new congested districts were not discrete entities, and more and more people outside them gradually became aware of the pressure of their novel, powerful, and alarming qualities. Even if he were not his brother's keeper, every man of property was affected by the multiplication of thieves; everyone who valued his life felt it desirable not to have a mass of carriers of virulent diseases too close at hand.

47

There were signs that some such dangers did exist and to look into their extent and to reveal their nature to a wider public were the tasks of the famous investigations, both public and private, of the eighteen-thirties and forties. The very titles of some of their reports make clear what were the major problems involved: *The Moral and Physical Condition of the Working Classes of Manchester*, the brief pioneer work of Dr. J. P. Kay; *The Health of Towns*; *The Sanitary Condition of the Labouring Population of Great Britain*. It was morality (or, more exactly, criminality) and disease that were causing concern. Overcrowding and congestion, poverty, crime, ill-health and heavy mortality were shown to be conditions commonly found together.

There was nothing new in the existence of congested criminal quarters. In this as in other matters it was the changed scale of things that gave to an old problem the appearance of something new. One of the most striking features of some of the large rapidly-growing industrial and commercial towns was the very high proportion of people they attracted who had no regular employment. They depended entirely on casual activities which might take any form that opportunity suggested. Pilfering and prostitution were occupations calling for little training and could be pursued extensively with little interference in the unregulated human agglomerations of the mid-nineteenth century. The opportunities for a predatory existence increased and there were many to make use of them, the more perhaps as the towns made so little provision for more decorous excitements. By the middle of the nineteenth century experienced observers took it for granted that there would be a congested quarter given up to dishonesty in any growing town. Merthyr Tydfil in the forties was a refuge for criminals from far and near. The clannishness of its immigrant population, said an observer, 'makes them oppose every obstacle to the detection of offenders, who flock to Merthyr from all parts of Wales. Scarce a day passes without constables from the country coming in search of criminals. The district called China is a mere sink of thieves and prostitutes, such as unhappily constitutes an appendage to every large town and is not peculiar to Merthyr. Few, if any, of the workmen live in it, unless, perhaps, a stray lodger here and there. . . . Drunken rows are frequent; and in these much cowardly ferocity but nothing like fair fighting is shown. Resistance, however, is seldom made to the police.'[1]

[1] *Commissioners of Inquiry into the State of Education in Wales, Report*, Part I (1847), appendix, p. 304.

Other centres of immigrant population exhibited similar phenomena, often on a vaster scale. Probably none were worse than the
great ports of the west coast. In 1840 a witness from Glasgow
expressed to the Health of Towns Committee his firm belief that in
that city penury, dirt, misery, drunkenness, disease, and crime cul-
minated to a pitch unparalleled in Great Britain.[1] And two years
later, Captain Miller, the superintendent of police there, described
the low quarters of Glasgow in these words:

'The houses in which they live are unfit even for sties, and every
apartment is filled with a promiscuous crowd of men, women and
children, all in the most revolting state of filth and squalor. In many
houses there is scarcely any ventilation; dunghills lie in the vicinity
of the dwellings; and from the extremely defective sewerage, filth
of every kind constantly accumulates. In these horrid dens the most
abandoned characters of the city are collected, and from thence they
nightly issue to disseminate disease, and to pour upon the town
every species of crime and abomination.'[2]

That the most dishonest quarters of a city were also the least
pleasant physically was a matter for no surprise; and that perhaps
reduced the force of the revelations about the moral condition of the
towns, though the propertied classes were not likely to ignore a
factor threatening social stability when they had seen and remembered
rioting at home both in town and countryside and had noted with
apprehension revolutionary outbreaks in half the capitals of Europe.
The possibility of an uprising remained as a shadow on the British
middle-class mind and a persuasion towards some measure of reform
until in 1848 Chartism petered out in the face of advancing prosperity.

But news of the excessive disease and mortality of the most confined districts really did strike with something of the force of novelty.
The first general investigation of the subject by a public body, the
Select Committee on the Health of Towns in 1840, led to a report
which carries the tone of men convinced by the facts about something which hitherto they had never suspected. The surprise was
echoed by subsequent non-professional investigators. The Royal
Commission of 1844–5, discussing Liverpool in its first report,
referred to 'the great extent of mortality, of which the local authorities
and the principal inhabitants appear to have been, up to a recent

---

[1] *Select Committee on Health of Towns, Report*, p. 62.
[2] Quoted in S. Laing, jun., *National Distress; its causes and remedies*, p. 11.

period, unaware'.[1] In its second report it made a similar comment in
a wider context, declaring that, until the publication of recent reports,
'the extensive injury to public health, now proved to arise from
causes capable of removal, appears to have escaped general observation'.[2]

There was plenty of evidence of the effect of the new towns on
health, and the presentation of some of it in statistical form was
beginning to be facilitated as the information obtained from the
decennial census was supplemented by that from the compulsory
registration of births, marriages and deaths, introduced in 1837.
This form of presentation, though sometimes misleading, gave an
appearance of objective precision which added weight to the evidence
in the public estimation.

Attempts had already been made, with limited data, to illustrate
in this way the increasingly lethal nature of the swelling towns. A
witness represented to the Select Committee of 1840 that the death
rate in Glasgow had been 1 in 39 of the population in 1821, rising
to 1 in 30 in 1831, 1 in 29 in 1835 and 1 in 26 in 1838, and that the
mortality of children under the age of ten had risen from 1 in 75
in 1821 to 1 in 48 in 1839.[3] Statistics in a more elaborate form were
soon available. Figures were put before the Commission on the
State of Large Towns purporting to show the differences in the
average age at death in families dependent on different occupations
in the same town and in different towns, and between families in
drained and undrained districts, and so on.[4] Crude comparisons of
this kind, taking no account of differences in family size and in the
age composition of different occupational groups, were not the
precise, incontrovertible things which superficially they appeared to
be. But they were vivid and striking, and probably few who read
them were aware of the errors which they might conceal. Moreover,
some of the differences in mortality which they displayed were so
large that errors of statistical method could have accounted for only
a small fraction of them. And already in the forties Dr. Farr was
producing for the Registrar-General more soundly constructed
comparative tables of the expectation of life which told a similar
story.

[1] *Royal Commission on State of Large Towns and Populous Districts, 1st Report*, p. viii.
[2] *Ibid., 2nd Report*, p. 1.
[3] *Select Committee on Health of Towns, loc. cit.*
[4] e.g., figures relating to Sheffield and Leicester in *Royal Commission on State of Large Towns, etc., 1st Report*, appendix, pp. 150-1.

There was also an enormous mass of qualitative evidence, from which any random selection was bound to give much the same impression. A responsible and unsensational doctor like Southwood Smith could thus describe to the Poor Law Commissioners the effects of part of the east end of London:

'Those neglected places are out of view, and are not thought of. . . . Such is the filthy, close and unwashed state of the houses, and the poisonous condition of the localities in which the greater part of the houses are situated, from the total want of drainage, and the masses of putrefying matters of all sorts which are allowed to remain and accumulate indefinitely, that during the last year [1839] in several of the parishes both relieving officers and medical men lost their lives, in consequence of the brief stay in those places which they were obliged to make in the performance of their duties.'[1]

The evil was not confined to a few or to obscure places. The proximity of royalty itself failed to touch it. Here is part of a report on Windsor made to the Poor Law authorities in 1842:

' Of all the towns visited by me, Windsor is the worst beyond all comparison. From the gas-works at the end of George-street a double line of open, deep, black and stagnant ditches extends to Clewer-lane. From these ditches an intolerable stench is perpetually rising, and produces fever of a severe character. . . . Mr. Bailey, the relieving officer, informs me that cases of typhus fever are frequent in the neighbourhood. . . . He considers the neighbourhood of Garden-court in almost the same condition. . . . The ditches of which I have spoken are sometimes emptied by carts; and on the last occasion their contents were purchased for the sum of £15 by the occupier of land in the parish of Clewer, whose meadows suffered from the extraordinary strength of the manure which was used without previous preparation.'[2]

Sanitary deficiencies were in fact very general. As it was put in 1845, 'the most important evils affecting the public health throughout England and Wales are characterized by little variety, and it is only in the degree of their intensity that the towns exhibit the worst

---

[1] Laing, *op. cit.*, p. 18. The death rate in Whitechapel was almost exactly double that in the parish of St. George's, Hanover Square.
[2] Poor Law Commissioners, *Report on an enquiry into the Sanitary Condition of the Labouring Population of Great Britain*, pp. 13–14.

examples of such ills'.[1] Scotland could have been added with equal truth.

But the intensity was a very important factor, which did much to colour contemporary views of the nature and prospects of the town as a social institution. It is interesting to see how people regarded the growing towns in the light of the shocking revelations about their condition. Some continued undismayed to regard the growth of towns as a continued sign of progress, carrying great hope for the future. They did not deny the existence of present evils, but regarded them as temporary accompaniments of growth, which were both removable and likely to be removed, and which were more than counter-balanced by great advantages in the urban way of life. Robert Vaughan, for instance, a Unitarian minister, appealed to the evidence of all recorded history to support a claim that the highest civilization was possible only in an urban milieu.[2] The new cities of his own day, it was true, did show peculiar evils, but these sprang only from the development of a new form of social existence.[3] Though the immorality of contemporary large towns was lamentable, it was opposed by a vast influence which likewise originated in the towns.[4] A similar, though rather more cautious attitude was expressed by Cooke Taylor. He pointed out the necessity of making the best of the situation, since it was the product of the factory system, which could not be abolished.[5] And he maintained that the situation, however fraught with danger, did hold something very good in prospect:

'It is scarcely possible to speak of the vast accumulation of masses of human beings in the manufacturing districts, "the crowded hives" as they have been called, without something like anxiety and apprehension. Our conceptions of them clothe themselves in terms that have something portentous and fearful. We speak not of them indeed as of sudden convulsions, tempestuous seas, or furious hurricanes, but as of the slow rising and gradual swelling of an ocean, which must at some future and not distant time bear all the elements of society aloft upon its bosom. We cannot disguise from ourselves, that in the development of such potent elements, there is much to fear, but there is also much to hope. The principles of safety are not

---

[1] *Royal Commission on State of Large Towns, etc., 2nd Report,* p. 75.
[2] R. Vaughan, *The Age of Great Cities* (2nd edn.), *passim,* especially pp. 114 *et seq.*
[3] *Ibid.,* p. 229.   [4] *Ibid.,* p. 297.
[5] W. Cooke Taylor, *The Natural History of Society,* vol. II, p. 263.

far to seek, and when they are secured, the principles of prosperity will develope [*sic*] themselves. That many will dissent from these views is highly probable: no new element of society was ever developed that did not excite alarm and produce peril; but that peril has ever been aggravated by the alarmists endeavouring to destroy the element instead of regulating its courses.'[1]

A commoner attitude was that no great general improvement in existing urban areas was immediately possible but that such reforms as were practicable should be introduced and steps taken to ensure that the old evils were not repeated in new areas. The Royal Commission of 1844–5 concluded that no rapid improvement in the condition of the buildings in the most densely crowded districts could be expected but that it would be comparatively easy to prevent the recurrence of similar evils in future.[2] It recommended new legislation to lay down general regulations about buildings and street widths, to bring common lodging houses under public inspection and control, to place the necessary arrangements for drainage, paving, cleansing and ample water supply under a single administrative body, with revision of local areas to conform with areas of natural drainage, and to give the central government power to inspect the execution of all general sanitary regulations in large towns.[3] These recommendations, though differently worded, resembled those of the Select Committee five years earlier. This had suggested a general act to apply to all future building, a general sewerage act, the appointment of boards of health in all towns above a certain size, and the appointment in large towns of an inspector to enforce sanitary regulations; within this general framework it suggested that special attention ought to be given to the pressure of crowded burial grounds amid populous cities, the need for an ample water supply, the reservation of open spaces in areas of new building, the inspection and regulation of common lodging houses, and the provision of public bathing places for the poor.[4]

Mild as these proposals might now seem they involved a radical departure from existing practice. The explicit grounds on which

[1] *Ibid.*, vol. II, pp. 274–5.

[2] *Royal Commission on State of Large Towns, etc., 2nd Report*, p. 59. The same argument was still being used in connexion with the Housing, Town Planning, etc., Bill of 1909, and that fact is a significant comment on the sanitary activity of the Victorian period.

[3] *Ibid., 2nd Report*, p. 6.

[4] *Select Committee on Health of Towns, Report*, pp. xv–xx.

their framers sought to justify them are valuable indications of the
terms in which urban problems and urban reform were seen. There
were two principal arguments. First of all, the existing condition of
towns created an economic loss, which adversely affected the whole
community. Attempts were made to express particular illustrations
of this quantitatively. For instance, 12,895 people had been patients
in Glasgow Fever Hospital in seven years and they were estimated
to have lost six weeks' employment each, which, at 7s. 6d. per week
totalled £29,004. To this had to be added the cost of attendance,
which was about £1 per case, where the patient recovered.[1] (The
heavy burden of funeral costs was another closely-related matter.
Chadwick put it at between £4,000,000 and £5,000,000 a year for
Great Britain as a whole.[2]) The general effect of the physical and
moral injury to the working classes was summed up in this way:
'The property which the country has in their useful labours will be
so far lessened, and the unproductive outlay necessary to maintain
and restrain them so far augmented.'[3] Secondly, towns in their
present state fostered unrest and defiance of the law, which threatened
the existence of the social structure. Remedial efforts were therefore
desirable on grounds both of humanity and expediency. The Select
Committee declared in 1840 that 'some such measures are urgently
called for, as claims of humanity and justice to great multitudes of
our fellow men, and as necessary not less for the welfare of the poor
than the safety of property and the security of the rich'.[4]

Property was a major consideration. The need to keep it inviolate
was not only an argument for social reform but also imposed several
limitations on the reform that might be attempted. The Select Committee of 1840 expected that the strongest objection that would be
made to a general building act was that it was an interference with
private property[5] and though it justified this interference on the plea
of the general good, it was careful to insist that it must be no more
than was strictly necessary for the promotion of public health.[6]

This attitude was only a reflexion of prevailing ideas. Examples
of the over-riding influence of the rights of property were constantly
occurring, in the field of public health as elsewhere. The influence

[1] *Ibid.*, p. xiv.
[2] Poor Law Commissioners, *op. cit., Supplementary Report on . . . the Practice of Inter-ment in Towns*, by Edwin Chadwick, p. 197.
[3] *Select Committee on Health of Towns, Report, loc. cit.*
[4] *Ibid.*, pp. xiv–xv.　　　　　　　　　　[5] *Ibid.*, p. xvi.
[6] *Ibid.*, p. xv.

was just as potent and obstructive in places which specially prided
themselves on their condition as in any others. Edinburgh in the
early nineteenth century may serve as illustration. The refuse of that
beautiful city was carried to the Water of Leith by small streams,
most of it by one known, for obvious reasons, as the Foul Burn,
which drained all the Old Town and part of the New. One tenant
through whose land the Foul Burn passed began to use it to irrigate
his fields and to collect some of its contents for manure.[1] When a
prosecution against the owner of this land, Lord Moray, to have
the practice stopped, was unsuccessful in 1809, almost all the landowners whose fields were crossed by any of these open sewers began
to follow suit. They found by experience that direct irrigation with
the excrementious fluid promoted very rapid growth and enabled
them to take off several successive crops of grass, which was highly
profitable. It also created a succession of stagnant, stinking marshes
which polluted the air for miles around.[2] Private individuals could
not afford litigation with the wealthy proprietors profiting from the
practice and the English remedy of indictment for nuisance did not
exist in Scots law. Consequently the evil continued unrestrained for
years, during which the incidence of fever in Edinburgh increased.
In 1832 the Commissioners of Police promoted a private bill, one
provision of which would practically have ended the nuisance by
permitting the Foul Burn to be diverted into a covered drain. But
they were thwarted. The interested landowners used their influence
to obtain an amendment stating that 'in making any main drain, or
sewer, or conducting drain, the water at present carried into any
existing outlet shall not be diverted therefrom'.[3] Such were the
difficulties of sanitary improvement, even in a centre of elegance and
even where Crown property, including the Palace of Holyrood, was
among that very adversely affected.[4]

Yet the revelations of the thirties and forties did lead to activity
of various kinds and in various quarters. There were new voluntary
bodies seeking by positive means to remedy specific deficiencies in
specific places, especially in London. Such bodies as the Metropolitan
Association for Improving the Dwellings of the Industrious Classes
and the Society for the Improvement of the Condition of the Labour-

[1] Edinburgh Commissioners of Police, *Papers relating to the Fetid Irrigations around
the City of Edinburgh*, p. 7.
[2] *Ibid.*, p. 8.
[3] *Ibid.*, p. 9.   [4] *Ibid.*, p. 11.

ing Classes, founded in 1841 and 1844 respectively and both providing model dwellings for the poor, or the Association for the
Promotion of Cleanliness among the Poor, which set up model baths
and wash-houses in the east end of London, may have been only
nibbling at the edges of an enormous problem, but at least they
brought positive action where none had existed before. There were
also new propagandist bodies, amplifying and spreading knowledge
of urban conditions, and campaigning for reform, including measures
by the government. Chief among them was the Health of Towns
Association, founded in 1844 by Southwood Smith, which was
specially influential because of its membership, which included the
Marquis of Normanby, Lord Ashley and that most pertinacious of
M.P.s in the cause of social reform, R. A. Slaney. Some of the
individuals concerned did their utmost to ensure that propaganda
was followed by action. Lord Normanby tried to do as a private
member what he had been unable to do as Home Secretary, and in
1842 reintroduced three bills into Parliament which would have had the
effect of implementing the principal recommendations of the Select
Committee on the Health of Towns, but he encountered considerable
opposition and the measures were dropped in 1843 in return for a
promise of a Government Bill which, however, was not produced.[1]

Then there were a few local authorities which were forced by
overwhelming circumstances to improvise new measures and to seek
and exercise new legal powers, which could serve as a model for
general use at some later date. Liverpool, than which no English
town was at this time worse afflicted, both physically and morally,
was a pioneer of such piecemeal improvement. Street improvement
there had been intermittently considered by the council since the
seventeen-seventies. A practical beginning was made in 1786 with
the first Liverpool Improvement Act[2] under which various street
widenings and extensions were executed in conformity with a prepared plan. In the same year it was decided that in future all leases
granted by the corporation should contain a provision voiding them
in cases where the tenants let or demised the cellars of the property
concerned as separate dwellings. Thereafter there was always a

---

[1] J. L. and B. Hammond, *The Bleak Age* (Pelican edition), pp. 206–8. The subsequent
pages give a good short account of the Parliamentary struggle for public health legislation in the eighteen-forties. For fuller details *vide* R. A. Lewis, *Edwin Chadwick and
the Public Health Movement 1832–1854*, Part One, and S. E. Finer, *The Life and Times
of Sir Edwin Chadwick*, Books Five and Seven.

[2] 26 Geo. III, c. xii.

standing clause to this effect in corporation leases, but it does not seem to have been very effective,[1] and in any case most property was not on land leased from the corporation. Liverpool Corporation was sufficiently concerned about town improvement for it to have a Select Committee of Improvements in the late eighteenth and early nineteenth centuries[2] and it promoted the planned extension of various quarters of the town. In 1826 it went on to obtain a new Improvement Act[3] for the widening of various streets, their rebuilding in accordance with prescribed architectural designs, and the improvement of the cemetery; and also to give powers to prevent nuisances and annoyance in the streets. It was then that the corporation first began to exercise limited supervision over private building in the town.[4] But attempts at town improvement were small before the thirties and forties, when the magnitude of the local problems both increased and was more fully examined. Much was owed to Joshua Walmsley, who was elected to the council immediately after the passage of the Municipal Reform Act. In order to produce evidence on which to base a demand for police reform he made a personal investigation of crime and its haunts in Liverpool. Of his inquiry he wrote:

'I went into damp, dark cellars, unfit for human habitations, where men and women lived huddled together. These were necessarily the headquarters of disease and crime . . . when I read my report on the state of crime in Liverpool, the council refused to believe it. The amount of vice in the town, I calculated, cost society upwards of £700,000 to maintain. There were more than 2,000 notorious male thieves, besides 1,200 boys under 15. There were several hundred receivers of stolen goods. Some laughed at the report, deeming such a state of things impossible, others contended that it must be founded on mistaken statistics.'

But the council agreed to set up a committee of inquiry, which found that Walmsley had, if anything, understated the facts. The official report was published and promoted discussion in Liverpool and far beyond.[5] In Liverpool itself a stimulus was given to the exercise of greater control over the condition of the streets and buildings and

[1] J. Touzeau, *The Rise and Progress of Liverpool from 1551 to 1835*, p. 586.
[2] Sir J. A. Picton, *City of Liverpool. Municipal Archives and Records from A.D. 1700 to the passing of the Municipal Reform Act*, 1835, p. 363.
[3] 7 Geo. IV, c. xxvii.   [4] Picton, *op. cit.*, p. 368.
[5] H. M. Walmsley, *The Life of Sir Joshua Walmsley*, pp. 80–2.

new powers were obtained for this purpose in 1842.[1] But within a
very few years the sanitary state of the town was reduced from the
chronic to the desperate, most rapidly in 1846 when there was an
influx of hordes of diseased and starving Irish, fleeing from the
famine. The corporation was forced hurriedly to seek further powers[2]
which enabled it, among other things, to appoint Dr. Duncan as the
first Medical Officer of Health in the country, to appoint the first
Borough Engineer, and to restrict more effectively the further
multiplication of its courts and cellar-dwellings.

There was also the Central Government, pressed by outside persons and bodies to authorize and, if need be, assist the towns to do
something for their own physical improvement, and finally urged
on by a more potent propagandist, the cholera epidemic of 1848.
Gradually the Government gave way to the pressure of circumstances
and there appeared the first general legislative measures of urban
reform: the Nuisances Removal Act of 1846;[3] The Towns Improvement Clauses Act of 1847;[4] then the Public Health Act of 1848,[5]
which had the appearance of a great victory: it set up a Central Board
of Health (unfortunately too like the Poor Law Commission, which,
having become discredited, had been superseded in the previous
year) and empowered it to set up local Boards of Health, either on
petition from the ratepayers or compulsorily when the mortality
reached a specified figure; to these local Boards was given authority
to deal with sewerage, water supply, the control of offensive trades,
the provision and regulation of cemeteries, and various other
matters; and at last in 1851 came the first housing acts, sponsored
by Lord Shaftesbury: the Common Lodging Houses Act[6] and the
Labouring Classes' Lodging Houses Act.[7]

In the middle of the nineteenth century it was obvious that there
was a tremendous amount of remedial work to be done in towns
before they could be healthy and pleasant, yet it seemed that there
was perhaps wide appreciation of the true nature of the problem and
the beginning of a serious attempt to deal with it in an informed way.
But as soon as one reads the sanitary literature over a longer period
it appears to be impossible that this can have been so. For its out-

[1] Liverpool Building Act (5 Vict., c. xliv) and Liverpool Improvement Act (5 & 6 Vict., c. cvi).
[2] Embodied in the Liverpool Sanitary Act (9 & 10 Vict., c. cxxvii).
[3] 9 & 10 Vict., c. 96. [4] 10 & 11 Vict., c. 34.
[5] 11 & 12 Vict., c. 63. [6] 14 & 15 Vict., c. 28.
[7] 14 & 15 Vict., c. 34.

standing characteristic is that the same unwanted characteristics of towns that were exposed in the thirties and forties were still being illustrated from just as abundant contemporary experience twenty or thirty years later, that the same reasons for reform continued to be preached, that similar remedies continued to be urged and their non-application noted. The knowledge of sanitary reformers widened and deepened and their instances multiplied, but the fundamentals of their doctrine remained unchanged because the situation with which they were dealing remained fundamentally the same.

No one did more to impress on his countrymen the insanitary nature of their towns than William Farr and nowhere can their failure to remedy this be better illustrated than from his writings, for he was appointed compiler of abstracts in the Registrar General's office in 1838 and, in that capacity, remained the most important source of sanitary information for forty-one years. In his report on the year 1841 he first tried to measure the expectation of life at birth. He pointed out that for England and Wales it averaged 41·16 years,[1] but whereas it was 45 years in Surrey, it was only 37 years in the Metropolis and 26 years in Liverpool.[2] Two years later he drew a similar unfavourable comparison for Manchester where the expectation of life at birth was 24·2 years against an average of 40·2 years for England and Wales.[3] The conclusions were obvious. Thirty years later he was still making the same sort of comparison and some of the figures involved were not drastically different. Sometimes he selected figures likely to have a special force or expressed them in a form especially suited to contemporary opinion. In his 1875 report he pointed out that for England and Wales the average infant mortality was 158 per 1,000 births and was 111 per 1,000 births for selected Healthy Districts,[4] but for the last three years it had averaged 218·9 per 1,000 in Liverpool, 217·3 in Leicester and 201·1 in Leeds;[5] and he commented:

'So unfavourable to infant life are the unsanitary conditions of large towns—especially Liverpool—that not only is the mortality at some months of age twice as high as it is in the healthy districts, but at 7 months of age and upwards it is three times as high. The mortality of infants by lung diseases in Liverpool is higher than in any other large town.'[6]

[1] W. Farr, *Vital Statistics* (ed. N. A. Humphreys), p. 467. [2] *Ibid.*, p. 454.
[3] *Ibid.*, p. 478. [4] *Ibid.*, p. 199.
[5] *Ibid.*, p. 192. [6] *Ibid.*, p. 200.

The following year he tried to measure the pecuniary loss to the community as a result of avoidable mortality, an argument to which a business age might well attach great weight. He capitalized annual income at 5 per cent interest for each year of life and in this way valued the population at £5,250,000,000. As the mean English lifetime was 40·86 years, but that given by the life-table for Healthy Districts was 49·0 years, by bringing England as a whole up to the standard of the Healthy Districts the economic value of the population would have been increased by £1,050,000,000.[1]

Chadwick was another sanitary reformer who, though he lived through nine decades of the century, never found any lack of errors to denounce and seek to remedy, and who found in the evidence of the sanitary condition of a town the true criterion by which to judge its quality as a town. In 1886, towards the end of his life, he made a statement which well summarizes the diagnosis of urban problems and the prescription for their treatment that he had been publicising for half a century:

'He would have the sanitary doctor inquire into the state of the intestine or sewerage of the place. Are the great canals properly purged and cleansed? Is the breath of the place sweet and wholesome? Is it free, or is it infested with vermin? Is the circulation of what goes in and out of the town orderly and regular? Is the water with which it is supplied of good and proper quality? Is the food sufficient in regard to quality and quantity? Is the place supplied with pure air or does mist hang over it morning and evening like a fog? Is the mental condition of the place good? Is it free of discontent, irritation, or excitement? Is the death-rate that of a healthy community, and is the hereditary history of the town of such a character as to be creditable to its constitutional qualities? In a word, is it a town that an insurance company could insure wholesale without weighting it with any excess on the normal premium?

If the answer to all these questions be in the affirmative, then the town may be pronounced healthy. If it fail to give so clean a record, then the sanitary doctor is to prescribe for it sanitarily, as the curative doctor might, in his way, prescribe for a sick man.'[2]

John Simon also, with a wider sympathy and less rigid outlook,

[1] *Ibid.*, pp. 60–4.
[2] B. W. Richardson, *The Health of Nations. A Review of the Works of Edwin Chadwick*, vol. II, pp. 317–18.

was in the second half of the nineteenth century constantly drawing attention to the persistence of similar problems and the neglect to apply known remedies for them adequately. He first came into prominence in 1848 when he was appointed medical officer of the City of London and from 1858 as chief medical officer first of the Medical Department of the Privy Council, then of the Local Government Board, and after 1876 as a private person, he was one of the leaders of the movement for sanitary reform. He pointed out the obvious things to which in the fifties and sixties few people were paying much attention: that the incidence of certain dangerous diseases varied widely between places characterized by very different physical conditions; that, for instance, in the epidemic of cholera in 1854 there were 2,000 deaths from the disease in Newcastle-on-Tyne and Gateshead, whereas in Tynemouth, eight miles away, where sanitary regulations and drainage had recently been greatly improved, there were only four;[1] that the death-rate from fever was always high where there was overcrowding;[2] that infant mortality was probably five times as high in the worst places as in the best.[3] Above all, he insisted on the extreme wastefulness of what was happening and its implicit threat to the national standard of life. 'Sanitary neglect', he declared, 'is mistaken parsimony. Fever and cholera are costly items to count against the cheapness of filthy residence and ditch-drawn drinking-water: widowhood and orphanage make it expensive to sanction unventilated work-places and needlessly fatal occupations. . . . The physical strength of a nation is among the chief factors of national prosperity.'[4]

That was in 1858, not the best of years commercially, but about this time national prosperity seemed generally to be very firmly established, in spite of what sanitary reformers had to say. That bit of their argument could therefore be, and was, ignored. In 1874 Simon was still pointing out the same wastefulness and the continuance in some places of absolute neglect. He claimed that a quarter of the annual deaths could be prevented if existing knowledge of the chief causes of diseases, as affecting masses of population, were reasonably well applied throughout England.[5] And he pointed out that 'the administrators . . . must begin by fully recognizing the real state of the case, and with consciousness that in many instances they

[1] Sir J. Simon, *Public Health Reports* (ed. E. Seaton), vol. I, p. 439.
[2] *Ibid.*, vol. I, pp. 447–50.   [3] *Ibid.*, vol. I, p. 460.
[4] *Ibid.*, vol. I, p. 486.   [5] *Ibid.*, vol. II, p. 447.

will have to introduce for the first time, as into savage life, the rudiments of sanitary civilization'.[1]

The writings and activities of Chadwick, Farr, Simon and many others, including, for example, the large number of men, both professional experts and philanthropic amateurs, who over a period of nearly thirty years from the late fifties addressed the Social Science Association, may be used to illustrate a variety of themes. But they make two things quite plain: that there was, to an extent unknown a generation earlier, an alert minority which had perceived the nature of some of the errors in the development and management of contemporary towns and was keenly anxious to have them corrected; and that, despite this, mid-Victorian society as a whole never came within sight of overtaking those problems.

It was not that nothing was done. Legislation on the subject of housing and sanitary affairs considerably increased. A mere list of the more important general acts in this field is a clear indication of this: in 1853 there was a new Common Lodging Houses Act;[2] in 1855 a Nuisances Removal Act[3] and another act[4] intended to facilitate the formation of companies for the erection of dwellings; in 1860 the Nuisances Removal Act was amended,[5] as it was again in 1863;[6] in 1866 was passed a further Nuisances Removal Act,[7] as well as the more famous Sanitary Act[8] which amended and extended the nuisance law, and two minor acts[9] dealing with the financing through the Public Works Loans Commissioners of new housing for the working-classes, a purpose which another act[10] in the next year was intended further to facilitate. All these came in the period between the two most famous of the early housing acts, that of Shaftesbury in 1851[11] and that of Torrens in 1868.[12] And there were also numbers of local acts bearing on the same problems. Under their provisions and those of legislation already in force various localities executed works for their own physical improvement.

Liverpool may be taken as an example, since its condition in the forties was so notoriously bad. In 1847, when its Sanitary Act came into operation, it included 1,405 streets with 53 miles 114 yards of sewers and drains, which, however, were outlets only for surface

---

[1] *Ibid.*, vol. II, p. 464.
[2] 16 & 17 Vict., c. 41.
[3] 18 & 19 Vict., c. 121.
[4] 18 & 19 Vict., c. 132.
[5] 23 & 24 Vict., c. 77.
[6] 26 & 27 Vict., c. 117.
[7] 29 & 30 Vict., c. 41.
[8] 29 & 30 Vict., c. 90.
[9] 29 & 30 Vict., c. 28 and c. 72.
[10] 30 & 31 Vict., c. 28.
[11] 14 & 15 Vict., c. 34.
[12] 31 & 32 Vict., c. 130.

water and were often badly made. In the next twelve years 258 new streets with an area of 40,128 square yards, were paved by the council at the expense of the owners, and 84,088 yards of footpaths were substantially flagged; 146 miles of new sewers were built at a cost of £215,231, many of the old sewers were reconstructed and ventilated and the gutters generally were remodelled; the water supply was increased, three public baths and two public wash-houses were provided and the slaughter-houses were improved by the laying-on of a water-supply and by the enforcement of periodical cleansing; large numbers of public conveniences were built throughout the town and 'had the effect of removing nuisances and enforcing decency'.[1]

In Liverpool the tradition of attempting to relate street improvements to some comprehensive plan still remained, at any rate into the eighteen-fifties. In the middle forties the Liverpool Health of Towns Association was urging the consideration of town planning. It had noted the example of Edinburgh New Town and the testimonies of Vetch and of Butler Williams and urged that work should be begun in Liverpool as early as possible on the lines which they advocated. There should be comprehensive rebuilding, beginning with the worst districts, and the further extension of the town should be carried out on the same principles as the rebuilding and in accordance with a fixed plan.[2] In 1850 the Corporation's Improvement Committee called for plans for improving the town and chose one by H. P. Horner. He pointed out that Liverpool had been built with little attention to the probability of its increase, and its outlying districts lacked good communications with the centre. His plan was concerned with the connexion of roadways not then linked, the straightening of inconveniently crooked roads, and securing a 'belt of garden or park land bounding the present extent of the town and insuring the interposition of a stretch of comparative country between the existing buildings and any more of a town character'. He proposed gradually to form nine parks, but the Corporation declined, on the ground of expense, to implement this part of the scheme.[3] But this plan made its contribution to the street improvements already noted.

Activities similar to those of Liverpool, though usually on a

---

[1] T. Baines, *Liverpool in 1859*, pp. 99–101.
[2] *The Liverpool Health of Towns' Advocate*, 1846, pp. 85–91.
[3] *The Builder*, vol. VIII, (1850), p. 532.

smaller scale and less related to a comprehensive plan, went on in many other towns. In this period, too, was constructed one of the major sanitary monuments of the century, the main drainage system of London, which the Metropolitan Board of Works completed in 1865.[1]

But all this legislation and all this activity in the sphere of local improvement went for little in the face of the manifold evils which already existed in the forties, without counting their magnification in the next quarter of a century. For one thing, this was the great era of permissive legislation; few of the powers conferred on local authorities by the sanitary enactments carried any obligation to enforce them and not all authorities felt interested in applying much that they were not obliged to do. Simon told the Sanitary Commission of 1869–71 that he believed the state of the law to be fairly adequate where it was applied,[2] but he had already expressed his views about the way in which it was carried out in his report to the Privy Council in 1868:

' If . . . we turn from contemplating the intentions of the Legislature to consider the degree in which they are realized, the contrast is curiously great. Not only have permissive enactments remained for the most part unapplied in places where their application has been desirable; not only have various optional constructions and organisations which would have conduced to physical well-being, and which such enactments were designed to facilitate, remained in the immense majority of cases unbegun; but even nuisances which the law imperatively declares intolerable have, on an enormous scale, been suffered to continue; while diseases which mainly represent the inoperativeness of the nuisance law, have still been occasioning, I believe, fully a fourth part of the entire mortality of the country.'[3]

The local improvements, too, left untouched far, far more than they remedied. Much as the streets and drains of Liverpool may have been improved in the eighteen-fifties it remained for long afterwards a very unhealthy city; in 1856 the average death-rate for the parish was still 29·9 and that of the most unhealthy ward 39·4 per 1,000.[4] Many things went by default, some were positively opposed. The

---

[1] H. Jephson, *The Sanitary Evolution of London*, p. 158.
[2] *Royal Sanitary Commission* (1869–71), *2nd Report*, vol. II, p. 241.
[3] Quoted in Jephson, *op. cit.*, p. 216.
[4] Baines, *op. cit.*, p. 104.

local medical officer, Dr. W. S. Trench, stated in 1871 that nothing had been done towards providing a hospital under section 37 of the Sanitary Act, 1866, and that he could not see his way to work such a hospital.[1] He also emphasized the difficulty of dealing with bad housing, especially cellars; if proceedings were taken against the occupiers they were so wretched that they were glad to be sent to prison; if the owners were prosecuted they claimed that they received no rent but could not prevent people from entering the cellars;[2] and so the evil persisted. Dr. Trench made many recommendations for improvement, but in 1884 the editor of the *Liverpool Daily Post* declared that only in the last nine months had there been any attempt to put them into effect, after they had been completely ignored for twenty years.[3]

This general inadequacy of urban reform in the mid-Victorian period is perhaps to be attributed mainly to two characteristics of the public at large: first, a zeal for economy in public administration and a somewhat narrow interpretation of what constituted economy; and second, a pervasive apathy about the whole subject of sanitary improvement, which seemed to be of relatively minor importance when set beside the contemporary achievements of industry and commerce.

The greatest influence of the insistence on public economy came from the manner in which it was measured and judged. Not merely was expenditure required to be remunerative but the profit must accrue to the same agency as incurred the expenditure and must be capable of precise measurement in the form of pounds, shillings and pence. If some town improvement could be represented satisfactorily in a statement of profit and loss by the body which effected it, all well and good. But vague claims of public advantage from public expenditure were not to be admitted without some more exact support. If the latter was not forthcoming, then town improvement, however pleasant, could not be set against the benefits of cheap government. For it was a tenet of the Liberal faith that expenditure by public authorities must always be kept to a minimum so that as large a proportion of income as possible should be left in the hands of those to whom it originally accrued and who knew best how to use it. Nowhere were what might be called the ideological obstacles

---

[1] *Royal Sanitary Commission, 2nd Report*, vol. II, p. 290.
[2] *Ibid., 2nd Report*, vol. II, p. 289.
[3] *Royal Commission on Housing of the Working Classes, Report*, vol. II, p. 499.

to urban improvement more clearly revealed than in one of the influential monthly organs of the Liberal press, which in 1858 devoted a long leading article to the subject of social reform:

'The social reformer in office is a dangerously popular man; because he is, in many cases, a dishonest one. He appears liberal that he may be all the more effectively obstructive and wasteful. *His political science is the science of guiding the sewage of the country in the way it should go*; it is the science of ramming theological dogmas, and a distasteful alphabet, down the starving throats of agricultural scarecrows; *it is the science of improving the architectural aspect of a city until it takes a foremost rank in the note book of the dilletante* [sic] *tourist*; it is the science of benefitting the metropolis at the expense of the general taxation of the country; it is the science of pacifying the cry for parliamentary reform, and the clamours of financial economists, with a pail of whitewash; but it is not the science of good, cheap, and honest government, which alone can make a country really great and respected, and a people really happy and prosperous.'[1]

No wonder the advocates of specific improvements were always acutely conscious of the need to demonstate that their schemes were profitable. When George Godwin wanted to strengthen the cause of sanitary improvement the best thing he could say was that 'good may be done and money made at the same time, or at all events not lost'.[2] Year after year the Social Science Association discussed topics in this field and consistently revealed a division of opinion about the way in which public funds might be used for such a purpose. The position was made plain after one paper in 1879 when the president, F. S. Powell, expressed the hope that it would be borne in mind in the discussion that any improvement must be made to pay, because they could never hope to have any sanitary improvements unless there was a commercial return.[3] When the Association discussed a paper which referred to the possibility of financial assistance being provided by the Government for the improvement of working-class housing, it was found expedient to draft a resolution which avoided mentioning that aspect of the question.[4]

---

[1] *The Financial Reformer*, Aug. 1858. Italics mine.

[2] G. Godwin, *Town Swamps and Social Bridges*, p. 20.

[3] *Transactions of the National Association for the Promotion of Social Science*, 1879, p. 474.

[4] J. Hole, 'Is it desirable that the State or Municipality should assist in providing Improved Dwellings for the Lower Classes; and, if so, to what extent and in what way?' in *ibid.*, 1871, pp. 524 *et seq.*

Insistence on the importance of a direct commercial profit from urban improvements continued to be strong even when these were being pursued more actively. When, in 1887, a pamphlet was published with the sub-title of 'Philanthropy and five per cent' it was intended as an attraction for investing capitalists, not as a denunciation of hypocritical charity.[1] An architect in the nineties found himself still forced to argue as strongly as ever against the same attitude. He repeated the old points about the wastefulness of existing conditions,[2] points that by then had become traditional, and noted that consciousness of this had brought about some reform: 'the fear of epidemics and consequent greater cost and higher rates has made the before-all-things money collecting Briton become willing that the human machine who *makes* his money should be better housed.' But the necessity of individual profit had caused the reform to be attempted in the least desirable way, i.e. by re-housing people in large blocks at very high densities.[3] And so back to the recurring question. 'It seems but idle mockery to talk about pure air and sound lungs. But try to think out a plan and you are met with the hard, impenetrable and unclimbable wall called, WILL IT PAY?'[4]

New arguments could be brought up by reformers within the terms of reference accepted by the exponents of public economy. Thomas Beggs, for instance, side-stepped the issue of commercial profit for an individual by concentrating attention on the provision of employment and of investment-opportunities and the increase in the national stock of real capital which sanitary improvements created.[5] Octavia Hill pointed out the common exaggeration of the cost of reforms because of failure to deduct the compensating increase in rateable values which they directly brought about.[6] And Simon, whose views seem to have become more radical as he grew older, formulated more precisely the old plea that the question of profit and loss ought to be judged in a wider context. He agreed that there ought to be no subsidy for housing because he had concluded that the housing problem was primarily one of low wages

---

[1] The National Dwellings Society, *Homes of the London Working Classes: Philanthropy and five per cent.*

[2] R. Williams, *The People the Nation's Wealth*, p. 7.

[3] *Ibid.*, p. 13.

[4] R. Williams, *The Face of the Poor or The Crowding of London's Labourers*, p. 8.

[5] T. Beggs, 'A Review of Sanitary Legislation in its Economical Aspects', in *Sessional Proceedings of the National Association for the Promotion of Social Science*, vol. IX, p. 36.

[6] *Royal Commission on Housing of the Working Classes, Report*, vol. II, p. 288.

and poverty[1] and any subsidy would, he believed, merely be passed on to employers of labour.[2] But, though money spent by the State to improve the conditions of the poor ought to be used in such a way as was likely to be remunerative, the measurement of the remuneration should take into account such things as the reduction in the cost of pauperism and the reduction in crime.[3]

Towards the end of the century a narrowly commercial attitude was no longer a major obstacle to the execution of some town improvements, but it did seriously influence and limit the type of work that was attempted. Apathy in the mid-Victorian period was an equally powerful influence but was to a considerable extent overcome rather more quickly.

Of indifference to town improvement in the fifties and sixties there is plenty of evidence, and in many cases it was reinforced by positive hostility from interested persons. George Godwin, writing in 1858, had something to say of the public attitude:

'It is truly remarked that if a single felon were known to die in England at the present day under circumstances which 85 years ago were the rule and habit of prison life, the whole strength of public opinion would express itself as against a murder. Yet outside the privileged area, fever continues its ravages. 17,000 or 18,000 victims of fever are annually slain,—the chief part from our labouring population,—and many more are laid prostrate by this cause for weeks and months, their families impoverished, and often brought to ruin and pauperism.'[4]

He went on:

'We come back to the old story,—the story we have told so oft,— the story which the world listens to, and, shrugging its shoulders, still disbelieves. Men must have pure air.'[5]

He had striking instances to give of obstinate refusal to recognize prominent but unpleasant facts. Like many contemporaries he pointed to the revolting condition of the Thames, which was a repository for refuse from gasworks, unwholesome factories, slaughter-houses, cow-sheds, stables, and breweries and for the drainage of graveyards, yet which, unfiltered, was the only drinking

[1] Sir J. Simon, *English Sanitary Institutions*, p. 434.
[2] *Ibid.*, p. 441.   [3] *Ibid.*, p. 454.
[4] Godwin, *op. cit.*, p. 69.   [5] *Ibid.*, p. 73.

water available for part of Rotherhithe; and he found intelligent men who would maintain that the Thames was salubrious.[1] He drew attention to the callousness in the siting of most offensive trades in residential districts. After describing one London example, Belle Isle, off Maiden Lane, where horses were melted down, he added:

'If, however, you venture . . . to mention to any manufacturer the complaints heard from the neighbours, you will probably be laughed at, and told, that "this is a *nuisance neighbourhood*. What business have you to interfere? Leave us alone—we neither hurt ourselves nor anybody else." Let us, however, say in reply, that what seems sport to him, is death to others.'[2]

A dozen years later the Royal Sanitary Commission sent out a questionnaire to local authorities about the condition of their districts and their activities in the field of public health. The tone of the replies varied greatly, but there were some which revealed an almost incredible complacency. Keighley, for instance, returned its death-rate as 29·15 per 1,000 for 1867 and 45·90 per 1,000 for 1868, figures which were believed to be exaggerated because the population had increased since the 1861 census, which was used in calculating them. It made no contribution to hospitals, it had no disinfecting apparatus, its house drains were not trapped, there were few W.C.s as the water supply was insufficient, its liquid sewage was drained into the River Aire. Yet the reply stated that there was no unhealthy district, that nuisance removal powers appeared to be sufficient and there were no defects in respect of private improvements.[3] This was an extreme example, but it pointed to a doubling of difficulty when such an attitude not only survived but survived within the cloak of authority.

Administrative weakness had long been an obstacle to the improvement and sanitary regulation of towns. So far as municipal corporations were responsible for it, this was recognized early in the nineteenth century and the Royal Commission of 1835 fiercely attacked their inactivity, not so much, however, because of its unhealthy consequences as because it involved the corrupt exercise of privilege. It concluded that few corporations admitted any positive obligation to expend the surplus of their income for objects of public advantage. 'Such expenditure is regarded as a spontaneous act of

---

[1] *Ibid.*, pp. 52–3. [2] *Ibid.*, p. 11.
[3] *Royal Sanitary Commission, 2nd Report*, vol. III, Part II, pp. 280–1.

private generosity, rather than a well-considered application of the public revenue, and the credit to which the Corporation in such a case generally considers itself entitled is not that of judicious administrators, but of liberal benefactors.'[1] The limits of what they were willing to do were serious. Plymouth Corporation was regarded as the best conducted in the west of England. But one of its chief sources of revenue was the supply of water to the town; it therefore in 1826 removed the six conduits from which water could be drawn free, alleging that they infringed its right of property in the stream and water.[2] The adequacy of the supply was apparently of less importance. In Newcastle-upon-Tyne there was a typical example of a job half done. There the Corporation paved the streets and laid kerb-stones but took no responsibility for flagging the footpaths, which was very indifferently done.[3] Distrust of the way a corporation managed its funds was also sometimes an obstacle to improvement, even when it professed good intentions. In 1822 the Corporation of Leicester sought to obtain a local act for paving, lighting, cleansing and sewering. But it was countered by a public meeting of householders which declared that the streets were filthy, neglected, repugnant to decent feeling, destructive to comfort and injurious to the health of the inhabitants; that the ample endowments of the Corporation ought to be applied to remedying this condition, but that the public would not stand an additional rate. So nothing was done.[4]

The weakness of municipal government was intended to be remedied by the Municipal Corporations Act of 1835 which applied to 178 of the 246 boroughs, the exceptions, apart from London, being mostly very small places. It gave to the reformed boroughs a very much more liberal constitution but beyond that did nothing to make them into more effective *administrative* instruments. There was less corruption, but otherwise borough government after reform consisted of a more or less different body of people doing the same things as before in the same way.

In any case the Corporation seldom had exclusive responsibility for the public services and sanitary condition of a town.[5] Sometimes this was shared with Improvement Commissioners, sometimes it was

---

[1] *Royal Commission on Municipal Corporations in England and Wales* (1835), *1st Report*, p. 45.
[2] *Ibid.*, *1st Report*, App., Part I, p. 591.   [3] *Ibid.*, *1st Report*, App., Part I, p. 1649.
[4] *Ibid.*, *1st Report*, App., Part I, p. 1921.   [5] *Ibid.*, *1st Report*, p. 29.

vested in Commissioners alone and always the powers of the latter were individually defined by a private act. The Municipal Corporations Act had made little difference to this condition of divided responsibility. The only function which was concentrated in the corporations and removed from other authorities in the same areas was the control of the constabulary. Every borough council was obliged to appoint a Watch Committee, which must appoint constables,[1] and as soon as this was done all provisions in local acts regarding the appointment, regulation, powers and duties of watchmen and constables, and rating for their expenses, ceased to be in force.[2] In addition, Commissioners or Trustees appointed in boroughs under local acts could, if they chose, surrender any or all of their further powers to the corporation,[3] but they were under no obligation to do so and there was no general rush by Commissioners to end their existence. Apart from this, borough councils were permitted, but not obliged, to fill in a few gaps in the sanitary regulation of their towns. They could make by-laws for the good government of the borough and for the prevention and suppression of nuisances which were not already punishable in a summary manner by an act already in force throughout the borough.[4] That was all.

There was further administrative weakness from the failure to match the spread of building with a corresponding expansion of local government areas. Some towns quite early in the nineteenth century had grown far beyond the area subject to the corporation,[5] so that large parts of them had no local government but that of the parish authorities and the county justices. Some substantial towns had never been incorporated and were handicapped because their old machinery for the enforcement of sanitary measures, such as the court-leet, had fallen into disuse.[6]

Many new general needs in local government naturally made themselves felt during the nineteenth century and were met for the most part by a series of *ad hoc* expedients. Individual measures some-

---

[1]. 5 & 6 Will. IV, c. 76, sec. 76.   [2] Sec. 84.
[3] Sec. 75.   [4] Sec. 90.
[5] *Royal Commission on Municipal Corporations in England and Wales* (1835), *1st Report*, p. 30.
[6] Poor Law Commissioners, *Rep. on San. Condn. Labg. Popn. of Gt. Brit.*, p. 370. A court-leet was still functioning in Manchester as late as 1846, after the town had been incorporated, but this was very exceptional (D. L. Keir, *A Constitutional History of Modern Britain*, p. 315). Moreover it was a very ineffective instrument. (A. Redford and I. S. Russell, *The History of Local Government in Manchester*, vol. I, pp. 187–8.)

times imposed order where none had existed before and thereby assisted in the increase of efficiency. The reform of London government in 1855 was such a measure since for the first time it recognized that there were needs common to a large metropolitan area and set up a body to deal with them, the Metropolitan Board of Works.[1]

But for the country as a whole the general result of changes in the mid-nineteenth century was to set up several networks of authorities, each responsible for only a very few functions and each with a different set of local boundaries. This multiplicity of bodies provided abundant opportunities for any apathetic one among them to disclaim responsibility. This happened in both small and large places. A Royal Commission found, for instance, in 1880 that at Cowbridge there was a corporation, which had spent money in draining part of the town, which, however, it declined to admit as part of its responsibility. Sanitary management vested in the Bridgend and Cowbridge Union and was unsatisfactory. There was also in the same place a Highway Board which would not cleanse the streets, though at one time it went so far as to order those inhabitants before whose houses filth had accumulated to remove it: some did and some did not, and the filth was left until it was dried up by the sun and blown away by the wind. The corporation, if it chose, could remove the filth and improve the sanitary condition of the town, but it claimed that it had other objects, that there was a Highway Board and a sanitary authority and that these matters should be left to those bodies. The Highway Board likewise refused to have anything to do with paving and the corporation occasionally dealt with this by paving and pitching at its own expense half the space in front of a house—but only if the house belonged to a corporator.[2]

In a small place like Cowbridge the worst effects of such chaotic administration were not felt but the similar experiences encountered in more populous places were fraught with greater danger. The metropolis itself was by no means free from them. In 1867, for instance, a ratepayer complained to the Home Office about certain sewerage deficiencies. The complaint was passed on to the Chiswick Commissioners and the Acton Board of Health. The former took steps to remedy the defect, so far as work in their area was

[1] Jephson, *op. cit.*, p. 83.

[2] *Royal Commission on Municipal Corporations* (1880), *Report*, Part I, pp. 29–31. Cowbridge was an unreformed corporation.

involved, but the latter declined to do so, claiming that responsibility lay with the Metropolitan Board of Works.[1]

If an authority chose to shelve or deny its responsibility it was unlikely that any superior body would succeed in forcing it to change its attitude. There were plenty of examples of recommendations from the Home Office being disregarded with impunity. A typical case occurred at Liverpool in 1866. A number of ratepayers appealed to the Home Office about the condition of Philip Street and other public manure wharves. A government inspector then recommended that the shipment of nightsoil from Philip Street wharf should be discontinued, but the Liverpool Town Council flatly refused to adopt the suggestion.[2]

If the administrative arrangements continued to be of great help to the proponents of inactivity, that was only to a small extent fortuitous. Failure to attempt a comprehensive reform of local adminstration was a symptom of the same attitude as led to the neglect of such administrative powers as did exist and which could have been used to effect a far greater improvement in urban conditions than was actually achieved. It was significant that measures of social improvement of all kinds went hand in hand with the reform of local government in the last quarter of the nineteenth century. The Public Health Act of 1875 was the first to put some semblance of order into the national sanitary administration by dividing the whole country into urban and rural sanitary districts with clearly defined duties and subject to the supervision of a single central department, the Local Government Board, which had been created in 1871; existing local authorities of one kind or another were fitted into the new pattern as far as practicable, the borough council, whenever one existed, being made the local sanitary authority, and existing Improvement Commissioners being similarly converted elsewhere.[3] Before the end of the century the boroughs, the counties, the county districts, the parishes and the metropolis all underwent substantial reform, so that a local government system was established which, though by no means uniform, was reasonably coherent and was capable of facilitating a wide range of activities.

In the last quarter of the century the prospects for town improve-

[1] *Royal Sanitary Commission, 2nd Report*, vol. III, Part II, p. 394. Both Acton and Chiswick were outside the metropolitan area defined by the Metropolis Local Management Act of 1855, but the sewers of Acton were connected to the main drainage system of London completed by the Metropolitan Board of Works.

[2] *Ibid.*, vol. III, Part II, p. 393. [3] Keir, *op. cit.*, p. 506.

ment were much better than they had been for several generations. On the whole the condition of most towns was still very nearly as bad as it had ever been. But recognition of their most pressing problems was much more widespread, there was growing willingness to do something positive about them (though there were still serious limitations on the type of action regarded as suitable) and a more effective administrative system was in course of creation.

Simon had already recognized a change in the public attitude and, writing of the year 1871 he declared that 'we now . . . were working amid general goodwill and amid a constantly increasing interest of the public in the matters which formed our sphere of duty.'[1] Even a little earlier there were signs of a change for the better in some quarters. By 1864 *The Builder*, edited by George Godwin, who had so thoroughly denounced the apathy and neglect of the previous decade, was declaring that 'the tide of improvement has sternly set in'.[2] It noted with pleasure that the government had at last partially accepted plans for a Thames Embankment, which its predecessors had been ignoring for forty years. But it recognized that a still stronger public opinion was needed if the scheme was to be successfully concluded. A year later it was welcoming the programme of improvements passed by Parliament, with the hope that they might enable London to bear comparison with Paris. It pointed out that even the recent improvements of London were mainly the work of large private estates, such as the Grosvenor, though some such estates remained sunk in inactivity; that where land ownership was minutely subdivided, private improvements were impracticable; and that the municipal authorities or Parliament must carry them out in the interest of the public.[3]

Occasionally there were almost prophetic suggestions, conceived on a magnificent scale. Such a one came from Godwin when, roused by the timidity of Parliament's attitude to London railway schemes, he proposed in 1864 the preparation of a Greater London plan, to cover the estimated expansion of the next hundred years, and 'designed and arranged for drainage and sewerage, water supply, intercommunication, and whatever may be the essentials in a city of immense population'. Such a plan would, he claimed, become necessary at last.

---

[1] Simon, *op. cit.*, p. 320. [2] *The Builder*, vol. XXII (1864), p. 94.
[3] *Ibid.*, vol. XXIII (1865), p. 152.

'The principles generally of planning the area of London; the spots which should be regarded as centres existing, and the directions that routes should take; the *degree* in which railways should trench upon open spaces, and upon those routes of the nature of streets which must always be required; and the several kinds of traffic to be provided for by the railways, as well as the species of engine and train best adapted to each kind, have never yet been considered as they should and might be by an architect or engineer, or by a commission well constituted and advised. Even Wren and Gwynn,[1] from whom much yet might be learned, considered in their plans, each, not the whole of the London of his time, and could hardly have foreseen the growth of a town district which seems likely to extend to Staines or Windsor, or the necessity for, and invention of, the appliances which now exist, for connecting quarters so far apart as those of the east and the west of the actual or future London. But to deliver over the metropolis of an empire, and home of at present nearly three millions of people, to the chances of its present agglomeration, on the assertion gravely made by some engineers, that it is impossible to foresee future requirements, as of railways,—but that circumstances must be met as they arise,—and allowing possibility for public good to be sacrificed to private ends, as those of speculators,—seem to us neither to be what should be regarded complacently, nor to be in the slightest degree necessary.'[2]

Such a proposal as this had no immediate practical result. It went far beyond those necessities which were beginning to be widely recognized. But in the extension of many smaller elements in sanitary activity and town improvement there was clear evidence that apathy continued to be dissipated. Some of the expected town improvements were indeed forthcoming, notably sanitary, though disguised in the architecture of increasing platitudinousness. And there were other sanitary gains. Inquiry in 1879, for instance, revealed that most towns of substantial size appeared to have secured a constant water supply of adequate quantity, though there were still some surprising exceptions.[3] Piecemeal improvement, the attempt to remedy some

---

[1] The author of *London and Westminster Improved* (1766).

[2] *The Builder*, vol. XXII, p. 161.

[3] G. P. Bevan, *The Statistical Atlas of England, Scotland and Ireland*, pp. 65–8. The towns which did not possess a constant water supply included Windsor, Birkenhead, Chester, Crewe, Exeter, Torquay, Bournemouth, Portsmouth, Hitchin, St. Alban's, Ashford (Kent), Beckenham, Chatham, Folkestone, Gravesend, Tunbridge Wells,

specific and glaring deficiency without considering very far how it was related to other defects, was all that had so far been attempted, but it had at last been carried far enough to yield useful, though moderate, benefits.

As experience accumulated, however, it was becoming clear that not only the scale of what had so far been done but also its very nature was inadequate. To build a new reservoir, to extend a sewer, to insist that the local slaughter-houses be regularly cleansed, all these were valuable services and, once they had been performed, were recognized as essential elements in the proper management of a town. But they had only a minor influence on the character and appearance of the town. They were services which had to be provided in much the same form everywhere. Every town, however, had its own local features, among them in most cases some district at least which it would have preferred to have quite otherwise in character and appearance. To make the desired change, even in a very limited degree, was impossible on the old lines; improvement had to be considered not in terms of single, separate services, but radically, so that in the extreme case it might have to involve a completely new beginning.

There was no sudden change in people's attitude to town improvement. All through the nineteenth century there had always been a few who had thought in terms of a thorough transformation of the urban environment. Towards the end of the century there were more, but still most of them did not contemplate changing a complete town, only limited districts. Within those severe limits, however, improvement in driblets was no longer the only alternative to gradual deterioration; there was still plenty of scope for the old reforms: putting a water-tap in a house, trapping the drains, sweeping the streets more often, and so on; it was also no longer out of

Colne, Haslingden, Rawtenstall, Barnet, Ealing, Hornsey, Bilston, Hanley, Longton, Stoke-on-Trent, Epsom, Guildford, Kingston-on-Thames, Hastings, Salisbury, Dewsbury, Heckmondwike, Llandudno and Swansea.

It is clear from the inclusion of such places as Bournemouth, Torquay and Tunbridge Wells in this list that places which even at this time took some care over their outward appearance were just as capable as less elegant places of neglecting the elementary needs of some of their inhabitants. There was no escaping this attitude. The most fulsome celebrants of contemporary civic progress could not ignore it; e.g. an almost blindly uncritical account of the growth, prosperity and achievements of Dundee in the nineteenth century found it necessary to quote a complaint of 1799 about the inadequacy of the water supply, and to point out that this inadequacy had continued for seventy years thereafter. (J. Thomson and J. Maclaran, *The History of Dundee*, p. 132 and pp. 155–6).

76

the question to recondition completely or to demolish and rebuild a house, a court, a street, a group of streets, nor was it out of the question to try to induce a shift of population from one district to another. There was in fact the beginning of a movement for town improvement which was something just a little more than a merely sanitary movement.

PART TWO

THE SEARCH
FOR A SOLUTION

CHAPTER IV

The Improvement of Central Urban Areas

THERE were three ways in which the physical structure of towns could be deliberately and fundamentally modified: the buildings and streets which already existed could be transformed in greater or less degree, either by complete demolition and reconstruction or by partial adaptation and renovation; or the whole business of town building could be begun afresh on previously unoccupied sites; or the formation of existing towns could be loosened by spreading their populations over wider areas of continuous building, in which any excessive compactness at the centre would be offset by more open development nearer to the fringe. In the nineteenth century, as in other periods, a great deal of change was continuously taking place in the appearance of the streets, the extent of the built-up area and the urban uses of land, without much consciousness of its relation to the character of the town as a whole. But even some of this unregulated change tended to conform to one or other of these three remedial patterns. And in the later years of the century, when awareness of the deficiencies of existing towns and of the need for some immediate improvement was more general than it had been, all three approaches to the problem of what was to be done about the towns were consciously used.

In improving the physical condition of towns from within, as they stood, sanitary measures of the kind mentioned in the preceding chapter were important. If refuse and excrement were carried away from the vicinity of buildings by a thorough system of drainage and sewerage and by regular collection and street-sweeping, instead of being left to eat into the walls and spread decay through whole blocks of buildings, if cleanliness were further aided by the paving of streets and by the provision of an adequate and constant water-supply, then there was the possibility of a marked change in both the appearance and durability of the streets and buildings of a district. Of two areas built of similar materials to similar designs the clean could be readily distinguished from the dirty by nose or eye. But however comprehensive such sanitary improvements might be they could do no more than make the best of what had already been built, and that best was often very bad. They could help to preserve the fabric of buildings but they could not turn bad material into good. They could not bring light and fresh air to buildings so arranged as almost entirely to exclude them. They could not increase accommodation in districts where there was not nearly enough for all whose employment kept them there. They could not provide space for the free movement of people and traffic where the necessary ground was already occupied by buildings.

It was thus necessary also for someone to pay attention to the number, quality and grouping of buildings if town improvement was to be maintained. But that necessity was not regarded as applicable to the buildings of a whole town. Most of the inhabitants were quite capable of looking after themselves and there was no desire to interfere with buildings in which business was conducted. From the eighteen-forties onwards, however, people were increasingly conscious that the districts inhabited by the working classes were overcrowded, dirty, squalid and decrepit and showed few signs of gradual improvement from within. This was something calling for special treatment, and for two generations the proper housing of the working classes was regarded as the central and dominating element in town improvement. Indeed, it would seem that to a great number of people the problem contained no other element. To the improvement of working-class housing numerous agencies, both public and private, addressed themselves, at first and for many years intermittently and on a very small scale, then gradually more and more comprehensively.

Deliberate efforts to improve the quality as well as the quantity of working-class housing were at first entirely in private hands. Private agencies, practically free of any regulation, provided all housing in the mid-nineteenth century, whatever its quality, and if any individual or group wanted the provision of something better or something as good at a lower price, the only way was for him or them to undertake the business. This was what was done by the philanthropic housing associations, chiefly in London, but also to a very, very small extent in some of the larger provincial cities. These

bodies, which were philanthropic in the sense of ensuring certain
minimum standards and of not raising rents to the maximum which
market conditions permitted, but not in the sense of subsidizing
reforms, began to appear in the eighteen-forties. The earliest were
the Metropolitan Association for Improving the Dwellings of the
Industrious Classes, founded in 1841, and the Society for the Improvement of the Condition of the Labouring Classes, founded in
1844.[1] The activities of such societies showed that no commercial
loss need be involved. The former of these associations, for instance,
opened its first block of dwellings in 1846, having constructed them
at the fairly low cost of £43 3s. 4d. per room; in 1870 this property
was yielding a profit of 5¼ per cent.[2] In the thirty years after the
beginning of the movement numerous similar bodies were created
to carry out the same kind of work. The most prominent among
them were the Improved Industrial Dwellings Co. and the Peabody
Trust. The former, which was founded by Sir Sydney Waterlow,
began to build in 1863 and its first dwellings, which contained 225
rooms, constructed at an average cost of £40 per room, yielded a
profit of 8 per cent.[3] It subsequently extended its activities by borrow-
ing capital at 4 per cent from the Public Works Loan Commissioners
on condition of not paying more than 5 per cent (tax free) to its
shareholders. This maximum was immediately achieved and maintained for several years.[4] The Peabody Trust was founded in 1862
with a donation of £150,000 by George Peabody. To this the founder
added £200,000 in 1866 and another £150,000 at his death, which
occurred a few years afterwards. The activities of the Trust began
slowly, however, and by 1870 it had housed only 400 families, at an
average cost of £113 per room and a profit of 2 per cent.[5] Other
housing societies operating in London in 1870 included the Marylebone Association for improving the dwellings of the working-
classes, which had been established in 1854, the London Labourers'
Dwelling Society Limited, founded in 1861, the Highgate Dwelling
Co. and the Strand Building Co.[6] Similar work had also been done
by various individuals, among them Lady Burdett-Coutts, who had
built property in Columbia Market,[7] a man named Hilliard, who

[1] Sir J. Simon, *English Sanitary Institutions*, p. 213.
[2] G. T. Robinson, 'On Town Dwellings for the Working Classes', in *Trans. Manchester Statistical Society*, 1871-2, p. 76.
[3] *Ibid.*, pp. 81-2. [4] *Ibid.*, pp. 82-3.
[5] *Ibid.*, pp. 73-4. [6] *Ibid.*, pp. 84-5.
[7] *Ibid.*, p. 74.

built model dwellings in Shadwell, and the Hon. Russell Gurney.[1] Practically every undertaking returned a steady, though not very large profit.

In comparison with the small beginning of the eighteen-forties there was a record of substantial progress by philanthropic housing societies. But in proportion to housing needs and to the extent of the building that was taking place contemporaneously what they achieved was negligible. Octavia Hill pointed out in 1875 that all the private efforts of benevolence in London in the previous thirty years had housed only 26,000 people, which did not much exceed the increase of London's population every six months.[2] The work continued, new societies were formed and the numbers accommodated increased, but they remained relatively insignificant. In 1884 it was estimated that 28 associations had incurred a capital outlay of £1,200,000 in housing 32,435 persons.[3] Development accelerated after that, and by 1905 the nine principal associations in London were accommodating about 123,000 people, the largest provision being made by the Artizans', Labourers' and General Dwellings Co. Ltd., which had opened its first building in 1868 and by this time had four estates, covering 280 acres, with accommodation for 40,000 people.[4] Outside London, the work of housing trusts remained so small as to be scarcely noticeable, though some building was done by the Manchester Labourers' Dwellings Co. and the Leeds Industrial Dwellings Co.,[5] and there had been ventures of very little profit by the Bristol Industrial Dwellings Co.[6] and the Newcastle Industrial Dwellings Co.,[7] among others.

The importance of the contribution made to city improvement by housing societies is difficult to assess. It can hardly lie in the amount of accommodation which they provided, for this was relatively small. Nor can it lie in their direct contribution to the removal of the worst

[1] *Ibid.*, p. 85.
[2] G. W. Child, 'How Best to Overcome the Difficulties of Overcrowding among the Necessitous Classes', in *Trans. National Assoc. for Promotion of Soc. Science*, 1878, p. 494.
[3] M. G. Mulhall, 'The Housing of the London Poor. Ways and Means', in *The Contemporary Review*, vol. XLV, p. 234.
[4] E. R. Dewsnup, *The Housing Problem in England*, p. 167.
[5] *Ibid.*, pp. 188–9. The Leeds Industrial Dwellings Co. was founded in 1876 and by 1900 owned 1,000 houses, many obtained by purchase, not as a result of new building. (B. S. Rowntree, *Poverty. A Study of Town Life*, p. 180.)
[6] *Royal Commission on Housing of the Working Classes, Report*, vol. II, p. 231.
[7] *Ibid.*, vol. II, p. 240.

housing and the most serious overcrowding. It is true that some of their building was on sites which had been cleared of extremely decrepit property and that what they erected there was of far better quality than what had been there before. But they were not providing improved accommodation for residents of the same area. Those who had been displaced crowded into the cheapest property near at hand and by the very fact of increased overcrowding tended to reduce its condition to that of the accommodation they had recently left. The housing societies did not cater for the very poor and therefore made no contribution to a major aspect of the problems of urban life. Sir Richard Cross's Committee of 1882 looked into this matter and concluded that 'the buildings of the Peabody Trustees appear to be somewhat beyond the means and unsuited to the wants and special callings of the poorer class of persons occupying areas with which it has been found necessary to deal under the Act of 1875'.[1] A large part of the population earned less than £1 a week, but in the eighteen-eighties the average earnings of the heads of households in Peabody buildings were about 23 shillings per week.[2] In the tenements of the Improved Industrial Dwellings Co. they were 28 shillings per week, and this company stated that it was impossible to house the very poor on commercial principles because their habits entailed too great an expenditure on repairs (up to 50 per cent of the rental instead of the normal 12 per cent), because of the expense of collecting rents from so many poor tenants, and because of the difficulty of getting prompt payment from them.[3]

Probably the greatest importance of the housing societies was in the attention that they attracted, which was out of proportion to the scale of their activities, and in the direction in which their influence was exerted. They recognized two powerful factors in the existing situation: that the density of population in towns was very high, and that all expenditure on improvements must yield a financial return to the body incurring the expenditure; and instead of trying to alter these factors, they acquiesced in them and tried to make the best of them. By so doing they contributed unintentionally to a lowering of standards among those concerned with the improvement of housing. They bestowed the hallmark of sanitary efficiency on high-density housing at a time when congestion was probably the most

[1] *Select Committee on Artizans' and Labourers' Dwellings Improvement, Final Report*, p. v.
[2] Presbytery of Glasgow Commission on the Housing of the Poor, *Report by William Smart on the Housing of the Poor in London*, p. 12.
[3] *Ibid.*, pp. 8–9.

G

serious of town problems; some of their spokesmen gloried in the huge numbers of people they could house upon an acre. And because the housing associations were able to produce a type of building which was commercially adapted to the means of one stratum of the population and was yet healthy, the belief spread that the whole housing problem might be satisfactorily solved by further modifications of the basic principle. In 1900 a group of architects put forward the view that high block buildings were the only practicable way of housing the poorest decently and that local by-laws which prevented the erection of such blocks were thoroughly deplorable.[1] They admitted that so far they had failed as a means of re-housing slums, but thought this could be remedied by adapting the buildings to the mode of life of the poor; they noted with approval one recent 'concession': the abandonment of the practice of including bathrooms; rigid economy was to be the first aim.[2]

But in another respect the influence of housing societies was helping to broaden ideas of town improvement. Their nineteenth-century answer to the housing problem was the accommodation of large numbers of people in blocks of associated tenements. The unit with which they had to deal was not the individual or the isolated family but a body of hundreds of people, and they had to make provision accordingly. Moreover, this need was increased because in many cases they were not putting up a single block but developing a substantial estate with groups of blocks. The practice of the Artizans', Labourers' and General Dwellings Co., for instance, was to build on estates of from 40 to 100 acres.[3] Consequently it was not entirely practicable to limit activity only to the provision of housing, though that was the main objective. Many of the societies built shops on their estates.[4] The Artizans', Labourers' and General Dwellings Co., at the beginning of its history was planning to develop an estate of 80 acres so as to include not only 2,000 dwellings, but also schools, baths and a lecture hall, with three acres of recreation and pleasure grounds in the middle of the estate.[5] A little later a student

[1] J. Honeyman, H. Spalding, W. E. Wallis and O. Fleming, 'Working Class Dwellings', in *Journal of the R.I.B.A.*, 3rd series, vol. VII, no. 11, pp. 249–50.

[2] *Ibid.*, p. 254.

[3] Presbytery of Glasgow, *op. cit.*, p. 10.

[4] Dewsnup, *op. cit.*, p. 167.

[5] Solly Collection, section 4, f. D.34. The Solly Collection of MSS., pamphlets, handbills and press-cuttings is housed in the British Library of Political and Economic Science at the London School of Economics. This entry is an undated but obviously early prospectus of the Artizans', Labourers' and General Dwellings Co., Ltd.

of the problem was commending to public notice the possibilities realized by M. Godin at Guise in France. In his *familistère* there were tenements of from two to five rooms, furnished bedrooms for single men and a variety of communal services including hot and cold baths, a laundry, a restaurant, a library, a reading room with daily newspapers, and a billiard room.[1] Even a convinced opponent of the system of blocks of model dwellings was prepared to make use of the possibilities they suggested for the orderly development of an estate and the satisfaction of the communal needs of its inhabitants. The architect, Robert Williams, declared categorically that model dwellings were not a solution of the housing problem, because they crowded people too closely together.[2] But he suggested that large municipalities might arrange associated homes in blocks not more than four storys high, each accommodating not more than twelve families, with at least half an acre of open space per block, and communal facilities for the whole.[3]

The type of activity undertaken by housing societies inevitably brought such considerations as these into prominence. By so doing they carried housing reform one step nearer towards town planning. Is it fanciful to suggest that there is a link between the work done by housing societies and philanthropists in the provision of estates of model dwellings and the extravagant plans for a new kind of town put forward in various forms in the last thirty years by Le Corbusier and his followers?[4]

Apart from the activities of the housing societies nothing fundamental to a change in the physical structure of existing towns was attempted even on a small scale by private bodies. There were, of course, various activities which modified the condition of urban housing without effecting any basic transformation. There was, for instance, the system of property management first put into operation by Octavia Hill in 1864[5] and still being extended forty years later.[6] She considered that 'the two improvements of people and dwellings

---

[1] W. Hardwicke, 'House Accommodation and Open Spaces', in *Trans. National Assoc. for Promotion of Soc. Science,* 1877, pp. 500-1.

[2] R. Williams, *London Rookeries and Colliers' Slums,* pp. 10–11.

[3] R. Williams, *The People the Nation's Wealth,* p. 11.

[4] For an exposition of their ideas see Le Corbusier, *Urbanisme,* esp. pp. 163–6 (1925 edn.), where increase of density and improvement of circulation are associated as fundamental principles.

[5] O. Hill, *Homes of the London Poor,* p. 17.

[6] In 1903 Octavia Hill's work expanded more than in any previous year. (*Vide* her *Letter to my Fellow-Workers* (1904), p. 2.

must go hand in hand'[1] and that therefore the problem of the housing of the lowest class could be dealt with only by the action of individuals.[2] So her method was to become the landlord of the houses of poor people and exert personal influence to help them to improve their own condition. Among other means she made a fixed allowance for repairs and improvements; if the tenants were not destructive, less needed to be spent on repairs and more was available for improvements, and the tenants themselves had the choice of what improvement they would have.[3] The limitations of what this system could achieve were obvious. It could increase the security and contentment of people brought in contact with it; it could reduce the degree of 'blight' affecting a particular property, but only to a trifling extent could it change the structural character of the property.

Then there were the building societies. They had a contribution to make because, by making it easier for the upper strata of the working class to purchase houses, they might facilitate the general reduction of overcrowding, thus retarding excessive deterioration in the quality of property. Moreover, where they were assisting the purchase of new houses they had a direct interest in ensuring that structurally they were of reasonable quality. Their activity was increasing rapidly in the late nineteenth century.[4]

On the whole, the building societies were concerned with the purchase of single houses by individuals. Conditions which they imposed could therefore not have a comprehensive influence on any district. There were, however, some societies which concentrated their activities more and played a less passive role. The Artizans', Labourers' and General Dwellings Co. was in a sense a combination of a building society with a housing association, for its activities included the acceptance of deposits from the public and the grant of advances to enable workmen to buy the houses that they occupied.[5] A few building societies were little more than estate development companies in disguise.[6] These, of which the 'Liberator' was the most notorious because it achieved the most spectacular failure, were in a

---

[1] *Royal Commission on Housing of the Working Classes, Report*, vol. II, p. 306.

[2] *Ibid.*, vol. II, p. 293.　　　　　　[3] *Ibid.*, vol. II, pp. 291–2.

[4] In 1872 the advances of building societies on mortgage were estimated at rather more than £16,000,000. By 1890 this had risen to £47,760,404. (Sir H. Bellman, *The Thrifty Three Millions. A Study of the Building Society Movement and the Story of the Abbey Road Society*, p. 32 and p. 329.)

[5] Solly Collection, section 4, ff. D.33 and D.34.

[6] *Quarterly Review*, vol. CLXXIX, p. 416.

position to determine the treatment of the estates for which they were responsible. There is, however, no clear evidence that the standards which they applied differed noticeably from those of other private builders; they were not really representative of the building society movement, and the latter cannot be accounted a major influence on the physical appearance of British towns in the late nineteenth century.

There was, however, a great deal of new building in towns during this period, most of it by private bodies. The quality and type of this building did much to determine the character of the town or district in which it was situated. The standard of quality depended in a large measure on the prevalent state of taste, conscience and the law, and also on the extent of the resources of those engaged in building.

The nineteenth century saw a significant change in the latter. In the eighteenth century it was rarely possible for a builder to exert much influence on the manner of laying out an estate, as few builders were in a position to undertake more than a few houses at a time and, indeed, the contractor arranging for every branch of building work was still a rarity. It was early in the nineteenth century that the large building employer with a permanent labour force began to emerge. Big builders of this kind, of whom Cubitt was the outstanding example, played a most important part in the creation of attractive new wealthy residential areas, which they often planned as a whole. But for many years the great mass of cheaper building was done by smaller men who leased land in very small lots and built without much reference to the layout of the neighbouring lots. These smaller men continued to predominate in the building trades. In 1833 the Operative Builders' Union was able to advance its claims successfully in Manchester by attacking the existence of the large general contractors and thus winning support from the more numerous small masters. In Liverpool there was then no general contractor for them to deal with.[1] But by the eighteen-fifties the large general builders were firmly established. In London they held all the big business; the old master carpenters were a vanished race and the master bricklayers and master masons had almost disappeared, displaced by the general building contractor.[2] This meant that in many

[1] R. W. Postgate, *The Builders' History*, pp. 72–3.

[2] *Ibid.*, p. 197. The preponderance of the general contractor was characteristic of the central districts rather than the suburbs. Even after 1900 small master builders and master workmen were still very numerous in the suburbs. (N.B. Dearle, *Problems of Unemployment in the London Building Trades*, p. 19.) For instance, the enormous amount of house-building in West Ham between 1880 and 1905 was mainly the work of small

districts even the lower grades of building were done on a larger scale than before. Larger estates were built as a whole and some sort of uniform plan, however crude, tended to be imposed on them by the builder himself, in his own economic interest.

The changing state of the law was equally influential. A limited amount of control over street widths, the heights of buildings and other matters affecting layout and structure, was exercised from the middle of the century in a few cities through by-laws made on the authority of local Acts of Parliament, but they were the exception, not the rule. The turning-point was the Public Health Act of 1875,[1] which first empowered the Local Government Board to permit sanitary authorities throughout the provinces to make building by-laws. Powers to make by-laws already existed in the metropolis as a result of other legislation.

The system of control through by-laws was by no means perfect. Many places had no by-laws and in 1885 the Royal Commission on Housing found it necessary to recommend that in London 'the vestries and district boards which have not already made and enforced by-laws should proceed to do so, although it is not likely that in all cases such action will be taken until the people show a more active interest in the management of their local affairs.'[2] For the provinces it recommended 'that in all urban sanitary districts the local authorities should be empowered to make by-laws . . . without any previous action on the part of the Local Government Board.'[3] The position improved as a result of amending legislation in 1890[4] and 1891.[5] Even where by-laws existed they were not always strictly enforced. It had been admitted in the eighties that in London, if a District Surveyor brought an action against anyone for infringement of the Building Acts, and the action was unsuccessful, he had to pay the costs out of his own pocket.[6] Thus official zeal was naturally much curbed.

builders with very little capital. (E. G. Howarth and M. Wilson (eds.), *West Ham, a study in social and industrial problems*, p. 12.)

[1] 38 & 39 Vict., c. 55.

[2] *Royal Commission on Housing of the Working Classes, Report*, vol. I, p. 29.

[3] *Ibid.*, vol. I, p. 30.

[4] 53 & 54 Vict., c. 59 (Public Health Acts Amendment Act) which applied to the provinces. It was still not compulsory for all local authorities to make building by-laws.

[5] 54 & 55 Vict., c. 76 (Public Health Act), which applied to London.

[6] J. Hamer, 'What are the best Means, legislative and other, of securing those Improvements in the Dwellings of the Poor which are essential to the welfare of the community?' in *Trans. National Assoc. for Promotion of Soc. Science*, 1884, p. 468.

Building regulations, whether embodied in Acts of Parliament or in by-laws, were not always very satisfactory in content and were hampered by the limits beyond which a large part of the public thought that regulation was not suitable. In London from 1855 until 1894 the statutory requirement for the amount of open space behind any building was related only to the length of the frontage.[1] When the London County Council sought to remedy this by relating the open space requirement to the height of the building the opposition included so eminent a body as the Royal Institute of British Archtects, which proposed merely that there should be a more generous area of open space in proportion to the frontage. Its memorandum included one most instructive suggestion: 'rights of light and air to be excluded [from the Bill], as they are in the nature of private property.'[2] Nevertheless the new principle was adopted in the London Building Act of 1894.[3]

Statutory or by-law control of new building in the late nineteenth century had many deficiencies which were only gradually removed and operated very unevenly over the country as a whole. But, in spite of this, nothing else made so much difference to the physical appearance and condition of British towns. Large parts of them were built under this régime and still survive. They seem a grim and depressing legacy, yet they represent a considerable advance on what came immediately before. The streets of this time were monotonous, but the monotony of order was an advance on the earlier monotony of chaos. They were devoid of all inspiration but at least they were sanitary, exposed adequately to air and moderately to light, and this was a result achieved widely and by deliberate provision, instead of occasionally and more or less by chance.

There was, of course, one other way in which public authorities could safeguard the quality of some of the new building which was needed. This was by undertaking it themselves. Local authorities had been given powers to build working class houses by Lord Shaftesbury's Act of 1851,[4] but the amount of new building for which they were responsible was quite insignificant. During the first thirty years in which the Act was in operation only Huddersfield, Liverpool, and Nottingham made use of the powers which it bestowed.[5] Even

---

[1] Williams, *London Rookeries and Colliers' Slums*, p. 37.   [2] *Ibid.*, p. 53.
[3] 57 & 58 Vict., c. ccxiii.
[4] 14 & 15 Vict., c. 34.
[5] E. Spencer, 'Artisans' and Labourers' Dwellings', in *Trans. National Assoc. for Promotion of Soc. Science*, 1881, p. 611.

then there was no certainty that such action would set any standard of quality. Huddersfield's first enterprise was simply to convert a warehouse into a block of dwellings in 1854.[1] Liverpool in the early eighteen-sixties built some large blocks of dwellings on its own estate and, though they yielded a profit of 4¼ per cent, one of its aldermen a quarter of a century later described the undertaking thus: 'the corporation at that time were very loath to go into it and they cheapened it down to the very lowest point; and the result is that our repairs account every year is much larger than it would have been had they spent a little more at the outset in having the buildings efficiently constructed.'[2]

Municipal building remained unimportant because it was regarded as undesirable and unnecessary. Some thought that housing problems could be solved without recourse to it. Octavia Hill told the Royal Commission of 1884–5 that Shaftesbury's Act was no longer needed now that the public mind was alive on the subject.[3] Others would not believe that there was a general shortage of accommodation. They pointed to the delay in the sale or letting of new houses built by private enterprise and took no account of the fact that differences in income could lead to a surplus of one class of house and a deficiency of another. The clerk to the Edinburgh City Improvement Trustees declared that they did not want to build houses; private enterprise supplied more than the demand.[4] In Glasgow the chairman of the committee of management of the City Improvement Trust thought that private enterprise was building in advance of the wants of the city.[5] He admitted that the working classes favoured municipal building, in the belief that they would get houses for very low rent, but declared, 'we know that we cannot do it, and sometimes in face of a little unpopularity we have to answer the question with a negative'.[6]

The persistent failure of private enterprise to put an end to the housing problem, however, gradually brought increased interest in the possibilities of municipal building, an interest doubtless encouraged by the expansion of municipal activity in other fields. The provisions of Shaftesbury's Act were re-enacted with amendments

---

[1] J. Hole, *The Homes of the Working Classes with Suggestions for their Improvement*, p. 54. A quarter of a century later Huddersfield was also building 100 self-contained cottages. (Spencer, *loc. cit.*)

[2] *Royal Commission on Housing of the Working Classes, Report*, vol. II, p. 497.

[3] *Ibid.*, vol. II, p. 292.   [4] *Ibid.*, vol. V, p. 23.

[5] *Ibid.*, vol. V, p. 54.   [6] *Ibid.*, vol. V, p. 57.

in the comprehensive Housing of the Working Classes Act, 1890,[1] and in the next ten years more use was made of them than in the previous forty. Some of these experiments received more publicity than any which had preceded them. One of the pioneers of municipal housing was Richmond in Surrey, which was able to build at only a moderate density, 22 houses per acre, and yet cover its expenses at rents of only 1s. 5d. per room per week.[2] It happened that one member of the council there, Alderman William Thompson, was a propagandist on a national scale for housing reform and the adoption of town planning, who made his local experience known to a wider public. Yet, in spite of its increase, municipal building to the end of the nineteenth and in the early years of the twentieth century, remained only a small factor in urban conditions. Hardly anyone regarded it as more than a small supplementary source of building suited to a narrow range of circumstances. Even the Fabian Society recommended that it should be undertaken only when it could be done at a fair profit.[3]

Most of the aspects of urban building so far discussed in this chapter have been concerned with the character of *additional* building. It is clear that, as in the past, this was carried out almost entirely by private enterprise to serve private interests and in accordance with personal taste, but that it was subject to an increasing amount of public regulation, which ensured certain minimum standards of structural soundness, ventilation, and avoidance of obstruction of traffic, light, and air. Thus a repetition of the worst evils of mid-nineteenth-century town building was avoided without any very high positive standards being enforced or encouraged.[4]

But there was another important question to be faced. Much of the very worst building of that earlier period still survived and was still in use. How was it to be improved, or demolished and replaced by something better? Something could be expected from the ordinary

---

[1] 53 & 54 Vict., c. 70.

[2] Fabian Society, *The House Famine and How to Relieve It*, pp. 23–4. This scheme is further discussed in Borough of Richmond (Surrey), *Housing of the Working Classes. Memorandum*.

[3] Fabian Society, *op. cit.*, p. 18.

[4] There was a good deal of levelling down as well as up. The minimum space requirements laid down in by-laws often became in practice a maximum allowance. The M.O.H. for Newcastle-upon-Tyne illustrated this from his own experience: 'these modern houses are systematically packed together as closely as ever the building regulations will allow. . . . The new Byker area is populated at the rate of 400 to the acre.' (*Royal Commission on Housing of the Working Classes, Report*, vol. II, p. 252.)

workings of commercial interest. Insanitary, decrepit houses, particularly in the most central situations, were sometimes demolished
because their sites could be more profitably occupied by shops,
offices or railway stations, and the new building that went on there
became subject to current regulations. Yet most of the worst
property survived without change of use or improvement of condition. Since it continued to yield them a profit as it was, there was no
incentive for its owners either to improve or remove it. Thus there
was one field in which general improvement could come only as a
result of public policy carried out by public authorities. In their
concern with the renovation and reconstruction of malignant property public authorities were immediately confronted by some of
the greatest opportunities and the most formidable difficulties in
town development.

Some local authorities obtained by private Act of Parliament
specific powers to demolish or reconstruct unhealthy areas. The
positive achievements under such powers were very restricted, for
the authorities were usually more concerned with demolition than
with reconstruction. In Dundee, a very seriously overcrowded town
where some of the main streets, flanked by five-story buildings,
were only from 12 to 25 feet wide, the Commissioners of Police
obtained a private act in 1871. Fourteen years later the local Police
Commissioner claimed that, as a result, the densely-populated parts
had nearly all been cleared of their unhealthy dwellings and new
wide streets, 40 to 60 feet across had been driven through them.
But the powers to build new dwellings to replace those demolished
had not been used.[1]

In Edinburgh a City Improvement Trust, which consisted of the
Corporation of Edinburgh and had statutory powers, began operations in 1867.[2] Its work was confined within the limits of what could
be done with a 4d. rate for twenty years and was also marked by the
same disregard for reconstruction. Though by 1885 it had dealt
with 17 areas and removed 2,721 houses it had erected only 340
new houses on the sites.[3]

[1] *Ibid.*, vol. V, p. 85. The completeness of reform is not borne out by later investigation. In 1905 the sanitary condition of some districts was so bad that there were 31
whole streets and blocks in 52 others to whose inhabitants the Prudential Assurance
Society would not issue life policies without a special enquiry (Dundee Social Union,
Report on Housing and Industrial Conditions and Medical Inspection of School Children, p. 5).
[2] *Royal Commission on Housing of the Working Classes, Report*, vol. V, p. 22.
[3] *Ibid.*, vol. V, pp. 22–3.

A City Improvement Trust had also been active in Glasgow since 1870, with powers derived from a private act of 1866. This, too, was concerned mainly with demolitions and street improvements rather than re-building.[1] It was also hampered because its activities were limited to areas specifically defined in the Act. Since the passage of the Act other areas had deteriorated, but there was no power to deal with them in the same way.[2] Thus, although between 1866 and 1885 over £1,600,000 was spent on improving the older parts of the city, with the imposition of a burden of £475,000 on the rate-payers,[3] it was clear that much remained to be done.

A small amount was also achieved in various places through the compulsory re-housing required by the Government in cases where either public or private bodies, for constructional purposes of their own, displaced population in crowded districts. In London, between 1884 and 1902, officially approved schemes displaced about 18,000 persons and re-housed nearly 15,000.[4] In the whole country, between 1886 and 1902, schemes approved by the Local Government Board under acts promoted by companies and local authorities provided for the displacement of 29,442 persons and the re-housing of 21,317.[5]

It is probably safe to assume that the condition of most of the districts affected was somewhat better after re-housing than before. But to the country as a whole these schemes made very little difference; valuable progress was being made in some districts under local acts, but most places had no legal powers to require or undertake reconstruction. Something more comprehensive was necessary for there were great numbers of houses and districts the reconstruction of which was clearly an urgent matter of public interest, while the interest of their owners was to do nothing about them. Octavia Hill used her own experience to put the situation in vivid relief in an essay called 'Why the Artisans' Dwellings Bill was wanted', written in 1874. She noted the impossibility of letting light and air into some of the courts she knew as long as the existing building layout was unaltered:

'The houses all round belonged to owners who had no interest in awarding a larger share of light and air to the dwellers in the

---

[1] *Ibid.*, vol. V, pp. 44–5.　　[2] *Ibid.*, vol. V, p. 45.　　[3] *Ibid.*, vol. V, pp. 44–6.

[4] *Joint S.C. of H. of L. and H. of C. on Housing of the Working Classes* (1902), *Report*, p. 19.

[5] *Ibid.*, pp. 134–9. The London figures cited above do not appear to be included in this total as the schemes concerned were under the supervision of the Home Office, not the Local Government Board.

court. Nor was there any means of compelling them to do so, since no Building Act lays down the amount of distance which must be allowed between the walls of buildings which have stood where they do now for many years. All that private effort unaided by statutory power could do to minimise the evil had been or might be done, . . . but who among us could ever move back that great wall which overshadowed the little houses and made twilight at mid-day? Who would give space to move the water further from the dustbins, and the drains further from the ground floor windows? Who could remove the house at the entrance under which the archway passed, or that at the end, and let a free current of air sweep through the closed court? None of us.'[1]

Only a public authority, armed with powers of compulsion, could deal effectively with such a situation. In the later nineteenth century two sets of measures were passed to assist local authorities in providing a remedy. First, there were the Torrens Acts which enabled local authorities to compel the owner of an insanitary house to demolish or repair it at his own expense. They took their name from the private member who promoted the first of the series, the Artizans' and Labourers' Dwellings Act of 1868.[2] Until 1890 it rested with the local authority whether it exercised the powers which they conferred or not. Then there were the Cross Acts, named after the Home Secretary responsible for the first of them, the Artizans' and Labourers' Dwellings Improvement Act of 1875.[3] They enabled local authorities to prepare reconstruction schemes for whole areas of insanitary property and they also were purely permissive enactments until 1885.

Both the Torrens Acts and the Cross Acts, as their titles indicated, were designed simply to assist in the maintenance of an adequate standard of working-class housing. Action under the Torrens Acts was concerned with too small a unit, the individual house, for it to make much difference to the state of a town as a whole, particularly as few authorities used the rebuilding provisions which were introduced in 1879.[4] But the Cross Acts had larger possibilities. In them for the first time local authorities were encouraged to plan in advance

---

[1] O. Hill, *Homes of the London Poor*, pp. 77–8.
[2] 31 & 32 Vict., c. 130.   [3] 38 & 39 Vict., c. 36.
[4] *Select Committee on Artizans' and Labourers' Dwellings Improvement, Final Report*, p. x. This was attributed to a misapprehension that in all cases the Cross Act provided a suitable alternative method.

the layout of limited areas under their control. This could not be called town planning, for the restrictions on what might be done were severe, but it was a step towards it. A reconstruction scheme could be carried out only where there was an area of definitely insanitary property. It need not, however, be absolutely limited to such an area. Neighbouring land could be included if this was desirable for the sanitary efficiency of the whole scheme. But the nature of the replanning that could be attempted was largely governed by an obligation imposed on the local authority to arrange for the provision of new accommodation, either within the area or close at hand, for at least as many working-class people as had been displaced by the scheme. The stringency of this obligation was relaxed a little by an amending act in 1879[1] which permitted the new accommodation to be built in any situation which was as convenient as the old. This was not as useful a concession as it might have been, because local transport was still inconvenient and deficient in quantity, and casual employment kept workers tied to a very limited area. Because they were housing measures first and foremost the Cross Acts could not do much to promote desirable changes of use in the land of different districts of a town.

Nevertheless, within these narrow limits, substantial improvement was possible in the physical condition of the worst urban areas. The actual achievement, however, was decidedly modest. A few considerable schemes were carried through, the largest in the period while exercise of the powers was still optional being in Birmingham, where, under the impetus of Joseph Chamberlain, civic improvement had become a major issue of local politics. This particular scheme affected 43¼ acres in a district of 93 acres. It involved making a wide new street through an insanitary district and continuing it into the best part of the town. As the corporation was able to acquire some of this better district and the effect of the continuation was to raise the value of property, it was able to recoup some of its loss on the insanitary part of the scheme. Moreover, as it did not need to acquire the whole district, but had power to select for purchase any 43 of the 93 acres, it was in a position to negotiate reasonable prices with property owners. Thus it was estimated in advance that the net financial loss on the scheme could be kept down to about £500,000, which meant an addition of 3d. or 4d. to the rates. In justification of this expense it could be pointed out that the death-rate in the eight

[1] 42 & 43 Vict., c. 63.

most unhealthy streets had been reduced from an average of 53·2 per 1,000 for the three years before reconstruction to 21·3 per 1,000 for the three years after it.[1]

In this Birmingham scheme astute attention to local conditions helped to reduce net expenditure, but most authorities found costs so heavy in proportion to what was achieved that they were disinclined to attempt very much under the Cross Act. One writer, reviewing the first six years of its operation, observed that when it was first passed local authorities regarded it as a great boon, but when the cost of strictly carrying it out became apparent, they sought relief from their responsibilities. In Brighton, Dover, and Hastings the Act was practically abandoned. Derby adopted an improvement scheme for 7½ acres at an estimated cost of £38,000 and obtained a confirmation Act from Parliament, but then declined to carry it out. Newcastle-upon-Tyne threw over a scheme because of the cost of rehousing displaced persons, but, with the approval of the Local Government Board, carried most of it through by means of a local Act, without provision for re-housing.[2] In 1881 the Chairman of the Commissioners of Sewers of the City of London commented sadly on two improvement schemes carried out by his authority: 'If we had given every man, woman and child £100 or £150 to start them in life somewhere else, it would have been cheaper to the ratepayers.'[3]

In London generally the cost of improvement schemes was exceptionally heavy and discouraged their application to anything near the extent that was desirable. Up to 1882 the Metropolitan Board of Works dealt with 14 areas covering 42 acres, inhabited by 20,335 persons in 5,555 separate holdings. Under these schemes it provided new accommodation for 22,753 people in 6,206 separate holdings and sustained a net loss of £1,115,836, apart from what it spent on the construction of new streets.[4] Altogether, until it was succeeded by the London County Council, the Metropolitan Board of Works

---

[1] *Royal Commission on Housing of the Working Classes, Report*, vol. II, pp. 444–7. The Birmingham improvement scheme was a long way from completion at the time of this report and its financial outcome still doubtful; all through the eighteen-eighties it was imposing a greater financial burden than expected. For a full account of the scheme and its finances *vide* C. Gill and A. Briggs, *History of Birmingham*, vol. II, pp. 77–82.

[2] Spencer, *op. cit.*, pp. 606–7.

[3] *Select Committee on Artizans' and Labourers' Dwellings Improvement, Interim Report*, p. 134.

[4] *Ibid., Final Report*, p. v.

proceeded under the Torrens and Cross Acts in 22 areas covering 59 acres and was obliged to pay over £1,500,000 more for property than it could obtain by its re-sale after clearance for the construction of artisans' dwellings.[1] In most of the great cities the situation was much the same. In Glasgow it cost £1,600,000 to deal with 80 acres of slums and Liverpool spent £130,000 on 4 acres.[2]

A combination of circumstances produced this situation, which was so discouraging for those interested in comprehensive town improvement. They may be summarized by saying that there were factors at work in determining the price at which local authorities could acquire property which had no part in settling the price at which they could sell it. The purchase price was raised because the value of the property was influenced by the competition of all types of commercial use for it, and in many cases also because of arbitrary additions in the assessment of compensation. The selling price was kept down because it depended on the effective demand for only one type of land use (working class housing), at least on most of the area, and that was not the most lucrative use. Moreover, although when it was purchasing property the authority had to compensate every interest which might conceivably be injured, when it was selling the property after improvement of the site it could not obtain payment from every interest which had gained by the improvement.

The purely commercial influences which tended to increase greatly the cost of town improvements are fairly obvious and can be illustrated briefly. They were due mainly to the growth in the size of the towns themselves. A central urban situation held many commercial advantages for a great many people engaged in very varied types of business. As the size of towns and the scale of business activity grew, competition for sites in the restricted central area increased and rents were steadily forced up. Many of the most insanitary housing districts survived in just such areas and whether the property in them was wanted by a private business or a public authority it could command a high price.

What was happening in the mid-nineteenth century can be illustrated by the following estimate of the course of rents in London:[3]

---

[1] Conference of Delegates on questions concerning the Housing of the People, *Report of the 'Financial and Compensation Committee' of the Conference*, p. 8.
[2] *Ibid., loc. cit.*
[3] Mulhall, *op. cit.*, p. 233.

Year	Population	Rent per house	Rent per inhabitant
		£ s.	£ s.
1831	1,655,000	31 6	3 15
1841	1,948,000	35 10	4 14
1851	2,362,000	40 1	5 2
1861	2,804,000	43 0	5 15
1871	3,254,000	51 0	7 1
1883	3,955,000	64 12	8 15

This does not reveal the full difficulties because a specially steep rise in values was concentrated in a comparatively small area. Before the end of the century land in the neighbourhood of the Bank was believed to be approaching £1,000,000 per acre in value.[1]

The same thing was happening elsewhere. In Liverpool about 1840 land could be obtained in Oldhall Street for about £2 10s. per square yard. Thirty years later it was costing four or five times that amount, while land rather nearer the Exchange was selling for £25 to £30 per square yard.[2] In Water Street also the value of property multiplied four or five times during the fifteen years before 1870.[3] There was an equally striking increase about the same time in land values in the commercial centre of Manchester, as shown by the following table:

Value of land per sq. yd. in certain streets in the centre of Manchester[4]

Street	1862 Minimum	1862 Maximum	1871 Minimum	1871 Maximum
	£	£	£	£
Market St.	25	40	70	95
Cross St.	10	20	65	85
Princes St.	10	18	32	45
King St.	10	15	35	45
John Dalton St.	10	12	30	45
Mosley St.	15	20	30	40
Oldham St.	10	15	25	40
Deansgate	5	12	15	40
Piccadilly	10	18	25	35
Corporation St.	5	15	12	35

In the face of such developments it is hardly surprising that town improvement should have been an expensive business. For not only

[1] B. F. C. Costelloe, 'The Housing Problem' in *Trans. Manchester Stat. Socy.*, 1898–9, p. 53.
[2] J. Stonehouse, *The Streets of Liverpool*, p. 25.
[3] *Ibid.*, pp. 58–9.
[4] H. Baker, 'On the Growth of the Commercial Centre of Manchester', in *Trans. Manchester Stat. Socy.*, 1871–2, p. 94.

were land values soaring but, competitively, a local authority contemplating an improvement scheme was worse situated than a private purchaser. The latter was rarely restricted in his choice of a site to the property of a single owner; he could play off one possible vendor against another, whereas the local authority usually wanted the whole of a compact area and, far from being able to bargain with competing sellers, was often confronted by an owner who knew that failure to acquire his property would wreck the entire project. The intended safeguard against the weakness of this position was the power of compulsory purchase given to local authorities, but that raised additional problems which will be considered a little later.

The additional financial difficulties caused by the obligation to sell cleared land for the erection of working class housing instead of for the most profitable commercial use were a constant source of complaint. The Metropolitan Board of Works, for instance, carried out an improvement scheme in Whitechapel and Limehouse and sold a site there to the Peabody Trustees for £10,000. If it had been empowered to sell the same site for commercial purposes it could have obtained £54,000 for it, so that an extra burden of £44,000 was thrown on to the ratepayers.[1] In 1882 the Metropolitan Board of Works estimated that altogether its expenditure on schemes under the Cross Acts had been increased by £560,000 because of its obligation to rebuild working-class dwellings.[2]

Apart from the weakness of their position in the property market, local authorities were further handicapped by public policy in the estimation of the extent to which public improvements injured private property and to which compensation ought to be paid to property-owners. Scarcely anything has so strongly influenced the power and will of public bodies to improve the distribution of land under their authority among its various uses, or to improve the quality of the property erected on it for one particular use, as the way in which the payment of compensation has been assessed, while the extent to which the collection of betterment has been permitted or been practicable has had a similar, though less powerful, influence. The development of practice regarding compensation and betterment is worth studying.

There can be little doubt that in the late nineteenth century the

---

[1] *Select Committee on Artizans' and Labourers' Dwellings Improvement, Interim Report,* p. 208.
[2] *Ibid., Final Report,* p. v.

assessment of compensation under the Torrens and Cross Acts was unreasonably favourable to property-owners and a serious drag on improvement. That was due partly to the provisions of the Acts themselves and partly to the way in which they were interpreted in practice, for the legislation left very wide scope for different interpretations of what ought to be considered when determining compensation, and for many years no amendment was made to clarify the position. A symptom of the Parliamentary attitude was the remarkable change in the Torrens legislation when, as a result of the amending Act of 1879, the owner of a condemned house could require the local authority to purchase it, a provision which remained in force until 1885.

Local authorities purchased by agreement if possible; otherwise they could purchase by compulsion at prices determined by arbitration. Prices paid by agreement were to a considerable extent determined by what both parties believed might be awarded if they took the matter to arbitration. The Select Committee of 1882 declared that the intention of the Cross Acts had been to guard against any excessive valuation of property but admitted that they had not in all cases done so, and attributed this failure to the inclusion in the 1875 Act of the words 'due regard being had to all circumstances affecting such value'.[1] This left a great many opportunities for adding to the valuation. In one town where the local authority had purchased property by agreement at nine or ten years' purchase an arbitrator awarded a price for similar property that represented sixteen years' purchase.[2] The Royal Commission on the Housing of the Working Classes went into the question and declared that excessive sums had been paid for land acquired both by agreement and compulsorily under the Cross Acts. It cited the example of a large area at Swansea, for which the price paid was more than one hundred times the annual rateable value.[3]

In fact the quest for compensation under the Housing Acts became the province of the racketeer. In all schemes there were deliberate attempts to obtain excessive compensation[4] and very many claims, especially in London, were completely fictitious. It was indeed alleged in the early years of the Cross Acts that only 3 per cent of

[1] *Ibid., Final Report*, pp. vi–vii.
[2] Spencer, *op. cit.*, p. 608.
[3] *Royal Commission on Housing of the Working Classes, Report*, vol. II, p. 706.
[4] *Select Committee on Artizans' and Labourers' Dwellings Improvement, Interim Report*, p. 139 and p. 179.

the small claims were genuine. After all, it was always worth trying because even if the claim failed altogether the claimant was granted £20 for costs,[1] which all added to the expense of an improvement, as well as increasing delays. And if the claim were successful, the success might be substantial. At any rate the prospect was sufficiently alluring for outsiders to try to buy up property as soon as they knew that it had been scheduled for inclusion in an improvement scheme.[2] It might well seem that the sweeping condemnation of the existing compensation system which was voiced in 1881 by the Chairman of the City of London Commissioners of Sewers was justified; he described it as 'a premium on evil-doing, a man gets a reward for letting his property be condemned'.[3]

Arbitrators defended themselves against charges of unfairness. Some suggested that the high costs were quite independent of any bias in their decisions. One of them, B. B. H. Rodwell, who was also a Member of Parliament, declared that 'there must always be pecuniary loss to any city or town by these improvements . . . and if you wait until you can recoup yourselves, you may go on and have another plague of London; you must make up your minds to pay for getting rid of this nuisance in some way or other'.[4] He stated that he based his provisional award on an examination of books and accounts and on income-tax assessments if they were available. Then he heard objections formally and made his final award on the basis of the evidence submitted, having himself made private inquiries about selling prices in the district.[5]

Critics, however, were sceptical of the amount of attention which most arbitrators paid to this last point. They contended that the evidence produced before arbitrators was concerned simply with local estimates of the value of property, not with actual selling prices.[6] Moreover, even if compensation were based on an examination of accounts, it did not follow necessarily that any particular account was strictly relevant to the question, or that calculations based on it were not exaggerated. One member of the Metropolitan Board of Works stated that 'when a house is declared to be more or less unfit for human habitation, a very small improvement is made by the owner of it, and he claims four or five years' additional value,

[1] Spencer, *op. cit.*, p. 610.
[2] *Select Committee on Artizans' and Labourers' Dwellings Improvement, Interim Report*, p. 139.
[3] *Ibid., loc. cit.*
[4] *Ibid., Interim Report*, p. 200.
[5] *Ibid., Interim Report*, pp. 179–80.
[6] *Ibid., Interim Report*, p. 165.

and gets it, so that it is a loss to the ratepayer instead of a gain'.[1] There was also the important question of compensation for loss of trading profit when business premises were taken over for an improvement scheme. The Select Committee of 1882 thought it doubtful whether the Cross Acts had intended that any compensation at all should be awarded for this reason, and said that certainly if the business could be set up again in the immediate neighbourhood, compensation should be confined to removal expenses.[2] But, in fact, it appeared to be the general rule that if a local authority wished to acquire property it had to buy out the trade interest.[3] Some arbitrators also apparently took the view that the very fact of compulsory purchase was a hardship which called for additional financial recognition. Critics claimed that 'an addition is made to the compensation money of ten, and in the country sometimes of fifteen or twenty per cent, according to the practice which has grown up under the Land Clauses Consolidation Acts,[4] in respect of the compulsory expropriation of the owner'.[5]

There were thus various additions to a basic estimate of compensation which was already high since, as it was put in 1890, 'owners of insanitary houses have obtained compensation based on the full nett income obtained from the property, when their rents have been swollen by the very overcrowding which has compelled public action to be taken, and their expenses have been kept down by the very neglect of repairs and sanitation by which the "insanitary area" has been created'.[6] The Cross Committee in 1882 recommended that if a house was beyond repair at a reasonable cost, its value should be only that of the land and materials, and the land should be valued

---

[1] *Ibid., Interim Report*, pp. 239–40.　　　　[2] *Ibid., Final Report*, p. vii.

[3] *Select Committee (H. of Lords) on Town Improvements (Betterment)* (1894), *Report*, p. iv and p. 17.

[4] 8 & 9 Vict., c. 18, and subsequent amending acts. Most of the provisions of the original act were still operative.

[5] Conference of Delegates on questions concerning the Housing of the People, *Report of the 'Financial and Compensation Committee' of the Conference*, p. 9. This conference was quite widely representative. The bodies which participated in it were the Allotments and Small Holdings Association, the London Liberal and Radical Association, the Mansion House Council on the Dwellings of the Poor, the Metropolitan Radical Federation, the National Reform Union, the Women's Liberal Federation, the Working Men's Club and Institute Union, the Financial Reform Association, the Political Committee of the National Liberal Club, the Leaseholds Enfranchisement Association, the English Land Restoration League and the Co-operative Union, Ltd. Among the members of this Financial Committee were R. K. Causton, M.P., R. T. Reid, Q.C., M.P., Graham Wallas and Sidney Webb.

[6] *Ibid.*, pp. 9–10.

only as subject to the evil surroundings in which it was there placed, and not as situated in a cleared space,[1] but no statutory revision was undertaken until 1890. Even then the change did not go as far as had been recommended eight years earlier. The Housing of the Working Classes Act simply laid down that an arbitrator must base compensation on the market value of the property, less deductions on account of the bad state of repair, the shortness of the term for which the property was held, and the fact that the property itself constituted a nuisance which the owner was liable to abate.[2] Not until 1919[3] was compensation policy adjusted to meet the criticism which had been put forward continuously since 1880 at least, and even then not all the loop-holes were stopped, while the problem itself had grown as the valuation of undeveloped land became a more important part of it.

Compensation policy remaining what it was, it was natural that the cost of town improvements continued high in the twentieth century. Financially the schemes of the London County Council were no less burdensome than those of its predecessor, the Metropolitan Board of Works. Between 1890 and 1914 it improved or reconstructed 40 acres of slums, at a cost to the rates of £750,000. In one area of 17 acres around Tabard Street the cost of acquisition was £14,000 per acre although almost all the property there was completely worn out.[4] The experience of Liverpool was similar. Between 1910 and 1912 the corporation reconstructed six areas there, covering between nine and ten acres. It displaced 3,268 persons and re-housed 2,828 at a total cost of £225,000, of which more than £100,000 was for the acquisition of land. One area of four acres contained 295 houses, of which 267 were insanitary, yet it cost £52,000 to acquire.[5]

Such high financial outlays would have mattered less if the financial return which they created had accrued to the spending authority. But that rarely happened. The intangible benefits of health

---

[1] *Select Committee on Artizans' and Labourers' Dwellings Improvement, loc. cit.* It is interesting to note that under a local act of 1867 Manchester had power to close houses unfit for human habitation, without paying compensation; but in fact until 1906 it always paid £15 to the owner of every such house demolished (E. D. Simon and J. Inman, *The Rebuilding of Manchester*, p. 10 and pp. 16–17).

[2] J. J. Clarke, *The Housing Problem. Its History, Growth, Legislation and Procedure*, p. 197.

[3] By the Housing, Town Planning etc., Act and the Acquisition of Land (Assessment of Compensation) Act (9 & 10 Geo. V, c. 35 and c. 57).

[4] Liberal Land Committee, *Towns and the Land*, pp. 28–9.

[5] *Ibid.*, p. 28.

and amenity which improvement schemes produced were to some extent shared by the community whose money was being spent, but the financially measurable increments of value passed mainly to the owners of neighbouring property, though local authorities ultimately gained from some increase in rateable values. There was no doubt that the usual effect of public improvements was to raise land values. Countless examples testified to this and just a few may illustrate what happened over and over again. In London, seven houses in Cannon Street were assessed at £2,770 before the construction of Queen Victoria Street in 1871; in 1875 they were assessed at £3,794, which, at 25 years' purchase, represented a profit of £25,600 to the landowners.[1] In 1896, as soon as the Blackwall Tunnel was under construction the value of the land in the neighbourhood rose from £5 to £300 per acre.[2] In Glasgow, the City Council paid £29,000 for 82 acres at Tollcross for a public park, and immediately the 12 acres adjoining rose in price from £350 to £500 per acre.[3]

Property owners accepted these windfalls gratefully and usually felt no obligation in respect of them. It is a rare mortal who can think of no good reason why he should deserve to have riches showered upon him; and some owners could reflect proudly on an astute purchase. In 1883 an improvement was carried out at Hyde Park Corner which greatly increased the value of the neighbouring houses. The whole cost of the scheme fell on the Metropolitan Board of Works, but the Office of Works invited the neighbouring owners to make a contribution in recognition of the benefit which they had received. All declined, except the Duke of Westminster who gave £3,000.[4]

The question was whether, in such circumstances, property owners should be compelled to make a refund. The proponents of the taxation of land values claimed that their schemes could avoid the the difficulty by obtaining for the public a share in all increments of land value.[5] But there were doubts about the equity of proposals which took no account of the way in which the increased value was created and they never had more than a very moderate amount of support. On the problem of adjusting the incidence of the cost of public improvements, opinion was divided among three main

[1] F. Verinder, *The Great Problem of Our Great Towns*, p. 3.
[2] *Ibid.*, p. 6.   [3] *Ibid.*, p. 7.
[4] *Royal Commission on Housing of the Working Classes, Report*, vol. II, p. 468.
[5] Verinder, *op. cit.*, pp. 22–3.

groups: those who preferred to attempt no adjustment, those who thought provisions for recoupment would be sufficient, and those who wanted power to collect betterment.

Recoupment was quite a simple matter. The essential thing was for an authority to be permitted to acquire more land than it needed for an improvement scheme. Thus the authority itself would be the owner of property adjoining the area of the improvement and undergoing an increase in value as a result of the scheme. From this increment in value the authority might recoup all or part of the loss which it sustained on the scheme itself. Within limits it was possible under the Cross Acts to adopt this practice, and it applied more extensively to some schemes executed under powers conferred by private acts. It seems to have had fairly satisfactory results in the large Birmingham scheme mentioned previously, but in most cases it was accounted a failure.[1] This apparently was mainly because the authority had to acquire all the interests of the property: freehold, leasehold, occupation interest, trading interest; whereas when it came to sell, it was disposing only of the freehold and leasehold.[2]

No exception was taken to the levy of one type of betterment charge. Where some necessary special service was provided and it was clear that certain people or the people of one particular district received additional protection or peculiar benefits from it, in a way that their neighbours did not, it had since the Middle Ages been the continuous practice to impose a special rate on them.[3] This was particularly important in the case of measures to guard against coast erosion or against flooding. Indeed, the first statutory provision for the collection of a levy of this type was in a measure of 1427 authorizing Commissioners of Sewers to supervise works for sea-defence,[4] and differential drainage rates have long been a normal feature of local finance.

But the recovery of incidental increments of value which had accrued to private persons as a result of public improvements undertaken quite independently of their special needs was rather a different matter and one on which there was a much larger body of hostile opinion. The principle was first applied in an act of 1662[5] which authorized an assessment on the owners of property which

---

[1] *Select Committee on Town Improvements (Betterment), Report*, p. iv.

[2] *Ibid.*, p. 17.

[3] *Expert Committee on Compensation and Betterment* (1942), *Final Report*, p. 106.

[4] 6 Henry VI, c. 5.

[5] 13 & 14 Chas. II, c. 2.

had increased in value as a result of street widenings in London. It was also applied in the rebuilding of London after the Great Fire but from 1670 it lapsed in England,[1] though it became firmly established in America. In Great Britain the principle was revived in the Edinburgh Improvement Act of 1827. Under that measure and a supplemental act in 1831,[2] which constituted Improvement Commissioners for twenty years, betterment continued until 1851 to be levied on different owners at different rates up to a maximum (applied in only one case) of 10 per cent of the feu duty.[3]

The power to levy a betterment charge lapsed in this case in 1851 but the principle was not forgotten again. Its first re-application in a general Act, though in a very restricted way, was in the amendment to the Torrens Act in 1879, when it was provided that the compensation paid to the owner of condemned property should be reduced by the amount of any betterment to property of the same owner arising from the execution of the same scheme. There was no provision for a betterment charge by direct levy. Six years later the Royal Commission on the Housing of the Working Classes considered the question. It heard evidence on the way in which betterment was charged in New York[4] and heard witnesses who argued strongly that the power to levy such a charge should be made general. Among them was the First Commissioner of Works, Shaw Lefevre, who flatly rejected the argument that if betterment could be charged there must also be such a thing as 'worsement' for which compensation would have to be given.[5] Nevertheless, the Commission was either unconvinced by the arguments or too strongly convinced of the extent of the opposition to their application, for it explicitly refused to recommend the levying of a betterment rate, on the grounds that the principle would be difficult to apply and that such a procedure might cause increased local opposition to improvement schemes.[6]

Various local authorities, however, continued to seek the right to recover betterment. The London County Council included a

---

[1] *Expert Committee on Compensation and Betterment, Final Report*, p. 107.

[2] 7 & 8 Geo IV, c. lxxvi and 1 & 2 Will. IV, c. xlv.

[3] *Select Committee on Town Improvements (Betterment), Report*, pp. 249–50. The commonest rate appears to have been 1½ per cent on the feu duty. (*ibid.*, p. 315.) The Uthwatt Committee in its historical review apparently overlooked this Edinburgh Act and attributed the revival of the power to collect betterment to the General Turnpike Act for Scotland in 1831 (1 & 2 Will. IV, c. 46).

[4] *Royal Commission on Housing of the Working Classes, Report*, vol. II, p. 531.

[5] *Ibid.*, vol. II, p. 474.   [6] *Ibid.*, vol. I, p. 48.

provision for this purpose in street improvement bills in 1890, 1892 and 1893, but it was rejected each time by Parliament.[1] Finally, Manchester Corporation obtained the right in a local Act in 1894, but did not use it.[2] The London County Council continued to be dissatisfied because enforced reliance on recoupment had involved it in loss and therefore it still asked for power to levy betterment as an alternative if it so desired.[3] The whole question was considered by a Select Committee of the House of Lords in 1894, but no clear recommendation emerged. The Committee merely said that the principle of recovering betterment was not unjust, but the effect of public improvements on land values was uncertain. If betterment was levied the owner should have due notice and power to require the local authority to purchase his property at what was its market value before the improvement; any 'worsement' which he sustained in respect of other property should be deducted from the betterment charge.[4] A provision for a direct betterment charge was granted, however, in the London County Council (Tower Bridge Southern Approach) Act, 1895.[5] And in 1909 the Housing, Town Planning, etc., Act[6] permitted local authorities to recover from an owner 50 per cent of the betterment to his property attributable to a town planning scheme. This was the first provision in a public general Act for the direct levy of a betterment charge since the seventeenth century. Provisions of this nature have remained part of town planning law ever since.

Thus very little help in the improvement of old urban centres came from the collection of betterment from private beneficiaries; for even when the principle had been conceded in town-planning schemes, this only affected land which was being newly developed; re-development remained for many years outside the scope of statutory town planning. But re-development, improvement from within by undoing past evil and putting something better in its place, was the obvious way of trying to remedy some of the most pressing problems of town life. In practice, the major effort was devoted to the rearrangement of estates and the rebuilding of the

---

[1] *Expert Committee on Compensation and Betterment, Final Report*, p. 108.
[2] Town Planning Institute, *Town and Country Planning Compensation and Betterment. Report of a Committee of the Institute*, p. 22.
[3] *Select Committee on Town Improvements (Betterment), Report*, p. 140.
[4] *Ibid.*, pp. iii–iv.
[5] 58 & 59 Vict., c. cxxx.
[6] 9 Ed. VII, c. 44.

property on them in order that the working classes might be better housed. This was a costly process, of which both the expenses and the rewards were very unequally distributed, and progress was very slow. If there had been nothing more to the improvement of central urban areas than knocking down old houses and building new ones in the same place the conclusion might well have been reached early in this century that this was a process which offered no prospect of great results within any foreseeable future, that the blighted areas of towns might as well be left to their fate and a fresh start made somewhere else. After all, there were other methods of housing the population.

But there were also other improvements to be effected in town centres. Not all the people of the town lived in positively insanitary areas, but they all needed certain services from the town. They needed to be able to move freely within it and they sought a certain amount of recreation and of open space. Decrepit, overcrowded, insanitary areas constituted not only intolerable housing conditions but also obstacles to traffic and to air. Even technically healthy districts were often unprovided with any open space for recreation and were served only by roads too narrow for the amount of traffic which used them. The increasing force with which these deficiencies presented themselves in the later nineteenth century took the problem of improving established towns beyond mere re-housing or slum clearance.

The attempt to provide increased open space was nothing new. Some attention had been given to it ever since the report of the Select Committee on Public Walks in 1833, but in most places much more was done in the last third of the nineteenth century than before to purchase and lay out public parks. Suitable land near the centre of a town was often expensive and sometimes the virtuous action of local authorities made it more so. After the Woolwich free ferry was established at the ratepayers' expense it was found to have increased by £3,000 the value of 11 acres required for public open space.[1] Some local authorities were able to create parks only near the fringe of their built-up areas, but nearly all of them managed to provide something somewhere.

Where public open spaces still survived from an earlier period there were at last numerous people prepared to take an active part in their preservation. The vigorous work carried on from the

[1] Verinder, *op.* cit., p. 6.

eighteen-sixties by the Society for the Preservation of the Commons in the Neighbourhood of London was a notable contribution.[1] The connexion between housing reform and the preservation and increase of public open space became clearly seen. Octavia Hill was an ardent worker for both causes. In 1883, when she wrote an appeal for funds to buy and preserve as open space the fields between Marylebone and Hampstead where the working people of Lisson Grove and Portland Town had been accustomed to stroll, she discussed the problem in a wider context. She pointed out that there was a need for places to sit in, places to play in, places to stroll in and places to spend the day in.[2] The preservation of Wimbledon Common and Epping Forest showed increasing recognition of the latter need, and the places saved by the efforts of the Society for the Preservation of Commons mostly ministered to the same purpose. Valuable as these achievements were, however, they were probably less urgent than the need to provide some recreational space nearer to the heart of cities. As Octavia Hill pointed out, many thousands of people never reached any open space and there ought to be places of happy out-door amusement close to the homes of those who had no gardens, no backyards, rarely a second room.[3] In London, many churchyards could be adapted as places to sit in[4] and there were many private open spaces. If the owners of the latter wished to make them available to the public the Metropolitan Board of Works had power under the Metropolitan Open Spaces Act, 1877[5] to accept them, but it could not use compulsion. There were some who believed that compulsory powers for this purpose, subject to the payment of proper compensation where the rights and privileges of private property were trenched upon, ought to be conferred by statute on local authorities,[6] but they did not have their way.

Nevertheless there was growing agreement with the conclusion expressed in 1877 by one writer who held such views:

'We are now in a position to affirm that it is an absolute sanitary necessity and duty incumbent upon the sanitary urban authorities to provide, purchase and utilise spaces for the people in all the highly

[1] An account of the activities of this Society is given in Lord Eversley, *English Commons and Forests*.

[2] Hill, *op. cit.*, p. 90.

[3] *Ibid.*, pp. 92–3.

[4] *Ibid.*, p. 91, and Hardwicke, *op. cit.*, p. 508.

[5] 40 & 41 Vict., c. 35.

[6] Hardwicke, *op. cit.*, p. 507.

populated districts of large towns. That adequate means for obtaining fresh air and recreation space should be open to all classes, and be especially maintained where they do not already exist for the use of the children of school age, and for the games and exercise of the young and growing-up generation. That seats should be provided, and in our treacherous climate shelter from weather, for convalescents, invalids and old or infirm persons.'[1]

In a quarter of a century that attitude gained official support, and in 1904 the recommendations of the Inter-Departmental Committee on Physical Deterioration included one to the effect that attention should be paid in building by-laws to the preservation of open spaces.[2] Another was that the duty should be imposed on local authorities of providing and maintaining open spaces in some definite proportion to the density of population and these should be furnished with shelters containing gymnastic apparatus.[3]

Most of the provincial centres of population were less fortunately served than London in the matter of surviving oases amid the desert of bricks and mortar. New public parks established in them were often some way from the centre. This was inevitable because of both physical and financial difficulties. What was less excusable was that often they were equally far from recent additions to the built-up urban core. Local authorities recognized that if their towns were to be satisfactory they must have improved buildings in sanitary streets and they must have more open space; they recognized that each of these reforms was complementary to the other. But they had not reached the stage of trying to effect them jointly. While in one district they were taking advantage of an opportunity to obtain land for a public park, they were at the same time in another district trying to ensure an adequate standard of building through by-law control, under which all the trees and grass disappeared and a new purely residential area appeared with no amenities or open spaces in the neighbourhood. Consequently, though there were considerable improvements in various aspects of urban development, they were not properly related to one another. One quarter received the benefit of one kind of improvement and continued to lack all the others, instead of these being so distributed as to benefit the town as a whole.

[1] *Ibid.*, p.'508.
[2] *Inter-Departmental Committee on Physical Deterioration, Report*, vol. I, p. 85.
[3] *Ibid.*, vol. I, p. 91.

The Improvement of Central Urban Areas

One improvement, the need of which made itself increasingly felt in the second half of the nineteenth century, was relief from the congestion of traffic in the streets. This congestion was probably worst of all in London, and it was there that it attracted most attention, but in some degree it became a problem in every large city. In the earlier stages of growth of most cities the volume of traffic was not such that great attention needed to be paid to it as new streets were built. That was so even in London. When Thomas Mozley, for instance, looked back on the London of his youth, he recalled that

'in 1820 Vauxhall Bridge, Waterloo Bridge and Southwark Bridge had all been completed and opened. It could hardly now [1885] be imagined how little use was made of them, so little traffic was there, and so much did people think of pence in those days. I must frequently have seen the two latter bridges in the middle of the day without a passenger on them, either on foot or on wheels. Enterprise and engineering were actually in advance of the public requirements.'[1]

By the middle of the century the situation was quite different. The paving of streets was extended and road surfaces were improved to bear a heavier weight of traffic, but apart from that people seem to have relied for improvement on the transfer of traffic away from the streets rather than on any change in the layout of streets. New railways, penetrating to the heart of the built-up area, certainly absorbed the longer-distance traffic and by the sixties were carrying much new suburban traffic. Yet this was not all relief for the central streets. Railways were often carried into cities by long viaducts of low arches which perpetuated existing street-widths. Their stations and sidings occupied residential land whose former occupants crowded into the immediate vicinity, and provided a demand for still more congested building, through which in future any new major thoroughfare could be driven only at great cost. And all the time, traffic between places separated by distances measurable in no more than hundreds of yards was increasing and could not be carried by the railways.

In London in the eighteen-fifties these difficulties provoked the revolutionary suggestion that additional local railways should be constructed underground. The construction of the first sections of the Metropolitan and the Metropolitan District railways in the next

[1] Rev. T. Mozley, *Reminiscences chiefly of towns, villages and schools*, vol. I, p. 360.

113

decade showed that this was a perfectly practical idea. Yet neither these nor the tube railways, which began to operate in the nineties, solved London's traffic problem. They merely reduced the rate at which it grew worse.

By the beginning of the twentieth century congestion in the streets had become so serious that urban transport was an important subject of discussion and inquiry. Much of this was concerned with facilities for extending the residential area, but there were other points as well. Realization grew that traffic delays imposed a serious economic cost on business in general. In 1905 a Royal Commission inquired into their extent at several points in London, with the results set out in the table below. The Commission concluded that

AGGREGATE OF STOPPAGES PER DAY OF TWELVE HOURS, 8 A.M. TO 8 P.M.[1]

JUNCTION	N.–S. TRAFFIC			E.–W. TRAFFIC		
	No. of delays	*Total time of delays*	*Total no. of vehicles*	*No. of delays*	*Total time of delays*	*Total no. of vehicles*
		hrs. mins.			*hrs. mins.*	
Piccadilly:						
St. James St.	214	3 41·4	5,018	230	1 47·3	15,456
Strand:						
Wellington St.	245	3 32·5	7,821	259	4 6·5	11,922
Ludgate Circus	297	3 41·2	13,728	301	4 42·6	9,228
Bank:						
Princes St.	337	6 5·3	3,059	—	—	—
King William St.	314	4 41·9	4,822	—	—	—
Queen Victoria St.	—	—	—	262	2 16·4	5,620
Mansion House St.	—	—	—	324	3 6·4	10,967
Threadneedle St.	—	—	—	324	5 5·5	5,459
Cornhill	—	—	—	315	5 1·4	3,216

improved transport in London was imperatively necessary, in the interests of public health and *for the prompt transaction of business*, as well as to make decent housing possible. It declared that the narrowness of the streets was the main obstacle to improvement and that a comprehensive plan for the improvement of streets and main roads should be prepared and continuously implemented as financial considerations allowed.[2]

At the same time others were beginning to complain of the lack

[1] *Royal Commission on London Traffic* (1905), *Report*, vol. I, p. 8.
[2] *Ibid.*, vol. I, p. 103.

of systematic planning in the provision of transport facilities.[1] Charles Booth in 1901 was advocating the refusal of powers to construct any more individual tube railways and the provision instead of a comprehensive, publicly-owned system for all London.[2] The significant word 'co-ordination' was beginning to be used when urban transport was under discussion.[3]

Those who were hopeful of easing the movement of traffic (it was mainly passenger traffic they were concerned with) by introducing more system into the routes and operation of public transport had the satisfaction of seeing some of their criticisms gradually met. But much less was done about the structure of the streets and roads themselves, to adapt them to the nature and volume of the traffic that had to use them. The Commission of 1905 pointed out that 'the difficulty is one of money and progress must be gradual'.[4] Often it seemed so gradual as to be almost imperceptible, both in London and in provincial towns. It was certainly more gradual than the increase of traffic congestion. In 1930 another Royal Commission was unable to find much evidence of improvement in traffic conditions in built-up areas:

'The case of London is, of course, the outstanding example. . . . What is true of London is true also of all, or nearly all, of the great cities of the United Kingdom . . . nothing has been done up to the present that touches more than the fringe of the problem in our great cities. . . . The cramped conditions that were sufficient for the London of a hundred years ago have been perpetuated, and even aggravated, in some cases of modern street reconstruction. This may have been due in some measure to the multiplicity of authorities . . . but in the main it has been the result of lack of vision in which everybody concerned must take a share of the blame. Many who read this Report will be able to recall a mass of mean streets that a generation ago occupied the area where the Strand and Fleet St. meet. They have been swept away and replaced by a noble thoroughfare [Kingsway]. This change epitomises the process we should like to see applied to London as a whole and other cities.'[5]

[1] *Vide*, e.g. A. R. Sennett, *Garden Cities in Theory and Practice*, pp. 1197–8.

[2] C. Booth, *Improved Means of Locomotion as a First Step towards the Cure of the Housing Difficulties of London*, p. 22.

[3] Browning Hall Conference, *Report of Sub-Committee on Housing and Locomotion in London*, 1902–7, p. 14 and pp. 16–17.

[4] *Royal Commission on London Traffic, loc. cit.*

[5] *Royal Commission on Transport* (1930), *Final Report, pp.* 60–1.

The Kingsway project was certainly exceptional. London had nothing else on the same scale. Few provincial cities attempted anything comparable. Street-improvement in the late-nineteenth and early-twentieth centuries was for the most part limited to the provision of a better surface, an occasional widening of some main thoroughfare, and the adoption of a rather wider standard than before for the layout of new streets.

Urban areas changed greatly in the half century before the First World War. For one thing they had to cover a much larger area in order to accommodate a very rapid increase in population. For another, there was much more conscious control over the manner of change. Local authorities were able and willing to spend far more on local services and there was something to show for it. Local indebtedness in England and Wales on account of public health rose from £57,566,000 (representing 7s. 11d. per £ of rateable value) in 1884–5 to £136,440,000 (representing 13s. 5d. per £ of rateable value) in 1905–6. In the latter year nearly half this indebtedness was for highways and public street improvements and for working-class housing.[1] Even where expenditure was devoted to other purposes it often had a great influence on the structure, condition and appearance of towns, especially that part of it concerned with such items as waterworks, tramways, and harbours. Between the years just mentioned local indebtedness increased altogether from £173,208,000 to £435,545,000.[2] In 1884–5 also the total amount of rates raised in England and Wales was £25,667,000, whereas just twenty years later it was £56,048,000.[3] In 1871–2 it had been only £17,646,720.[4]

The major change was that towns had become physically much healthier and socially much more attractive than they had ever been. A Parliamentary Committee of 1906 which drew attention to the overwhelming superiority of life in the towns to life in the country was witness to the accomplishment of a profound change.[5] Yet the change was very incomplete, the new state of affairs very imperfect, the manner of achieving further change haphazard. Some of the worst evils of mid-nineteenth-century towns had been removed.

[1] Local Government Board, *Statistical Memoranda and Charts relating to Public Health and Social Conditions*, p. 90.

[2] *Ibid., loc. cit.*   [3] *Ibid.*, pp. 94–5.

[4] *Royal Commission on Local Taxation* (1901), *Final Report* (*England and Wales*), Appendix, p. 75.

[5] *Select Committee on Housing of the Working Classes Acts Amendment Bill* (1906), *Report*, p. xxiv.

Essential services and a few desirable amenities had been provided by most towns in some way, often not the best way, in some place, often not the most convenient. As new quarters had been added to towns sufficient control had been exercised over their construction to avoid the most lethal mistakes of the immediate past; those less deadly had been perpetuated and multiplied. But progress had been slow and costly. The deficiency of quality in urban conditions had been openly recognized as a deficiency and the incompleteness of remedial achievement was apparent to all. At the end of this period it was still possible to describe conditions in Scotland in these drastic terms:

'. . . unsatisfactory sites of houses and villages, insufficient supplies of water, unsatisfactory provision for drainage, grossly inadequate provision for the removal of refuse, widespread absence of decent sanitary conveniences, the persistence of the unspeakably filthy privy-midden in many of the mining areas, badly constructed, incurably damp labourers' cottages on farms, whole townships unfit for human occupation in the crofting counties and islands, primitive and casual provision for many of the seasonal workers, gross over-crowding and huddling of the sexes together in the congested industrial villages and towns, occupation of one-room houses by large families, groups of lightless and unventilated houses in the older burghs, clotted masses of slums in the great cities. . . . To these . . . add . . . ramshackle brick survivals of the mining outbursts of 70 years ago in the mining fields, monotonous miners' rows flung down without a vestige of town-plan or any effort to secure modern conditions of sanitation, ill-planned houses that must become slums in a few years, old houses converted without necessary sanitary appliances and proper adaptation into tenements for many families, thus intensifying existing evils, streets of new tenements in the towns developed with the minimum regard for amenity.'[1]

England and Wales on the whole were not as bad as that, but there also much remained in the environment that was thoroughly deplorable. A possibility of radical change in urban conditions had been perceived, very tentative steps had been taken towards realizing it, and consciousness of their severe limitations was spreading. There was an incentive to devise some more comprehensive method of control and reform.

[1] *Royal Commission on Housing in Scotland* (1912–17), *Report*, p. 346.

CHAPTER V

The Creation of New Model Villages and Towns

PART of the explanation of the unsatisfactory nature of nineteenth century towns lies in the piecemeal nature of their development. When a town was required to serve some new function the ways in which it could be adapted were seriously limited by the type of building and layout already in existence. The way in which towns grew has already been discussed and it is clear that it was such as to make a well-designed town almost an impossibility. But the difficulties were aggravated because an industrial town was usually not developed in the first place as an industrial town. It was perhaps a village or a local market suddenly invaded by factories and then engulfed by a rapid flood of cheap housing. That was, of course, not true of all industrial towns. Some of them were physically as well as socially new, and their development was a sign of lost opportunity. But the standard was set by places which were characterized by successive graftings of something newer and different on to something older. The tenacity of what had already been created, however faulty it was subsequently recognized to be, made it difficult to re-shape a town once it was firmly rooted. The slow progress achieved in the effort to improve towns from within was discussed in the last chapter. What some keen reformers most wanted was a chance to begin again from scratch and build towns well-suited to life and work, avoiding past errors, without the handicap of having first to remove the physical embodiment of those errors.

Ideal new towns for an industrial era might be elaborate plans in the minds of theorists reacting against the contemporary environment, or they might be creations made manifest in bricks and mortar and in the lives of citizens. The opportunity for a successful fusion of theory and practice varied greatly at different times. It was probably greatest in the early days of factory industry. Once the factory system had become thoroughly established, new model towns appeared mostly in the realm of theory rather than practice, but there were occasional individual attempts to create new industrial settlements; and eventually, as the deficiencies of existing towns became more widely realized, resettlement of industry and population on new sites, at any rate on a small scale, became recognized as one practical contribution to urban improvement. The possibility of such resettlement was never quite forgotten in the nineteenth century, though it was not prominent, and there was a body of thought, writing and practice which makes a clear and unbroken, though tenuous chain, linking the new towns begun after the Second World War with some of the small, carefully-regulated settlements of the early factory system.

For there were some who realized that factory work imposed a new way of life, implying ideally a new kind of environment which could be created only by deliberate effort, and occasionally the effort was made. It was easier then to achieve something positive, for two reasons. First of all, economic conditions sometimes made the foundation of new settlements unavoidable. The very nature of early factory operation, with its dependence on water-power, which was often most conveniently obtained in sparsely-populated localities, and its need for an adequate supply of cheap labour, frequently forced employers to initiate or participate in the formation of new communities. And secondly, if any social reformer wished to adapt an existing settlement to permit a more wholesome life in changed conditions, the scale of urban activities had not become so great as to make a reversal of the course of development almost impossible. Outside London there were very few large centres of population. In 1801 there were in Britain only twenty towns with populations of more than 20,000,[1] and the small rural industrial community was ready to hand as a convenient exemplar for any attempts at social improvement.

The effect of these two favourable sets of circumstances may be illustrated from the experience and achievements of Samuel Old-know and Robert Owen, the one building a new community round a new factory, the other using the industrial village as an experimental cell for schemes of social improvement which he hoped would be of general application.

[1] A. F. Weber, *The Growth of Cities in the Nineteenth Century*, p. 43 and p. 58.

Oldknow was active at Marple from 1790 onwards. The work of building his Mellor factory attracted additional population to the district, but once the spinning mill was in production the demand for labour was for that of women and children. Oldknow preferred to try to build round his factory a community of contented families and therefore deliberately sought to create employment for heads of families. He employed colliers, lime-burners, builders, and farm-labourers on his estate, and provided work for other labourers in building roads and bridges and making other public improvements.[1] Financially, it was not a very successful experiment, mainly because those enterprises which arose from Oldknow's desire to build a community, and which had no necessary connexion with cotton-spinning, absorbed an amount of capital on which he could not afford to continue paying interest.[2] Consequently, like many others, he had to rely on increasing the import of parish apprentices.[3] But the experiment draws attention to the inevitability of a new kind of small community growing up wherever the new factories were established and to the possibility of regulating the conditions of that growth.

Owen came to a rural industrial establishment at a rather later date in its history. David Dale had built his factory at New Lanark in 1784, attracted by the water power of the Falls of Clyde, and had been almost obliged to build houses and let them at low rents in order to induce labour to settle in what was then a rather remote and thinly-peopled district.[4] Owen took charge of this establishment from 1799, and his most successful social experiment, which provided a living example to his contemporaries and guidance for the development of his own theories, was thus carried out in a setting of a kind which had already arisen in many places in response to the industrial requirements of the time. His great achievement was to transform the character of his village without injury to the business on which it depended. In the first thirteen years of his management the proprietors received over £50,000 in addition to 5 per cent on all their capital; more than 2,000 persons were supported without employment for four months at a cost of over £7,000; the output capacity was increased more than five-fold; the village was extended to accommodate an additional population of between 1,100 and

---

[1] G. Unwin and others, *Samuel Oldknow and the Arkwrights*, pp. 162–7.
[2] *Ibid.*, p. 175.   [3] *Ibid.*, p. 170.
[4] R. Owen, *A New View of Society* (Everyman's Library), pp. 26–7.

1,200; and many special comforts were provided for the inhabitants.[1]
A few years later, Owen was buying food, fuel, and clothing to
resell to his workers at cheap but unsubsidized prices.[2] In 1816 he
supplemented these reforms by opening the 'Institution', the educational centre of his village, on which he placed his highest hopes of
guiding his people into the way of perfectibility.[3] New Lanark,
under Owen, became something more than a compact community
living, at the indulgence of its employer, in greater comfort and
happiness than most others. It was all that, and it was also the transformation of a common contemporary pattern into a form which
was intended to be an example for the reorganization of communal
life throughout the world.[4] Owen planned to accommodate everyone
in symmetrically-built villages of 1,200 persons each, at an estimated
cost of £96,000 per village.[5] In fact, never being able for long to
keep on good terms with any set of partners, he was obliged to quit
New Lanark itself, and in spite of many efforts, was never able to
create anything which could replace it as a model.

Owen's plans for the establishment of a complete system of small
industrial communities fell into neglect by reason not only of their
unpractical nature but also of their very association with what were
widely considered his subversive doctrines of social organization.
By the thirties and forties, when the wider adoption of steam power
had made local diffusion of industry a matter of option instead of
necessity, the only significant examples of factory villages were those
which, like New Lanark, depended on a business that had obtained
a firm and prosperous foundation in the early days of expanding
factory production. None of these embodied comprehensive schemes
of social reform like New Lanark, but the opportunity existed for a
mill-owner to take on the position and responsibilities of local squire,
and in some places he did so with a zealous care for the welfare of
his workpeople, building comfortable cottages for them and providing schools for their children. The dangers of such dependence of
workers on their employer were plainly enough revealed by the
repeated inquiries into the truck system, but employer-landlords could
and did confer real material benefits where they chose to do so.

[1] R. Owen, *A Statement regarding the New Lanark Establishment*, pp. 9–10.

[2] R. Owen, *A New View of Society*, p. 32.

[3] R. Owen, 'An Address to the Inhabitants of New Lanark', reprinted in *A New View of Society, and other writings* (Everyman's Library), p. 98.

[4] *Ibid.*, p. 106.

[5] *Weekly Dispatch*, 29th June, 1817.

Cooke Taylor, an acute though not unprejudiced observer, found that Henry Ashworth's employees at Turton counted it a privilege to rent one of his cottages, 'that it was in fact a reward reserved for honesty, industry and sobriety'.[1] He was able to contrast the strong sense of community which he found at Turton and similar places with the extreme non-intercourse which he considered the greatest evil of large towns such as Manchester.[2] There seems little doubt that the inhabitants of these factory villages were more conscious of the relative comfort of their conditions than of the weakness and perhaps indignity of their status. And when Egerton and Turton under the paternal sway of the Ashworths, or Styal under the Gregs is seen against the revelations of the Health of Towns Commission the preference appears inevitable. But it was a preference that for most people was irrelevant. Many industrial villages had swollen into substantial towns, losing their original character in the process, and it was the towns which were growing and which offered the chance of employment; some existing factory villages may have maintained their existence as such, but they were survivals, not young and vital creations, and their relative importance was declining.

Cooke Taylor himself did not accept this view at the time. In 1840 he wrote: 'Before the progress of manufacturing industry met the severe interruption from which it now suffers, it was daily becoming what might perhaps be termed *sporadic*; new mills, instead of being crowded together in streets, were chiefly erected in villages and suburbs, affording employers opportunities of coming frequently into personal communication with their workpeople and exercising a healthy control over their domestic habits and private morals.'[3] And doubtless there were others who believed that the great cities were ceasing to be in the van of industrial progress, like Disraeli's manufacturer who told Coningsby that if he really wanted to see life he should be visiting not Manchester but Bolton and Stalybridge. But the few instances to which Cooke Taylor could refer do not seem adequate to support the weight of his generalization, and subsequent development abundantly confirmed that the trend was strongly in favour of the large town and against the village as an industrial centre.

The inadequacies, and even horrors, of the growing towns, together with distasteful elements in the triumphant *ethos* of bourgeois

[1] W. Cooke Taylor, *Notes on a tour in the Manufacturing Districts of Lancashire*, p. 32.
[2] *Ibid.*, pp. 164–5.   [3] *Ibid.*, p. 140.

society did, however, produce a reaction in a few idealists, who demanded a different sort of community with its nature expressed by a different physical environment. Their schemes remained purely hypothetical, but they kept alive the tradition of reform. Some of them were based mainly on moral and religious considerations, others were primarily concerned with architectural attractiveness and physical comfort. Among the latter was a proposal in 1845 by a London architect named Moffatt to house 350,000 persons at an estimated cost of £10,000,000 in garden villages within ten miles of London.[1] Two years later an association purchased a site at Ilford and invited the public to subscribe £250,000 in £5 shares, to be used for the erection of 800 to 1,000 cottages, provided with main services and with schools, churches, open spaces and public gardens. This plan was for the creation of a dormitory suburb, rather than an industrial village, one of its features being that the payment of rent should cover the provision of a return ticket to London.[2] It is thus an interesting illustration of the early realization that the railway could make possible a widened choice of residential site.

The projects which sprang from strong moral considerations and a concern, like Owen's had been, with general social regeneration were often more elaborate and detailed. Among the most interesting was the plan for a Christian Commonwealth prepared by Minter Morgan and a group of Anglican clergy. This scheme dates from the late eighteen-thirties and was the subject of propaganda in the forties, though a complete account of it did not appear in print until 1850. It was conceived in deliberate opposition to the prevailing spirit of *laissez-faire*. Morgan declared that political economy obscured the perception of moral truth and the laws of justice;[3] that competition was a kind of civil war, promoting national antipathies; that a system could not be the best when it permitted, as *laissez-faire* did, the maintenance of distilleries, gaming-houses and brothels;[4] and that the pursuit of wealth ought not to be the major aim as hitherto it had been.[5] He recognized that the whole of society could not be changed at once but thought that a beginning could be made with the unemployed of the working-class.[6]

[1] A. W. Brunt, 'Experiments Sixty Years Ago', in *The Garden City*, New Series, vol. I, p. 131.
[2] *Ibid., loc. cit.*
[3] J. M. Morgan, *The Christian Commonwealth*, p. 3.
[4] *Ibid.*, pp. 16–17.   [5] *Ibid.*, p. 41.
[6] *Ibid.*, p. 42.

The scheme put forward by Morgan and his colleagues was for a Self-Supporting Institution for three hundred families. These would be housed in four-roomed cottages placed in the centre of not less than 1,000 acres of land; the chief employment would be agriculture, combined, at the discretion of the Committee of Management, with handicrafts and mechanical pursuits. Land would be taken on lease, not purchased, at the outset and Morgan thought that the capital cost could thus be kept down to £45,800. This he brought up to £60,000 to allow for the purchase of food and clothing in the first year. The annual value of produce he estimated at £18,632 (apparently taking no account of differences in the productivity of different soils) and expected an annual surplus of £4,172 after payment of all expenses, including interest at 5 per cent on £60,000.[1] There were to be no beer-shops or 'other pernicious excitements',[2] but for leisure there would be lectures, reading-rooms and music, and in summer cricket, botanic gardens and other recreations.[3] The benefits claimed for such a colony were: parental care, ministerial solicitude, superior education for adults as well as children, religious exercises, regular occupation, early association of ideas, the force of habit, discipline equal to that of the army, greater inducements to good, less incentives to vice, support and comforts in old age, protection of children on the death of parents, increasing attractions of the Institution, freedom from depressing anxiety, influence of gardens and of natural scenery, the pursuits of science, libraries and lectures, ultimate proprietorship.[4] Morgan attempted to launch a 'Self-Supporting Village Society' for the purpose of collecting and imparting information on the subject and encouraging any experiments which seemed to have a prospect of success.[5] He himself tried wherever possible to interest influential people in his scheme, both in Britain and in France, which he visited for this purpose and also in order to study a few special educational colonies[6] in 1845.

It is obvious that Morgan's project had much in common with those of Owen. One of his chief supporters, James Silk Buckingham, made it clear that the similarity was not accidental. In 1846, when he spoke at a public meeting to popularize the idea of the Self-

[1] *Ibid.*, pp. 44–7. [2] *Ibid.*, p. 66.
[3] *Ibid.*, p. 64. [4] *Ibid.*, pp. 88–9.
[5] J. M. Morgan, *Letters to a Clergyman on Institutions for Ameliorating the Condition of the People: chiefly from Paris, in the Autumn of* 1845, pp. 106–7.
[6] Notably one conducted at Petit-Bourg by M. Allier for 130 boys (*ibid.*, pp. 30–3) and one at Mettray for 306 boys (*ibid.*, pp. 70–6).

Supporting Institution, he declared that, twenty years earlier, he and Morgan had agreed that Owen's plan was practicable, but had failed because of the omission of religious instruction and public worship. Similar colonies, like that of the Rappites in Ohio, where this omission had not been made, had, he claimed, succeeded and there was no reason why such a community should not succeed in England.[1] He added that there was a strong connexion between architecture and morals, because if a man lived in a village or the open part of a large town, where all his movements were seen and known, he would be a much better man than in 'a crowded and crooked-lane neighbourhood; and if a man did wrong under such circumstances, no one would speak to him; he would find the place insupportable and would be compelled to go away.'[2]

Buckingham himself published in 1849 an elaborate proposal involving the formation of a public company to build an entirely new town, Victoria, with every advantage of beauty, security, healthfulness and convenience, with its inhabitants divided in due proportions between agriculture and manufacture, and between the possessors of capital, skill and labour.[3] This also was a detailed conception of social organization on the Owenite scale. The city was to be about one mile square, to have a population of not more than 10,000 and to be surrounded by about 10,000 acres of agricultural land;[4] manufactures and handicrafts were to be placed at the edge of the town,[5] and obnoxious trades placed by themselves at a distance;[6] the natural increase of the population was to be accommodated, not by expanding the town, but by building new settlements of a similar kind.[7] An elaborate code of behaviour was prescribed, insisting, among other provisions, on the complete exclusion of all intoxicants, tobacco, weapons of war and explosives.[8] Buckingham estimated that it would cost £3,000,000 to build his town and another £1,000,000 to provide for the employment of all its inhabitants. To offset this, he claimed that by demonstrating a means of absorbing all the unemployed it would save half the poor-rates and half the expenditure on prisons and penal colonies (a joint saving of about £8,000,000 per year), not to mention the £30,000,000 or more which he believed to be the annual English expenditure on

---

[1] *Ibid.*, pp. 154–5.   [2] *Ibid.*, pp. 156–7.
[3] J. S. Buckingham, *National Evils and Practical Remedies*, p. 141.
[4] *Ibid.*, p. 142.   [5] *Ibid.*, p. 143.
[6] *Ibid.*, p. 151.   [7] *Ibid.*, p. 152.
[8] *Ibid.*, p. 144.

intemperance.[1] But, although Buckingham offered salvation to the entire public, neither his nor any of the other schemes mentioned had attractions for the private investor. Railways appeared a far more promising investment than model towns, and only by the provision of capital are castles in the air brought down to earth.

In fact none of these projects of the eighteen-forties bore any practical fruit, but at the same time one or two industrialists who had accumulated capital reserves did decide to devote part of them to building new and healthier villages for their workpeople. An early example was Bessbrook in Ireland, which was begun in 1846 by Messrs. Richardson, who employed 2,500 people in their linen mills. They built four-roomed cottages to let at 3s. per week, and two-roomed cottages at 1s. 6d.; they provided schools, churches, an institute with meeting-hall and library, and a temperance hotel. The superior quality of the village depended almost entirely on the efforts and interest of the Richardson family, and when it passed from their ownership its model characteristics were allowed to decay.[2] In England, a creation of this period which enjoyed some contemporary fame was the small village built in 1853 at Bromborough for the workers at Price's candle factory. But neither of these can compare, in the scale of achievement nor in the attention which they attracted, with Saltaire, which calls for fuller consideration.

Saltaire was a product of the attractive eccentricity often found in early-Victorian individualism. Its creator, Titus Salt, was a notable example of one of the ideals of the time, the 'self-made man', who had risen to fortune as a woollen manufacturer by the exercise of energy, foresight, and skill. He had originally planned to retire at the age of fifty, but as that time drew near he resolved instead on another project, which was both a hobby and a business: to replace his existing mills in Bradford by one enormous factory, larger than all of them together, and to build round it a new town for his workpeople.[3] He selected a site which was crossed by both canal and railway and entirely free from buildings, save for an old water-mill[4] and began building his factory in 1851. His enterprise caught public attention both by its novelty and its magnitude. The new factory, which was opened in 1853 on the proprietor's fiftieth birthday,

[1] *Ibid.*, pp. 154–5.

[2] J. E. Budgett Meakin, *Model Factories and Villages: Ideal Conditions of Labour and Housing*, pp. 419–20.

[3] R. Balgarnie, *Sir Titus Salt, Baronet: His Life and its Lessons*, p. 114.

[4] J. Burnley, *Sir Titus Salt, and George Moore*, p. 44.

covered 6¼ acres[1] and employed some 3,000 people.[2] It was an object of wonder and speculation. 'In *The Times* and *Daily News* the expense of this gigantic undertaking is set down at half a million of money; but it is locally estimated at much less.'[3]

Although the factory preceded the other buildings, and for a time the workpeople were conveyed to and from Bradford by special train,[4] a plan for a complete town existed from the beginning, and Salt's orders were known before the factory was opened. 'The architects are expressly enjoined to use every precaution to prevent the pollution of the air by smoke, or the water by want of sewerage, or other impurity. . . . Wide streets, spacious squares, with gardens attached, ground for recreation, a large dining hall and kitchens, baths and wash-houses, a covered market, schools and a church; each combining every improvement that modern art and science have brought to light, are ordered to be proceeded with by the gentleman who has originated this undertaking.'[5] Over the next twenty years the plan was gradually realized. The first concern was to provide houses for at any rate a substantial proportion of the workpeople, amenities and institutions being left until later. For over-lookers, parlour houses with from three to six bedrooms were built at a cost of about £200 each (excluding land, roads and drainage), and ordinary workmen's cottages were built for £120 each. Rents ranged from 2s. 4d. to 7s. 6d. per week and returned approximately 4 per cent on capital outlay, which is less than would have been expected of normal commercial investment.[6]

The founder also bore the cost of most of the public buildings of his town. In 1859 a Congregational church was completed at his sole expense[7] and nine years later a Wesleyan chapel was built by public subscription on a site given by him for the purpose.[8] Temporary accommodation was provided for elementary schools from the foundation of the town, and in 1868 permanent buildings were erected at a cost of £7,000.[9] Salt also paid careful attention to the needs of public health; he installed a thorough and complete drainage

---

[1] A. Holroyd, *Saltaire and its Founder*, p. 11.

[2] Balgarnie, *op. cit.*, p. 135.

[3] *The Manchester Guardian*, 21st September, 1853.

[4] Burnley, *op. cit.*, p. 49.

[5] *The Manchester Guardian*, 21st September, 1853.

[6] J. Hole, *The Homes of the Working Classes, with Suggestions for their Improvement*, pp. 67–8.

[7] Holroyd, *op. cit.*, p. 17.   [8] *Ibid.*, p. 18.

[9] Balgarnie, *op. cit.*, p.136.

system (a comparative rarity in 1860); he built an accident infirmary and a dispensary and issued disinfectant to the people during the cholera epidemic;[1] and in 1863 he opened a set of baths and wash-houses.[2] In fact, he provided the equipment which in the next forty or fifty years all towns gradually realized that they must provide for themselves. He also followed a long tradition of English philan-thropy by building and endowing 45 alms-houses, whose inmates received 7s. 6d. per week if they were single, or shared 10s. per week if they were a married couple.[3] One more of Salt's innovations deserves passing notice: the factory canteen which sold meat for 2d., soup for 1d., tea or coffee for ½d., and offered free cooking and accommodation to workpeople who preferred to bring their own food.[4] With true nonconformist zeal, Salt banned all public-houses, but tried to replace them by the gift in 1871 of a club and institute, which had a library and reading-room, two rooms for use as an art school, a lecture room and laboratory for science, a main concert hall, a committee room, a bagatelle room, a billiards room, a gym-nasium, a drill room and an armoury.[5]

In this same year, 1871, Saltaire as planned by its founder was completed by the opening of a 14-acre park.[6] At that time the town consisted of four main thoroughfares, twenty-one other streets and four squares, with 820 dwellings for a population of 4,389. It hardly conformed to the ideas of later town planners, for the residential area was only 25¾ acres,[7] the density being 32 houses and 170 persons per residential acre, or 89 persons per gross acre. But by the stan-dards of its time it was a notable achievement in the improvement of living conditions, and it was widely recognized as such. Salt had been invited to enter his town for a prize at the Paris Exhibition of 1867 but declined to do so; not long afterwards his work was publicly acknowledged by the bestowal of a baronetcy. A contemporary verdict was given by the *Birmingham Post*: 'Saltaire is not a fortuitous collection of dwellings gathered by chance around the manufactory where their occupants are employed. It is the result of thought and design, the realisation of a great idea. . . . It has at least shown what

[1] *Ibid.*, pp. 224–5.

[2] Holroyd, *loc. cit.*

[3] Balgarnie, *op. cit.*, p. 145.

[4] *Ibid.*, pp. 233–4. This canteen had another characteristic familiar to the present day: £50 a year was realized towards its upkeep by the sale of its waste to pig-keepers.

[5] *Ibid.*, pp. 226–9.

[6] Holroyd, *op. cit.*, pp. 30–1.　　　　　　　　　[7] *Ibid.*, pp. 15–16.

can be done towards breaking down the barrier which has existed between the sympathies of the labourer and the employer. The founder of Saltaire has taught us that there are noble duties which the capitalist can perform, and that in discharging them he may elevate himself to a glorious position without interfering with the prosperity of his business. No finer picture could be imagined by the dreamer who would think of a probable future of progress for mankind, than that of a city where education is open to every child, —where labour is respected,—where intemperance is banished,— where the graces of life and the higher intellectual pleasures are open to the enjoyment of all,—and where misfortunes are tempered by forethought and kindness.'[1]

Saltaire was acknowledged to be a model, but it was not a model that was copied. In the twenty years when it was being built, in- dustrial prosperity came easily enough for the reform of industrial conditions to be left aside, and the private philanthropy that con- cerned itself with the homes of the people found far more than it could cope with in the centres of the great towns. Outside the large cities, efforts to improve the physical environment were, with this one exception of Saltaire, not only few but feeble.

The principal towns of the country were already in existence and urban development was almost entirely based on established centres. The few exceptions to this process, such as Middlesbrough, occa- sionally showed signs, in the very early stages of their growth, of more orderly arrangement, but, as their scale increased, the mani- festations of order diminished and their features had more and more in common with those of other industrial towns.[2] Some of the new towns created to serve the railways have already been discussed; some, like Swindon, did not begin too well; others, like Crewe, soon left behind their early days of moderate order and beneficence.

In some virtually new towns increased amenities, and, in parti- cular, improved housing, were provided as the most effective means of attracting labour from elsewhere. That was so, for example, at the decayed port of Grimsby, which was deliberately revived by the Manchester, Sheffield, and Lincolnshire Railway Company. This company began to build a new dock there, complete with warehouses

---

[1] Quoted in *ibid.*, pp. 31–2.

[2] For brief comments on the nature of nineteenth-century development in Middles- brough *vide* R. Glass, *The Social Background of a Plan: a study of Middlesbrough*, esp. pp. 10–13 and 45–8.

and sidings, in 1846.[1] Development was further stimulated by two of the chief members of the company, the chairman, the Earl of Yarborough, who built an hotel,[2] and E. W. (afterwards Sir Edward) Watkin, who was anxious to make it an important fishing port. He found it very difficult to induce fishermen to settle there until in 1860 he began to build houses, which were quickly occupied and paid him 4 per cent.[3] Similarly the Duke of Newcastle was able, by building houses of better quality than was usual in the district, to obtain sufficient labour for his new coal mine at Shireoaks, which was opened up gradually between 1857 and 1861; and the proprietors of the Kiveton Park collieries provided houses and playing-fields for their workers.[4]

Mining industries were among the few which continued to give rise to new settlements, and mining communities, because of their frequent isolation, were specially susceptible to the good or evil effects of the policy adopted by the employers to the general life of the village. But it does not appear that that policy usually produced much positive benefit. One of the few exceptions to this state of affairs in mid-Victorian times is to be found in the history of the London Lead Company, which, under the influence of its Quaker outlook, was still maintaining a tradition, begun more than a century earlier, of steadily improving the material equipment for the social life of its miners among the northern fells. From the end of the eighteenth century it had been providing shelter and services for a community of nearly 4,000 people where no such provision had existed before.[5] At Nent Head, near Alston, it had built a small new village which it enlarged in 1825, and though the improvement of its material condition was slow (it was only in 1850 that a proper water-supply was laid on) it appears to have been steady. The company built cottages which it let at £4 to £6 per annum and provided sites free for public buildings, besides bearing a substantial proportion of the cost of their construction.[6] The scattered disposition of

---

[1] Manchester, Sheffield and Lincolnshire Railway Co., *A Description of the New Docks at Great Grimsby*, p. 5.

[2] *Ibid.*, p. 10.

[3] R. J. Simpson, 'In what way can healthy Working Men's Dwellings be erected in lieu of those removed for carrying out Sanitary or Municipal Improvements or for other purposes?' in *Trans. Natl. Assoc. for Promotion of Social Science*, 1874, p. 617.

[4] *Ibid., loc. cit.*

[5] A. Raistrick, *Two Centuries of Industrial Welfare: The London (Quaker) Lead Company, 1692–1905*, p. 21.

[6] *Ibid.*, p. 24.

its workings made it desirable for it to provide better living conditions at more than one site and it did something to further this aim at Garrigill, Dufton, and Hilton and at Masterman Place, adjoining Middleton-in-Teesdale, by building cottages to let at low rents and by providing an adequate water-supply.[1] These were unspectacular efforts but they contrast with the general absence of worthwhile achievement in this field.

New industrial villages of the type of Saltaire were almost unknown. A second Yorkshire manufacturer, Edward Akroyd, built a suburb for his workers around his factory at Copley, near Halifax, with allotment gardens, a recreation ground, a church and a village school, of which one classroom served also as a public library and news-room.[2] This was no doubt an industrial setting rather better than the average of the time, but it was not very satisfactory. The houses, though soundly constructed and provided with adequate sanitation, were all built back to back, and each successive block was built more cheaply than the last in order to maintain a return of 4½ per cent on capital without raising rents to a level that strained the workers' means.[3] Akroyd had been influenced by the activities of the Halifax Union Building Society, which was founded in 1845 and for which he had acted as a trustee.[4] He used this experience in establishing the Akroydon Building Association[5] to operate a scheme for the creation of a second Halifax suburb, Akroydon. This project, which was only partly carried out, was separate from any industrial undertaking and was intended to assist working men to build houses on land which Akroyd had bought, and to purchase them through the Halifax Permanent Benefit Society. Akroyd provided plans, defrayed all contractual expenses, guaranteed the fulfilment of the contract within the estimated price, and in some cases guaranteed the first three years' subscriptions to the building society. All this he did with the expectation that in a few years his ground rents would rise to a profitable level.[6]

By the eighteen-seventies, though there was more active interest in the condition of towns, there was no exodus from them and out-side them little attention was given to sanitary reform. Saltaire had

---

[1] *Ibid.*, pp. 29–30.
[2] Hole, *op. cit.*, p. 70.   [3] *Ibid.*, p. 71.
[4] J. W. Alderson and A. E. Ogden, *The Halifax Equitable Benefit Building Society*, 1871–1921, p. 6.
[5] *Ibid.*, p. 7.
[6] Hole, *op. cit.*, pp. 72–5; O. Hobson, *A Hundred Years of the Halifax*, pp. 33–4.

lost the attraction of novelty and no similar private venture had followed it. The spread of cities began to be a serious threat to farmland and to open spaces, but it was nobody's business to organize any part of the overflow into new and distinct communities. There was need for a fresh example and an effort to supply it came from George Cadbury. Like Salt, he was seeking room to expand his business and found that purpose better served by leaving Birmingham and building on an unoccupied site of his own choice, which he named Bournville. But Bournville was the outcome of a wider conception than Saltaire. It was never intended to be an 'employer's village', but was a full-scale experiment in community planning, aiming to include workers of all classes; in fact, about 50 per cent of the occupied population have been employed elsewhere than at Cadbury Brothers' factory.[1] Bournville was to be not only part of an improved system of industrial organization, but also a social example of general significance, and, to make it effective as such, Cadbury was determined to show that it could be made to pay.[2] In the long run he succeeded, but the many years of preparation when expenditure was being incurred without apparently hastening very much the day when a return could be expected would have deterred the ordinary commercial investor. The factory and a few cottages for those workmen whom it was essential to have close at hand were built in 1879, but it was not until 1895, when he had acquired 120 acres, that Cadbury really set to work to build a village[3] and even then progress was not rapid. There was the persistent problem of a free market that if land in one district is sought in bulk, the price is forced up throughout the neighbourhood; consequently it was necessary to lock up capital by purchasing small, scattered areas as opportunity arose and building on them only when a compact portion had at last been acquired. That was one reason why it took another twenty-five years to round off the Bournville Estate.[4]

Nevertheless, the building of the village gradually went ahead, and by 1900 Cadbury owned 330 acres, had erected about 300 houses in small groups along tree-lined roads, and had laid out open spaces. He was aware of some of the dangers of excessive paternalism and in 1900 he renounced all financial interest in the undertaking, transferring ownership of the land and houses to an independent body,

[1] Bournville Village Trust, *Sixty Years of Planning*, p. 26.
[2] *Ibid.*, p. 7.   [3] *Ibid.*, pp. 10–11.
[4] Cadbury Brothers, Ltd., *Bournville Housing*, p. 5.

the Bournville Village Trust, on terms which ensured that all profits could be devoted to the further improvement and extension of the village.[1] After this, Bournville was responsible for its own development, but of course it was in more favourable circumstances than an ordinary town. Current charges on capital had to be met (the Trust aimed at a profit of at least 4 per cent)[2] but there was no claim for arrears in respect of the many years in which the founder had tied up capital without return; no commercial venture could have been deliberately financed on these lines. Moreover, Cadbury and his family and firm continued to make various contributions. In 1906 elementary schools were given to the village by Mr. and Mrs. Cadbury;[3] in 1919 a Bournville Works Housing Society was formed to assist the workpeople to buy houses and was financed by the firm.[4] Bournville was neither a purely commercial venture nor a piece of undiluted philanthropy; but it successfully took root and grew and became strong enough to stand by itself.

The foundation of Bournville was followed by another notable undertaking, the building of Port Sunlight, which was begun in 1888. Once again the creation of a model village was part of a scheme which included the expansion of an already-established business. In this case the association of the village with the firm was as close as it possibly could be. Port Sunlight was not, like Bournville, an attempt to demonstrate one practical answer to the housing problems of great cities, but rather it was a pioneer extension of its activities in labour-management by a growing industrial firm. W. H. Lever was very interested in schemes of profit-sharing but was anxious to devise one which should be independent of any individual, and the building of Port Sunlight was the plan he chose.[5] 'Prosperity-sharing' was the name he gave to his idea. He made his intention quite plain in his speech at the formal opening of the village in 1890: 'Our idea', he said, 'before we took the land at Port Sunlight, was that profit-sharing should be so managed that those who take the profits are those who are working at the works, and what we propose to do with the proportion of profit devoted to the workers is to apply it to the building of houses to be let at a reduced rental. We propose that those who have been longest in our service should have the

[1] Bournville Village Trust, *op. cit.*, pp. 11–13.
[2] Cadbury Brothers, Ltd., *loc. cit.*
[3] Bournville Village Trust, *op. cit.*, p. 32.   [4] *Ibid.*, p. 21.
[5] 2nd Viscount Leverhulme, *Viscount Leverhulme by his Son*, p. 53.

greatest claim. We desire to encourage permanency in the people around us and we consider that by these arrangements the profits which are to be shared will always remain with the workers for the time being and not be divided up and squandered.'[1]

The village grew up on the lines implicit in this idea. Houses of sound quality were built and amenities provided on a generous scale; by 1904 two schools, a men's social club, a junior social club, an open-air swimming bath, an open-air theatre, a technical institute, Sunday schools and a church had all been provided; there was even a village inn, temperance at first, which Lever had consented to have licensed, after 80 per cent of the adult population had voted in favour of this step.[2] But all these things were offshoots of the firm. The village was managed by a special department of the firm and the tenants for many years could air their complaints only to the firm's estate manager.[3] Provision was made, it is true, for houses to be let at rents increased by $33\frac{1}{3}$ per cent to persons not on the staff of Lever Brothers Ltd.,[4] but in fact twenty years after its foundation Port Sunlight had not enough houses for the families of half the firm's employees.[5]

The contribution which the firm made, in addition to the vision and energy of W. H. Lever himself, was that no interest was charged on the capital outlay, no overheads were charged in respect of salaries and office accommodation for the estate management department, and in the earlier years temporary losses on income account were accepted, although rents were adjusted to keep such losses to a minimum. A surplus was realized for the first time in 1907, when about half the total deficit of the previous five years was recouped.[6] At that time, when the total capital outlay was £498,526,[7] the waiving of interest amounted in effect to a bonus of about £8 per employee,[8] but the limitation and variety of accommodation meant that this bonus was not altogether evenly distributed. The firm considered itself amply recompensed by the improved quality of its labour, and certainly the growth of the business suggests that its expenditure on the village was no drag on its prosperity. On the other side, the health and vital statistics that Lever was fond of

---

[1] *Ibid.*, pp. 54–5.   [2] *Ibid.*, p. 91–7.
[3] W. L. George, *Labour and Housing at Port Sunlight*, p. 208.
[4] W. H. Lever, *Inaugural Address to the Birkenhead Congress of the Royal Institute of Public Health*, appendix, p. xxxi.
[5] George, *op. it.*, p. 205.   [6] *Ibid.*, p. 96.
[7] *Ibid.*, p. 93.   [8] *Ibid.*, p. 195.

quoting are clear testimony to at least one kind of benefit which the workers derived.

Port Sunlight and Bournville were not quite the solitary expressions of an individual's idea that Saltaire had been. By the eighties, changes in the environment and location of industry had become at least a topic for occasional discussion. In most of the basic industries profits were not so easily obtained as in the recent past and the urgent importance of efficient and healthy labour was, as a direct result, beginning to be more widely recognized. At the same time landowners were faced with the new problem of agricultural depression and the gradual ebbing of population from the villages. It was in this setting that there was founded in 1883 a Society for Promoting Industrial Villages[1] whose members included social reformers and a few industrialists. The original president was Sir George Campbell; the Rev. Henry Solly was chairman of the council, and among the vice-presidents were Lord Shaftesbury, Lord Aberdeen, Professor Foxwell and Samuel Morley; the members of the council included James Hole, who was secretary of the Associated Chambers of Commerce, Benjamin Jones of the C.W.S., and Walter Hazell of the printing firm of Hazell, Watson & Co.[2] The objects of the society were entirely propagandist and it never intended to participate in any financial schemes or undertakings requiring capital.[3] Its viewpoint can best be illustrated from one of a series of pamphlets published under its auspices, where it was stated that 'the true answer to "The Bitter Cry" of outcast London and other great towns is to be heard in the dreary half-populated rural districts of the kingdom. The one evil must redress the other and the formation of Industrial Villages, on the plans recommended by the Society will, we believe, best secure the object'.[4] The proposals for the villages were quite imposing to read. Cottages were to be well-built, well-drained and well-ventilated, with legal safeguards against overcrowding and sub-letting; a surrounding belt of land was to be reserved in perpetuity for co-operative or cottage farming and allotments, with provision for sports grounds and children's playgrounds; every cottage was to have a small garden plot; there were to be schools of

[1] Solly Collection, section 4(b), f. D.181.
[2] *Ibid.*, f. D.57.   [3] *Ibid., loc. cit.*
[4] H. Solly, *Industrial Villages: a Remedy for Crowded Towns and Deserted Fields*, p. 3. Page references are to the edition printed by J. S. Durant. Another issue of the same date (1884) and from the same publishers (Swan, Sonnenschein) but printed by Sampson and Davey has different pagination.

three grades, a public hall, public libraries, art galleries and museums
where practicable, provident dispensaries and sanatoria, public baths
and wash-houses, and co-operative stores; social clubs and coffee
taverns would be provided, but public houses were, of course,[1]
prohibited.[2] It was all, no doubt, very beneficent, but the only plan
for its realization was that 'we trust and believe that many benevolent
and public-spirited men will devote capital and energy to the
successful prosecution of our plans'.[3]

There were some associated with the Society who were conscious
of its lack of practicality, and in 1887 an attempt was made to launch
a company called the Improved Villa and Cottage Homes General
Land and Building Company Ltd. According to a leaflet which it
issued, its objects were:

'to acquire Freehold, Copyhold or Leasehold Agricultural and other
land suitable for the promotion and formation of Industrial Villages,
and the erection thereon of Factories, Workshops, etc. (with or
without the working plant), also for Allotments, Farming, Gardening, or for Building purposes, and of land situate within easy access
of the Metropolis, and other great centres of industry where there
is an undoubted demand for increased House Accommodation; to
develope [sic] the same for use; and to erect Villa and Cottage Residences thereon for letting, or to sell the same at sums payable by
weekly, monthly, or quarterly instalments, according to an equitable
scale to be arranged. The cost of travelling to and from business (at
least once daily, and at such times as may suit the resident's own
convenience) may be included in the rent, or in the instalments of
purchase money if desired.'[4]

The prospectus stated that

'special attention will be given to sanitary arrangements. . . . Closets,
traps, drains, etc., in or near the houses will be well constructed and
arranged. The same attention will be given to the construction and
ventilation of sewers, and to the distribution of gullies, etc., in the
roads. It is proposed to plant trees along the roads, and everything

[1] 'Of course' is correct. The temperance outlook is one of the common strands
running right through the history of Victorian schemes for the reform of housing and
of urban living conditions generally. It persisted in the garden city movement of this
century.
[2] Solly, op. cit., pp. 9–10.   [3] Ibid., p. 15.
[4] Solly Collection, section 4 (b), f. D.223.

possible will be done to make the estates healthy, pleasant and attractive.'[1]

The company's authorized capital was £100,000,[2] but in a letter dated 28th March 1888, Henry Solly was informed that practically nothing was being done about it[3] and it appears to have gained no support.

All that remained was propaganda. The Society for Promoting Industrial Villages had a genuine case to state and was not alone in its advocacy. The economist, Alfred Marshall, for instance, was drawing attention to the way in which the crowding of industry in towns had raised workshop rents, which in turn kept wages down, and he was recommending on economic grounds that the home industries of London should be transferred to districts in the country where rents were lower.[4] And one manufacturer told the Society that he found urban expenses growing; he was paying £400 a year for the amount of water which, twenty years earlier, had cost him only £25, and rents and rates were also up, whereas, in the country, land was more readily obtainable and labour was cheaper, because of the decline of agriculture.[5] But, in spite of having a valid text on which to preach, the Society seems to have achieved few conversions, although it cast its net quite widely, sponsoring lectures to such various bodies as Trinity College, Cambridge, and the Guild of Co-operators, Uppingham School and the Fabian Society.[6] Its resources were very restricted and in its early years it was financed almost entirely by Samuel Morley,[7] who died in 1886. Its cash-book in the following years shows the small scale of its activities: for 1886–7 subscriptions totalled £49 15s. and receipts from publications seven shillings; for 1887–8 subscriptions were £50 0s. 6d., receipts from publications and expenses repaid, £1 13s. 4d.[8] Apart, however, from the handicap of small resources, the Society also suffered from a readiness to accept trivialities as evidence of the success of its efforts, and from a certain preciosity of outlook. It believed that there was a growing taste for hand-made goods and that this favoured its work, and it put on record as a notable achievement that it had

[1] *Ibid.*, f. D.224.   [2] *Ibid.*, f. D.223.
[3] *Ibid.*, f. D.226.
[4] A. Marshall, 'The Housing of the London Poor. Where to house them', in *Contemporary Review*, vol. XLV, pp. 226–9.
[5] Society for Promoting Industrial Villages, *3rd Annual Report*, p. 21.
[6] *Ibid., 2nd Annual Report*, p. 10.   [7] *Ibid., 2nd Annual Report*, p. 5.
[8] *Ibid., 3rd Annual Report*, p. 52.

persuaded two London firms to take in work done by rural crafts-men.[1] The only new enterprises which it was able to claim owed their foundation partly to its influence were the Prescot Watch Company, a factory for light iron goods at Earlsfield, and a co-operative small-holding group which surely reached the nadir of nomenclature with its title of the Total Abstainers' Industrial Farm.[2]

Clearly, the Society had not fully thought out the problems to which it addressed itself. It was incapable of promoting a vigorous movement and it quickly withered away. A meeting was called in September 1889 to discuss its liabilities and arrange for winding up[3] and two months later an appeal was made to members to send donations to pay off the outstanding debt of £32 17s. 11d.[4] The disappearance of this rather pathetic society was due as much to its own internal weakness as to public apathy on the question of the diffusion of population and industry. Apathy there certainly was, but it was in fact a little less complete than formerly, and perhaps the propaganda of the Society for Promoting Industrial Villages, which had attracted a certain amount of favourable press comment, had contributed a little towards the creation of a more encouraging environment for subsequent developments.

It was in the next few years that Port Sunlight and Bournville became firmly established, and there was increasing attention by employers to the physical conditions and amenities of working life, which in a few cases extended to the direct provision of improved housing.[5] Another stimulus came from the publication in 1898 of Ebenezer Howard's book *Tomorrow*, and its practical sequels, the foundation of the Garden City Association and of First Garden City Ltd., the public company which enthusiastically set about the build-ing of a new town. These events, which will be discussed a little later, carried the question of building new towns almost on to a different plane. They suggested that changes could be effected which few people had hitherto regarded as at all practicable. Doubtless this encouraged people to continue with smaller enterprises more strictly in the tradition of Bournville and Port Sunlight, which seemed less visionary than they would have done a few years earlier.

New individual enterprises in village-building were undertaken by employers. A rather exceptional case was the Foyers Estate at the

[1] *Ibid.*, 3rd *Annual Report*, pp. 10–11.   [2] *Ibid.*, 3rd *Annual Report*, pp. 4–6 and 14.
[3] Solly Collection, section 4 (b), f. D.200.   [4] *Ibid.*, f. D.204.
[5] On this topic generally, *vide* Meakin, *op. cit., passim.*

head of Loch Ness, acquired in 1895 by the British Aluminium Co., which wished to harness the power of the waterfalls there. The remoteness of the situation made it necessary for the firm to provide housing, and though its earliest building was unremarkable in quality it subsequently accepted advice from Mrs. G. F. Watts, who took a special interest in the district, and from the Garden City Association. Houses were placed away from the works, and the firm provided shops, a school and a workmen's club, with library and baths.[1]

A larger undertaking also arising from the need to settle population on a new site was the Woodlands Colliery Village, near Doncaster. In 1906 the Brodsworth Main Colliery Co. sank a new pit and planned in connexion with it a complete village of 1,000 houses. A large private house on the estate was to be converted into a club with a fishing lake and park, and central sites were reserved for public buildings and a co-operative store. One of the directors, A. B. Markham, who was the chief promoter of the scheme, himself bore the cost of a set of public baths.[2] Work on the project began in the summer of 1907 despite opposition within the company. The necessary capital was raised by 5 per cent debentures so that there was little margin for profit. In fact, the total cost averaged about £200 per house and as rents ranged from 5s. 3d. to 6s. 9d. per week, the net return after allowance for depreciation, management and payment of fixed interest charges should have been of the order of 1½ per cent. In spite of this low return, however, the scheme went on, and by 1912 the village had grown to 653 houses.[3]

At this period and in rather similar circumstances, there was the first example of a local authority establishing a model village for its employees. The Birmingham Corporation built a new waterworks in the Elan Valley and spent an additional £20,000 on the provision of a village for the staff. The housing was, by prevailing standards of what was suitable for the working classes, exceptionally good, every house having four bedrooms and a bathroom. A school with accommodation for 120 children and serving as an assembly hall for general use was also provided.[4]

[1] W. M. Morrison, 'Foyers Industrial Village' in *The Garden City*, vol. 1, pp. 8–9. The parallel with the experience of the new cotton factories a century earlier is worth noting.

[2] P. B. Houfton, 'A Model Mining Village', in *Garden Cities and Town Planning*, New Series, vol. III (1908), pp. 126–7.

[3] *Ibid.*, 'The Woodlands Colliery Village', in *ibid.*, New Series, vol. II (1912), pp. 37–9.

[4] J. J. Clarke, *The Housing Problem. Its History, Growth, Legislation and Procedure*, p. 81.

Other new industrial villages of the early years of this century had rather different associations. Earswick, the creation of a trust founded in 1904 by Joseph Rowntree, was obviously based on the example of Bournville. It was close to the works of a growing firm of chocolate manufacturers whose profits made possible the foundation of the village; but like Bournville it was not confined to the employees of the factory. Earswick resembled Bournville also in being administered by a trust and in its financial arrangements. Cadbury, after more than twenty years of individual effort, had handed over his land and buildings without charge to a trust; Rowntree formed a trust at the outset and gave it funds to begin its work. The interest on this gift and the receipts from rents formed the trust's entire income, which was more than enough to meet all charges on it.[1] This arrangement made it possible for the trust to let three-bedroom cottages with a minimum of 350 square yards of garden for 4s. 6d. per week (excluding rates) and still have sufficient funds to continue building.[2]

The last notable example of the period was something of a hybrid in that while it was nominally an independent village it was in fact to a large extent the private preserve of one large manufacturing firm. Hull Garden Suburb, which was opened in 1908, was built and owned by the Hull Garden Village Co., whose dividends were limited to 3 per cent and whose chairman, Sir James Reckitt, held two-thirds of the total share capital of £200,000. The estate covered 140 acres and nearly half was to be sold for the erection under restrictions of 400 to 500 houses, the directors being willing to sell land at cost price to any company or society intending to assist working men to own their houses. On the rest of the estate one-half to two-thirds of the houses were reserved to be let to employees of Messrs. Reckitt, who had 3,300 workers in four factories close to the village. Living conditions were excellent and rents, which (excluding rates) ranged from 4s. 6d. to 8s. per week, were reasonable. But it was not entirely an altruistic project and it is interesting to note that Sir James Reckitt, in his oddly contradictory speech at the opening ceremony, revived the argument of social reform not just for its own sake but as a preservative of the existing order: 'The only object in view', he said, 'is the betterment of our neighbours,

---

[1] G. B. Brown, 'The Joseph Rowntree Village Trust', in *The Garden City*, New Series, vol. I, p. 197.
[2] *Ibid.*, p. 169.

and to enable them to derive advantage from having fresh air, a better house, and better surroundings. I . . . urge people of wealth and influence to make proper use of their property, to avert possibly a disastrous uprising.'[1]

Meanwhile the garden city movement was making striking progress. It owed its origin to Ebenezer Howard's book, *Tomorrow*, which was afterwards revised and reissued under the title *Garden Cities of Tomorrow*. Howard's plan was for the purchase of an estate of 6,000 acres at £40 per acre (the average current price for agricultural land),[2] the construction in the middle of it of a complete town for about 30,000 people and the reservation of the rest of the estate for agriculture.[3] The financial aspect was worked out in some detail;[4] essentially the scheme depended on the recoupment of increased land values as a result of urban development. The profit thus obtained would be used first to pay interest on the capital borrowed for the purchase of the land and preparation of the site, and the surplus that still remained would be applied to further development.

There was little in Howard's proposals that was very original. The most unusual suggestion was that when a garden city had grown to its full size of, say, 32,000 it should then grow by establishing another garden city beyond its own zone of country until gradually a cluster of garden cities had come into existence.[5] But even this had been anticipated long before by Owen and it attracted little public attention in Howard's lifetime. Howard himself stated that his project included the type of organized migration which Alfred Marshall had mentioned and a model city as outlined by Buckingham, though, quite rightly, he claimed that his proposals were far less rigid than Buckingham's.[6]

But the proposals were comprehensive; they were reasonably free from crankiness; and they were launched in an atmosphere less un-

---

[1] *Garden Cities and Town Planning*, New Series, vol. III (1908), p. 97.
[2] E. Howard, *Garden Cities of Tomorrow* (ed. F. J. Osborn), p. 50.
[3] *Ibid.*, pp. 54–5. [4] *Ibid.*, pp. 64–82.
[5] *Ibid.*, p. 142.
[6] *Ibid.*, p. 119. The term 'garden city' was also not original, though Howard gave it a rather more precise meaning than it had had (a precision soon dissipated by many who claimed to be acting under the influence of his ideas). The term was perhaps first used by Alexander T. Stewart to describe a model estate which he laid out on Long Island, New York, in 1869. (C. B. Purdom (ed.), *Town Theory and Practice*, p. 16.) Bournemouth was described as 'the Garden City of the South' by the Lord Mayor of London when he opened a new pier there in 1880. (C. Mate and C. H. Riddle, *Bournemouth: 1810–1910*, p. 161.)

receptive than at any previous time. Howard's personality and enthusiasm, too, were of great help in the practical furtherance of his idea. In 1899 the Garden City Association was formed to discuss and publicize his project.[1] Three years later a public meeting sponsored by the Association agreed unanimously to register a small company with an authorized capital of £20,000 for the purpose of prospecting, securing an option on a suitable estate and preparing a scheme.[2] This company was known as the Garden City Pioneer Company. Before the end of 1902 all its capital had been subscribed and by April 1903 a suitable estate at Letchworth had been bought privately from fifteen different owners for £155,587, i.e. £40 15s. per acre.[3] In September a new company, First Garden City Ltd., was registered with an authorized capital of £300,000 to undertake the creation of the city, the shareholders in the pioneer company being given equivalent holdings in the new company.[4] The original directors of the latter were mostly successful business men, half of them successful industrialists, and its structure was fairly orthodox, except that dividends were limited to 5 per cent cumulative, any balance of profit left after meeting interest on capital had to be devoted to the benefit of the town and its inhabitants,[5] and, in the event of winding up, shareholders were to be entitled to no more than the return of their capital plus a bonus of not more than 10 per cent plus any arrears of dividend.[6]

Interest in the scheme was widespread and in 1903 it was discussed by the Economic Section at the annual meeting of the British Association. In the course of a very favourable review, one speaker pointed out that the scheme would not be proved a failure if it failed to meet its preference dividends in the early years; the full dividend could not be paid until the capital value of the estate had greatly increased and, as that could be achieved only gradually, it might well be that there would at first be no dividend at all.[7] There was the weakness of the scheme as a commercial attraction. A quick

[1] D. Macfadyen, *Sir Ebenezer Howard and the Town Planning Movement*, p. 37.
[2] Garden City Association, *Garden Cities. Report of a public meeting at the Holborn Restaurant*, 2nd June, 1902, pp. 11–12.
[3] Macfadyen, *op. cit.*, p. 39.
[4] C. B. Purdom, *The Building of Satellite Towns*, pp. 57–8.
[5] F. J. Osborn, *Green Belt Cities: The British Contribution*, p. 58.
[6] G. M. Harris, *The Garden City Movement*, p. 47.
[7] H. E. Moore, *The Economic Aspect of the First Garden City. An address to the Economic Section of the British Association*, 1903, pp. 8–9. In fact, no preference shares were issued until 1916.

return could be obtained only by capital expenditure on a scale beyond the resources of the company in its earlier years and the development of Letchworth Garden City was hampered both as a social and a financial enterprise by a serious shortage of capital. Probably few, if any, of the pioneers foresaw how long it would be before risk-bearing capital received any reward. No dividend was paid until 1913, when 1 per cent was paid; then there was nothing more until 1918 when 2½ per cent was paid, and the maximum permitted level of 5 per cent was not reached until 1923.[1] The financial position was, however, continuously improving, interest on loan capital was always met[2] and, as development proceeded, more and more security was created for further loans, which could be applied to the quickening of further development.

In spite of financial handicaps the creation of a new town went ahead steadily. In a very few years from its commencement it had been convincingly demonstrated that this was no barren Utopianism; what had once been just an idea was established as a living town of people and buildings. Before the garden city was begun the population of the estate was 400; by the outbreak of the First World War it was about 9,000, and over £600,000 had been spent on new buildings.[3] It was intended above all to promote better living conditions for working people than could be found in the old cities (though it was not conceived as either a purely residential or a one-class town) and it had proved possible for private enterprise to provide these on an economic basis:[4] all speculative building of shops and houses was left to private building firms.[5] It was, moreover, a town that was not just a dormitory; it had its own shopping facilities and its own occupations. An adequate supply of shops was deliberately encouraged by the leasing of sites at specially low ground rents while population and turnover were low;[6] and firms in a wide variety of industries, especially engineering, were attracted.[7] Most of them found industrial conditions very advantageous, though the type of industrial development which was possible was to some extent restricted by the small size of the town, which could not supply sufficient labour for very large establishments.[8]

The achievement at Letchworth did not, however, lead to any

---

[1] Purdom, *op. cit.*, p. 138.   [2] *Ibid.*, p. 137.
[3] *Ibid.*, p. 81.   [4] *Ibid.*, p. 66.
[5] Osborn, *op. cit.*, p. 65.   [6] *Ibid.*, p. 84.
[7] Purdom, *op. cit.*, pp. 109–10.   [8] Osborn, *op. cit.*, p. 79.

immediate attempts to copy it elsewhere. On the whole, the public was less interested in the fact that it had proved possible to establish a new town than in the adoption in that town of new kinds of house design and street layout. The latter appeared to be a means of improving residential conditions that could be adopted anywhere on any scale which local circumstances and the available finance made appropriate, whereas the foundation of new towns was something which could be undertaken in only a limited number of places and which was bound for a long time to be a costly enterprise, whatever the ultimate rewards might be.

Just as in the case of the rebuilding and redesign of congested areas of established towns, so also the attempt to relieve urban conditions by accommodating industry and population in self-contained settlements on new sites was gravely restricted by the heavy expenditure which was involved. It is significant that the most notable nineteenth-century efforts to set up such settlements were invariably associated with business expansion by prosperous firms. Enterprise of this nature required not only an abundant interest in the project and belief in its value, but also the possession of substantial capital reserves and of sufficient income from other sources to make it possible to forgo for several years any appreciable return on the investment of these reserves. Since public organization for social enterprises was quite outside prevailing ideas for most of the period, an industrial firm which had prospered for several years and put an appreciable proportion of its profits to reserve was the only interested body capable of providing the necessary finance.

Of course, more firms had sufficient means to found a new settlement than actually did so. Most of them had no incentive to do this; rather the reverse. Such activity not only involved the question, 'What sort of town shall we have?' but immediately brought forward the further question, 'Where shall we have a town, whatever sort it is; where shall we locate a particular industry?' And that was of vital importance not merely to the new town itself but to the whole region in which it was situated, perhaps to the whole country. What was most desirable for that region or for the country was not necessarily what seemed at the moment to be the interest of the particular industrialist with whom rested the power of decision. But in the late nineteenth century, though part of the public was beginning to grope its way towards an idea of some kind of town planning, hardly anyone had a notion of the relevance of regional or national planning.

Firms located themselves where they thought best among the sites available to them and usually they settled in the midst of a large town. By so doing they kept more easily in contact with their customers, suppliers, and competitors; they gained access to a convenient reserve pool of labour; they obtained for a relatively low charge the advantage of such public services as existed and thus conserved their capital for direct use in their own business. The real cost of public services was almost certainly lower in substantial towns than in villages,[1] and, in any case, a large part of their cost in the former was borne by householders; the overhead burden imposed on an industrialist by charges for public services was probably less than proportionate to his share in the imposition of costs on the community. If he settled on a new site he was likely to have to lock up capital in providing services for himself and perhaps in housing as well. Thus industrialists had strong reasons for contributing to the expansion of large towns rather than to the establishment of a multiplicity of industrial villages. The creation of new model villages and towns therefore made hardly any of the contribution which it was potentially capable of making to the better distribution of various social and economic activities among different districts of a large region. Howard, for instance, had envisaged his garden city as a means of transferring occupations and people out of London,[2] but that aspect of it had little immediate appeal or practical influence.

The more easily recognized advantage of new settlements, the opportunity of creating a town of improved design, was realized in some, but by no means in all instances. Where a new village was built as part of a scheme to achieve improved living and working conditions, some care for the design and layout of buildings and streets was usual; but where a village was newly built because there was no alternative, its design was often as careless as that of any existing settlement. The location of some industries, of which the chief was coal-mining, was fixed within narrow limits by natural conditions, and the workers engaged in them had to be accommodated in comparatively small, isolated groups. There were a few attempts to build in these circumstances villages which would be

---

[1] The comparative costs of such services in large towns and in villages were never thoroughly investigated. In 1910 a study of all the county boroughs suggested that the cost *per caput* of nearly all public services was lowest in towns with populations of about 90,000. *Vide* C. A. Baker, 'Population and Costs in Relation to City Management', in *Journal of the Royal Statistical Society*, vol. LXXIV, p. 75.

[2] Howard, *op. cit.*, pp. 154–9.

healthy and comfortable living places, but most mining settlements were far from being models of what was desirable. The squalid physical environment of the working classes, which became best known in the great towns, was repeated with the same vivid abjectness in the mining valleys of South Wales[1] and in colliery villages elsewhere. Not all colliery companies had capital to spare for purposes only indirectly connected with mining enterprise, but often enough new mines were opened by firmly-established companies, which, when they were bringing into existence a new community, could have afforded to invest the capital necessary to ensure that it was at least done decently. The usual practice, however, was for the colliery company to leave the provision of houses to a speculative builder, lease them from him for twenty or thirty years, and sub-let them to its employees.[2] The results were often very bad in quality.

The type of development, however, which became best known at Bournville, Port Sunlight, and Letchworth Garden City was in marked contrast with what could be found within the nineteenth century town. It was a type of improvement that gradually caught the public fancy, but it was applied neither to the establishment of new self-contained settlements nor to the remodelling of old ones, but to the vast spread of a new kind of suburb around old centres which themselves changed relatively little.

[1] A brief and vivid account of housing conditions in this district in the eighteen-nineties is given in R. Williams, *London Rookeries and Colliers' Slums*.
[2] Houfton, *op. cit.*, p. 38.

CHAPTER VI

Suburban Development

OR a town to grow by the gradual accretion on its fringes of new quarters which served at first only a limited function and which eventually were absorbed as an integral part of the town itself was no new thing. It was common on the continent of western Europe in the later Middle Ages.[1] There was equal lack of novelty about the desire felt by some people to be of a town but not resident in it. In England perhaps the unusual number of large old houses in the Home Counties[2] is testimony of this. The aristocrat engaged in the pleasures or duties of the capital, but keeping apart from the herd, was sometimes the suburbanite of an earlier day.

Whether a person could indulge a fancy to live on the outskirts of town depended on two sets of circumstances: the frequency and urgency with which he had to go to town, and the cost and speed of travelling to and fro. Before the nineteenth century the necessities of daily work meant that all but a very few had to be on the spot for most of their time and only those could travel to residences outside the town who could afford to keep their own means of conveyance. The growth of the middle class in the course of the nineteenth century notably increased the number of those who could keep a horse and carriage and the safety of whose employment was not endangered by a lack of rigid time-keeping. For employers of the second generation and for professional men the solid Victorian villa in its garden on the edge of the town became a natural habitat.

[1] H. Pirenne, *Medieval Cities*, *passim*.
[2] This may perhaps be illustrated by the number and nature of the buildings in the Home Counties found worthy of record by the Royal Commission on Historical Monuments, particularly the great preponderance of examples of domestic as compared with ecclesiastical building among the most striking monuments. *Vide* e.g. the Commission's *Report on the Historical Monuments of Middlesex, passim.* (For the purposes of this report a monument ceased to be historical if it was built after the accession of George I.)

A more striking development took place in the late nineteenth and the first half of the twentieth century, when not hundreds but millions of people, drawn from a wide range of occupations, moved into suburban residences. Two major questions are posed by this change: what new social and economic conditions made it practicable, and what sort of places came into existence?

There were, of course, strong forces of repulsion from town centres. The constant influx of population caused congestion in central districts to become so acute that they became less and less desirable to stay in, and at the same time it made it inevitable that the buildings of the town should spread over a wider and wider area. But in the course of that surface expansion no care was taken to keep places of residence and employment in convenient proximity to one another, and whether families could benefit themselves and contribute to the relief of urban congestion by moving outwards as the town spread out was determined by the speed, convenience and expense of public transport; the hours, conditions and security of employment; the level of income; and the relative cost of urban and suburban accommodation.

It was probably the improvement of transport which focused attention on suburban development as a most desirable means of curing great cities of their dreadful congestion and their soaring rents. Technical change and the growth of population had made it practicable to introduce relatively cheap public local transport, by railway or by horse-omnibus, and the person who lived in one district and worked in another was no longer bound to furnish his own means of conveyance. Statutory requirements on a railway to provide special trains at cheap fares for workmen were first imposed in the eighteen-sixties in respect of several London suburban lines. The obligations imposed on the Great Eastern Railway, in particular, led to the rapid development of certain districts at the north-eastern edge of London. The Cross Committee was told in 1881 of a large daily influx of workers to central London from West Ham and Edmonton, and heard that thousands upon thousands of working-class houses were being built in West Ham, mostly for occupation by people employed in London.[1] The following figures show how

---

[1] *Select Committee on Artizans' and Labourers' Dwellings Improvement, Interim Report*, p. 230. The increase of factories in West Ham and the opening of the Royal Albert Dock about this time suggest that this statement was probably much exaggerated.

the population of Edmonton and Walthamstow grew with the increase of workmen's train facilities:[1]

Year	EDMONTON		WALTHAMSTOW	
	Population	Workmen's trains	Population	Workmen's Trains
1851	9,708	—	4,959	—
1861	10,930	—	7,137	—
1871	13,860	Trains just started	11,092	Trains just started
1881	23,463		21,715	
1883		3 trains instead of 2		3 trains instead of 2
1891	36,351	5 trains instead of 3 in 1890	46,346	6 trains instead of 3 in 1890
1901	61,892	7 trains in 1890	95,131	8 trains in 1899

But trains were often inadequate and inconvenient. A Soho painter and plumber told the Cross Committee:

'At the time I used to have to go out to Alexandra Palace, the trains used to be overcrowded of a morning, and I know what an evil it is to lose a train. In my case I had either to walk or lose a quarter; and if you are on a job, and lose a couple of quarters in a week, they will take another man on.'[2]

And many suburban districts were not served by workmen's trains at all. Both the Cross Committee in 1882[3] and the Royal Commission on the Housing of the Working Classes in 1885[4] had recommended that other London railways should be obliged to run workmen's trains on similar terms to the Great Eastern. But twenty years later there was still no other workmen's service to equal the Great Eastern's in cheapness and frequency, though there had been a great increase in the provision of workmen's trains on other lines.[5] The working classes crowded into those few suburbs which had cheap transport[6] and the increase in the daily movement

[1] *Royal Commission on London Traffic, Report*, vol. I, p. 14.
[2] *Select Committee on Artizans' and Labourers' Dwellings Improvement, Final Report*, p. 126.
[3] *Ibid., Final Report*, p. x.
[4] *Royal Commission on Housing of the Working Classes, Report*, vol. I, p. 51.
[5] Browning Hall Conference, *Report of Sub-Committee on Housing and Locomotion in London*, 1902–1907, p. 6. The extent of some of the other workmen's services and the fares charged are discussed in H. J. Dyos, 'Workmen's Fares in South London, 1860–1914' (*Journal of Transport History*, vol. I, pp. 3–19).
[6] *Royal Commission on London Traffic, Report*, vol. I, p. 15.

of the working population went on. The changing life of the City of London was a witness to this. The night population of the City fell from 74,897 in 1871 to 50,526 in 1881, a decrease of 32·5 per cent, while the day population rose from 170,133 in 1866 to 261,061 in 1881, an increase of 53·4 per cent.[1] But much of this movement depended on pedestrian or horse-drawn transport and it has been suggested that between 1860 and 1890 the London suburbs were built up practically to the maximum that could be served by horse-drawn transport.[2] No other city was so afflicted by the problem of scale as London was, but similar problems of rather less acuteness existed elsewhere.

What fundamentally changed the situation and made people look to the prospect of further suburban extension on a vast scale was the coming first of the electric tramway, then the electric railway and, in the early years of this century, still at the stage of promise rather than performance, the appearance of the motor-bus. Anyone could see what had happened in those suburban districts which had already been reasonably supplied with transport. Now that there was the prospect of a rapid increase in transport facilities it was assumed that similar development could be readily promoted in other districts. Better transport and suburban building became the most prominent demand of housing reformers. The Fabian Society, after reviewing in 1900 the various panaceas for the housing of the poorest classes, concluded that

'the solution of the problem lies in the direction of providing cottages as far away from population centres as is possible, and in providing at the same time cheap and rapid means of transit to and from work for those whose business lies at the great centres of industry. In this way lower rents are obtained as well as gardens and fresh air; and that new form of overcrowding in so-called "model-dwellings", with all their repulsive features, is avoided.'[3]

Charles Booth at the same time was declaring that the chief methods of curing overcrowding which remained to be tried were the acquisition of vacant land for the construction of houses, and the promotion of cheap and speedy means of access to districts where

---

[1] Corporation of London, Local Government and Taxation Committee, *Report on the City Day-Census*, 1881, pp. 7–8.
[2] F. J. Osborn, *London: An Awful Warning to Glasgow* (typescript), p. 2.
[3] Fabian Society, *The House Famine and How to Relieve It*, p. 43.

land was available for building, or some combination of these two.[1]
He urged the construction, preferably by the London County Council, of a large and complete scheme of underground and overhead
railways and surface tramways, extending beyond the existing metropolitan boundaries to wherever the population might go. The result,
he expected with a confidence that events have appallingly justified,
would be the spread of London in all directions.[2]

There were strong reasons for such an expectation. In London
the public for a generation had rapidly been increasing its use of the
improving but not very adequate public transport. The number of
passengers carried by local railways, tramways and the two principal
bus companies rose from 269,662,649 in 1881 to 847,212,335 in 1901,
an increase in the average number of journeys per head from 56·6
a year to 128·7 a year.[3] In the first few years of the twentieth century
there was a very great increase in locomotive facilities in London[4]
and the outward drift of population which had been expected as a
result was very much in evidence. Around the City, the poor were
displaced by warehouses, the artisans by the poor, the lower middle
and the middle class by artisans. The rich remained in some central
areas, such as Mayfair, but artisans moved out beyond them to North
Paddington, Hammersmith and Fulham, the middle class farther
afield to Highgate, Hampstead, Putney, Wimbledon, Wandsworth,
and Brixton, or beyond.[5] On the whole, the house in its own grounds
was tending to disappear and be replaced by the rows of new streets,
suited to middle-class purses, which were appearing in large numbers
in Clapham, Brixton, and Streatham.[6] As the means of transport
were extended, so the course of development changed. Hammersmith, for instance, had been very popular with the lower middle
classes, but part of the demand for new residences there was diverted
to Acton and Ealing when these were connected with London by
tram and tube.[7]

Even further out, better transport was exerting the same influence.
The Board of Trade reported in 1909:

'Good train services have a powerful effect in promoting the
development of residential districts. Examples of this are to be seen

[1] C. Booth, *Improved Means of Locomotion as a First Step towards the Cure of the Housing
Difficulties of London, p.* 13.
[2] *Ibid.,* pp. 15–17.
[3] *Royal Commission on London Traffic, Report,* vol. I, p. 6.
[4] Browning Hall Conference, *op. cit.,* p. 6.   [5] *Ibid.,* p. 18.
[6] *Ibid.,* p. 8.   [7] *Ibid.,* pp. 9–10.

in the neighbourhood of Dollis Hill, between Willesden Green and Neasden, where the Metropolitan Railway Company have opened a new station; at Harrow where there is now a ten-minute service of trains; at Wembley Park; at Golder's Green, and in other directions. The railway companies are alive to the advantage which they may derive from the development of residential areas, and lose no opportunity of providing facilities calculated to further it. The increase of season ticket traffic between London, Southend and Westcliff furnishes a striking instance of what may be done by a cheap and fast service suited to the needs of business people. Building is active in this and in other parts of the area served by the London, Tilbury and Southend Railway. . . . The areas served by the joint lines of the Metropolitan and Great Central and the Great Western and Great Central Railways afford further examples of the stimulus to building which good train services are able to give.'[1]

There were signs of a suburban exodus even from the poorest districts. In 1902 the Town Clerk of Shoreditch was looking to the further improvement of railway services and housing on the rural fringes of London for a solution of the housing problem of his borough.[2] In support of his faith in this development he pointed to the large numbers who already came into Shoreditch daily by rail; he noted that it was as quick and as cheap to travel by the Great Eastern Railway from Enfield to Shoreditch as it was to go from one end of Shoreditch to the other by tram, and that, as a result, Enfield was becoming built up.[3]

That this process of residential diffusion had been steadily maintained was a sign that great changes had taken place in the working conditions and perhaps also the incomes of a large part of the population. That in the opening years of this century there was a confident expectation that the process would continue implied a belief that many more had benefited from these changes than had yet taken advantage of them to move their place of residence. A good deal of attention has been given to working hours and wages in the late nineteenth and early twentieth centuries[4] and, though the total

---

[1] Board of Trade, *Report of the London Traffic Branch*, 1909, p. 52.
[2] *Joint S.C. of H. of C. and H. of L. on Housing of the Working Classes, Report*, p. 72.
[3] *Ibid.*, pp. 74–7.
[4] *Vide*, e.g., A. L. Bowley, *Wages and Income in the U.K. since* 1860, and, for a recent discussion, W. W. Rostow, *British Economy of the Nineteenth Century*, especially chapter IV and appendix.

magnitude of the change cannot be stated with any great exactitude, its direction is unquestionable. The reduction in hours was perhaps especially influential on suburban development. In 1886 it was estimated that hours of work had fallen on an average by three to four per week since 1870.[1] People had a little time to spare for daily travelling which they had not had previously. Moreover, as the nineteenth century wore on it seems probable that the relative importance of casual work in the economic life of the great cities slowly declined. Both this change and the increasing importance of skilled and non-manual occupations meant that for a larger and larger proportion of people the allocation of time in daily life became reasonably predictable, a circumstance favourable to the dissociation of places of employment and residence.

Changes in the level of incomes also affected the ability of people to live at some distance from their work. There were complaints by working men in the eighteen-eighties that, though they would prefer to live in the suburbs, they could not afford to do so. One who worked in Soho and had tried living in Battersea declared that it was too expensive; he saved in rent but increased his expenses by more than this saving because of the cost of travelling and meals out.[2] Another drew attention to the lack of opportunities in the suburbs for women to supplement their husbands' earnings[3] and there appeared to be a widely-held belief that it was cheaper to live in London than outside it.[4]

The fact that so many more people were able to move out of the great cities into suburbs during the next thirty years, and to remain there, is evidence that they were able to afford it. To demonstrate conclusively that the rapid growth of suburbs was dependent on an increase of personal incomes it would be necessary to show that the majority of people who moved into suburbs had recently experienced an increase of income. It is impossible to do this, but the indirect evidence strongly suggests that suburbanization was a sign of growing wealth. A very rough indication of this can be obtained from the value of residential property as reflected in the figures of rateable value per head of population. In 1894 the average for the County of London was £7 17s. 5d. and the highest values were naturally

---

[1] Rostow, *op. cit.*, p. 92.
[2] *Select Committee on Artizans' and Labourers' Dwellings Improvement, Final Report*, p. 124.
[3] *Ibid., Final Report*, p. 122.   [4] *Ibid., Final Report*, p. 85.

in the parishes with a high proportion of business premises. But it is significant that the lowest figures were all for parishes in the urban core largely given up to residences and domestic occupations, whereas the figures for the outer parishes were nearly all either up to or above the average, despite the unimportance of business premises there.[1] The lowest figures were:

	£	s.	d.
Mile End Old Town	3	9	6
Bow	3	8	4
Bethnal Green	3	7	2
Bromley (by Bow)	3	5	3
Plumstead	3	5	3
Mile End New Town	2	14	1

The figures for the outer parishes were:

	£	s.	d.
Hampstead	9	16	4
Kidbrooke	9	12	10
Eltham	8	15	7
Lee	8	2	5
Penge	7	7	5
Streatham	7	1	11
Hammersmith	5	10	10

Although it would appear that in the new suburbs some better property was being built, presumably for people able to pay for it, suburban development involved economies in certain directions. In particular, it was almost invariably possible to build houses of similar quality more cheaply in new suburbs than close to town centres, because of the much lower price of land. It was for this reason that so many enthusiasts for housing reform selected building in suburbs as the most satisfactory solution of existing difficulties; they already had bitter experience of the way in which high land values hampered the provision of decent accommodation within large towns. But the economy of cheap land was one which was rapidly reduced as the suburbs were built up. Already in 1881 an architect and surveyor pointed out that, though it would be worthwhile for the Metropolitan Board of Works to purchase land in the suburbs, land was not substantially cheaper until some distance from the town centre.[2] Four years later, the surveyor to the London School Board stated that in suburbs 'you may take it that as the houses grow

[1] London County Council, *London Statistics*, 1894–5, p. 723.
[2] *Select Committee on Artizans' and Labourers' Dwellings Improvement, Interim Report*, p. 125.

you are able to get about the same price for the land that you had been able to obtain for the portions nearer to London twelve months before'.[1] Land at the outer edge of London varied in price from £2,000 to £4,000 per acre and was obtainable more cheaply only in districts beyond the reach of a railway station. There were, in fact, zones of higher and lower land value. As one went north or north-westward from London land fell in value just beyond the metropolitan area, then rose again in the areas 'suitable for gentlemen's residences', and eventually fell again at an appreciable distance from London.[2]

The steady rise in land values tended to spread building farther and farther out from the city. But the advantage of cheaper land was not all lost. Many people obtained new houses in suburbs before they were caught by rising land values, and where public authorities undertook rehousing they were able to do it much more cheaply in the suburbs than in central areas. That is clearly illustrated by the early schemes of the London County Council. Between 1890 and 1895 several schemes were carried out in central districts and the average cost per head of persons in occupation was £131 8s. in respect of land and buildings, or £64 1s. in respect of buildings alone. The corresponding figures for the first suburban schemes (at Tooting and Tottenham) were, up to 1904, only £74 8s. for land and buildings, but £60 0s., nearly as much as in the centre, for buildings alone.[3]

Such economies did not need to be confined to residential building. But it has already appeared how strong were the reasons which attached most industrial undertakings to the centres of towns.[4] Most of them were as little inclined to move into suburbs as into new detached settlements. A few did so, however, and, just as there were residential estates in the suburbs quite separated from places of work, so also there were various examples of businesses moving to the outskirts of a town while their employees retained their old dwelling places. In Glasgow by the mid-eighties, for example, a number of factories had been re-located near the edge of the city, including the Singer sewing-machine works which settled at Kilbowie, but the workpeople concerned tended to remain in the city.[5] The whole

---

[1] *Royal Commission on Housing of the Working Classes, Report*, vol. II, p. 196.
[2] *Ibid., loc. cit.*
[3] *Royal Commission on London Traffic, Report*, vol. I, pp. 12–13.
[4] P. 145, *supra.*
[5] *Royal Commission on Housing of the Working Classes, Report*, vol. V, p. 48.

movement was extremely haphazard, for at the same time many other people were going to live in the Glasgow suburbs,[1] whether these were conveniently placed for their work or not.

The prospect of a much-increased suburbanization of industry was foreshadowed by the coming of the trading estate. The pioneer enterprise of this kind was Trafford Park Estates Ltd., which was formed in 1896 to acquire Sir Humphrey de Trafford's private estate. The opening of the Manchester Ship Canal and the construction of Manchester Docks alongside this estate had made the owner anxious to sell it and also made it specially suitable for industrial development.[2] In the early stages of development about 2,000 houses were planned on 79 acres of this estate by a company associated with the Westinghouse Company.[3] About 700 houses were actually built, but subsequently only industrial building was undertaken. The estate, when acquired, covered 1,200 acres and contained no buildings except Trafford Hall and two farm-houses. The estate company provided or arranged for roads, statutory railways, gas, water, electricity and other factory facilities, including very cheap rail haulage from every factory on the estate to Manchester Docks. In 1904 it obtained an Act of Parliament which enabled all kinds of industrial facilities to be granted on, under and over the roads in Trafford Park. Thereafter the estate was gradually occupied by a large number of firms until by 1938 there were about 200 of them, employing 50,000 people.[4]

Trafford Park, however, remained for many years an exceptional enterprise.[5] It was only in the period between the two World Wars that the trading estate became an accepted feature of industrial life. There were, of course, other examples earlier of large factories being set up in suburban districts and some of them, as for example, the jam factory of W. P. Hartley at Aintree, were associated with experiments in improved housing in the vicinity.[6] But in the general pattern of urban history these were of minor importance. Suburban

---

[1] *Ibid.*, vol. V, p. 46.

[2] D. G. Wolton (ed.), *Trading Estates. The Growth and Development of the Modern Factory Unit*, p. 23.

[3] J. E. Budgett Meakin, *Model Factories and Villages: Ideal Conditions of Labour and Housing*, p. 421.

[4] Wolton, *op. cit.*, pp. 23–5.

[5] It was not the only trading estate founded before 1914. A few others, which were less favourably situated, collapsed. (W. G. Holford, 'Trading Estates' in *Journ. of the Town Planning Inst.*, vol. XXV, pp. 152–3.)

[6] Meakin, *op. cit.*, p. 422.

spread was a major feature, but it was a spread overwhelmingly for residential purposes, and this was what primarily determined its character.

Although the growth of residential suburbs eventually came to be regarded as the chief source of hope for the rapid provision of better living conditions, it appears that when the movement began to attain importance it was having rather different results. The Social Science Association discussed this subject in 1879 and almost every speaker agreed that suburban districts outside town boundaries were a threat to health. The advantages of country air were being offset by faulty building, bad drainage, and insufficient water supply.[1] This was attributable partly to the lack of legislative authority over the suburbs. Urban areas were beginning to impose minimum standards on new building within their boundaries by means of by-laws, but suburban areas in what were administratively rural sanitary districts were not subject to similar control. The Association therefore proposed that both the municipal area and the suburban districts should be brought within the control of one sanitary authority.[2]

The provision of healthier and pleasanter suburbs was partly dependent on changes in local government boundaries and on the gradual tightening of public health law. But the minimum standards imposed in this way were not high and even thirty years after the Social Science Association's resolution there were still some who complained that the common result of opening a new area for building was to convert it into a jerry-built district as cheerless and chaotic as the previous one developed.[3] On the whole, however, there was some improvement in the standard of suburban development. In the early years of this century, if people wished to cite the errors of past suburban development they usually chose their examples from what had been done twenty or thirty years earlier.[4]

Various influences were at work to bring about some improvement. Changes in the income and social standards of suburban dwellers had their influence on the type of building and layout for

[1] *Transactions of the National Assoc. for Promotion of Soc. Science*, 1879, pp. 454–63.

[2] *Ibid.*, pp. 462–3.

[3] J. S. Nettlefold, *Slum Reform and Town Planning. The Garden City Idea applied to existing Cities and their Suburbs*, p. 2.

[4] *Vide*, e.g., speech by John Burns, Pres. of L.G.B., on the second reading of the first Town Planning Bill in 1908, where he took as typical of the evils of city expansion without planning, Edmonton, Tottenham, West Ham, Bermondsey and Rotherhithe, (*Parl. Debates*, 4th series, vol. 188, col. 957.)

which there was a good market. So had the type of social position to which these people thought it suitable to aspire. Increasingly was a suburban residence a cherished symbol of respectability. Not without reason did a corner of Fulham cast off its plebeian associations and adopt the name of West Kensington.

A gradual but cumulative influence was also exerted by various private experiments in suburban improvement. Of these, probably the earliest of any importance was the creation of Bedford Park at the western edge of London in 1877. This was a commercial enterprise undertaken by Jonathan T. Carr and executed in accordance with designs made by Norman Shaw. Bedford Park, in its origins, showed the diluted influence of Morris's views on art and society, although its designer had no sympathy with Morris himself. But it was an attempt to provide pleasant residential conditions on economical lines for people of quite moderate incomes, and it has stood the test of time.[1]

Bedford Park attracted a fair amount of contemporary attention and it provided certain new standards for suburban development. A little later, new manufacturing villages such as Port Sunlight and Bournville were also setting new standards of layout and many people who were not concerned to promote the establishment of new, self-contained, detached settlements were willing to see these standards applied to suburban extension. In particular, a few new suburbs began to appear which were characterized by a more open type of development and the provision of gardens for small houses.

Among the movements associated with the changing character of residential suburbs one of the earliest and most influential was that for co-partnership housing. In an organized form it began in 1888, when Benjamin Jones, manager of the London branch of the C.W.S. and one of the original members of the council of the Society for Promoting Industrial Villages, then approaching dissolution, founded Tenant Co-operators Ltd. This company made little progress until the turn of the century when it appears to have been stimulated by the public interest which the garden city movement roused. By 1914 Tenant Co-operators Ltd. had, by purchase or erection, established estates at Upton Park, Penge, Camberwell, East Ham and Epsom.[2] The co-partnership method was to raise capital from both investors

---

[1] Bedford Park is discussed in S. E. Rasmussen, *London. The Unique City*, pp. 266–7, and Sir R. T. Blomfield, *Richard Norman Shaw, R.A. Architect*, 1831–1912, pp. 33–6.

[2] E. G. Culpin, *The Garden City Movement Up-to-Date*, p. 49.

and prospective tenants and to limit interest to 4 per cent or 5 per cent. The tenant members' share of the profits was credited to them in shares, not in cash, and any surplus profits after payment of the maximum interest on capital were paid to the tenants as a dividend on rental[1] corresponding to the dividend on purchases in consumers' co-operative societies.

The example of Tenant Co-operators was followed in the early years of this century by a number of similar societies, of which the best known was probably Ealing Tenants Ltd., which was founded in 1901 and which concentrated on a single estate at Brentham.[2] Very soon some of the various co-partnership societies found it desirable to form a federation, which took the name of Co-Partnership Tenants Ltd. The steady growth of the movement is illustrated by the increase in the value of the property belonging to societies affiliated to Co-Partnership Tenants. In 1903 this was only £10,237, in 1905 £36,390, and in 1907 £204,639.[3] By the end of 1911 the figure had reached £1,005,000,[4] but after that the rate of progress slackened and the value in 1914 was £1,250,000.[5] By that time there were fourteen associated societies: Anchor Tenants Ltd. (Leicester), Brentham Garden Suburb (Ealing), Burnage (Manchester Tenants Ltd.), Fallings Park Tenants, Garden City Tenants, Greta Hamlet, Hampstead Heath Extension Tenants Ltd., Hampstead Tenants Ltd., Second Hampstead Tenants Ltd., Harborne Tenants, Liverpool Garden Suburb, Oakwood Tenants Ltd., Sevenoaks Tenants Ltd., and Stoke-on-Trent Tenants Ltd.[6]

The co-partnership movement was primarily concerned with housing rather than town planning. Indeed, no fewer than five of the fourteen societies just named were providing houses within the framework of development schemes prepared and controlled by other organizations. But they were not dealing with individual houses; they concentrated their activities on substantial estates in suburban districts and they made their own contribution to estate planning. It was their practice to lay out an estate as a whole with ten or twelve houses per acre, good private gardens, and public

[1] H. Vivian, *Co-partnership in Housing in its Health Relationship*, pp. 5–6.
[2] Vivian, 'Garden Cities, Housing and Town Planning', in *Quarterly Review*, vol. CCXVI, p. 512.
[3] Vivian, *Co-partnership in Housing in its Health Relationship*, p. 7.
[4] Vivian, *Quarterly Review, loc. cit.*
[5] Culpin, *op. cit.*, p. 50.
[6] *Ibid.*, pp. 51–6.

tennis courts, bowling greens and children's playgrounds.[1] They were also early supporters of the principle of 'social mixture' and claimed that, as on their estates they deliberately provided houses of varied size and rental, they helped to create a more socially diversified community.[2]

One of the major processes to which the co-partnership societies contributed was the transformation of the suburb into the garden suburb. This change was mainly the result of the impact of the garden-city movement on a situation in which economic and technical factors had rendered suburban expansion the easiest means of improving living conditions. The argument was obvious. In the ordinary course of commercial activity new suburbs were springing up every month; in building and layout they left much to be desired. At the same time a garden city was being built which was a handsomer, more salubrious place than the towns which had grown up in the last sixty or seventy years. But new towns were costly rarities. Therefore such attributes of the rarity as could be extracted and applied separately must be bestowed on the common novelty, the suburb. So 'suburban housing on garden-city lines' became the fashion.

The project which did more than all others to set the fashionable seal on this prolific hybrid was the Hampstead Garden Suburb. The promoters of the scheme had notable aims in matters both of social relationships and amenity, as is shown by a statement of their viewpoint issued in July 1905:

'We desire to do something to meet the housing problem, by putting within reach of working people the opportunity of taking a cottage with a garden within a 2d. fare of Central London, and at a moderate rent. Our aim is that the new suburb may be laid out as a whole on an orderly plan.

We desire to promote a better understanding between the members of the classes who form our nation. Our object therefore, is not merely to provide houses for the industrial classes. We propose that some of the beautiful sites round the Heath should be let to wealthy persons who can afford to pay a large sum for their land and to have extensive gardens.

We aim at preserving natural beauty. Our object is so to lay out the ground that every tree may be kept, hedgerows duly considered,

[1] Vivian, *Co-partnership in Housing in its Health Relationship*, p. 5.
[2] *Ibid.*, p. 8.

and the foreground of the distant view be preserved, if not as open fields, yet as a gardened district, the buildings kept in harmony with the surroundings.'[1]

The instigator of the scheme was Henrietta Barnett, supported by Earl Grey, Sir John Gorst, Sir Robert Hunter, Herbert Marnham, Walter Hazell and the Bishop of London. In 1905 they secured an option on a site of 256 acres owned by the Eton College Trustees, and after much propaganda they succeeded in raising £202,000.[2] Then in March 1906 they formed the Hampstead Garden Suburb Trust, with Earl Grey as President and Raymond Unwin as architect. In May 1907 work on the construction of the suburb began.[3]

As there were certain novelties in the type of development which was proposed a private Act was necessary and was obtained in 1906.[4] The most important provisions in it which differed from or supplemented general building law were :

(i) the average proportion of houses must not exceed eight per acre;

(ii) on every road there must be a space at least fifty feet wide between houses on opposite sides of the road, free of any buildings, except walls, fences and gates;

(iii) the company could make by-laws to regulate any gardens, recreation grounds or open spaces which it provided for common use;

(iv) the operation of local by-laws was suspended as far as concerned the layout and making of roads in the case of culs-de-sac of limited length and subject to certain safeguards.[5]

The last was a particularly important point because it permitted savings in the cost of making roads which did not have to carry much traffic. It provided a useful argument against those potential critics who might claim that the low-density garden suburb was too expensive.[6]

[1] Hampstead Tenants Ltd., *Cottages with Gardens for Londoners*, pp. 6–7.
[2] Dame H. Barnett, *The Story of the Growth of the Hampstead Garden Suburb*, 1907–28, pp. 5–6.
[3] *Ibid.*, p. 8.
[4] 6 Ed. VII, c. cxcii.
[5] Hampstead Garden Suburb Trust, *The Hampstead Garden Suburb. Its Achievements and Significance*, p. 5.
[6] On the subject of costs and possible economies in the layout of low density suburban estates *vide* R. Unwin, *Nothing Gained by Overcrowding, passim.*

Most of the directors of the Trust were unwilling for it to undertake building, and so in 1907 a Garden Suburb Development Co.
was formed which spent nearly £250,000 but ceased operations in
the middle of the First World War.[1] Much of the rest of the building
was carried out by various co-partnership societies specially founded
for the purpose. Hampstead Tenants Ltd. was registered in 1907,[2]
Second Hampstead Tenants Ltd. in 1909,[3] Hampstead Heath
Extension Tenants Ltd. in 1912,[4] and Oakwood Tenants Ltd. in
1913.[5] The co-partnership societies not only built up much of the
Trust's estate but also, through their federal body, Co-Partnership
Tenants Ltd., extended the suburb, by arrangement with the Trust,
on land which they themselves leased from the Ecclesiastical Commissioners.[6] The Trust itself erected homes for its own staff and
also certain public buildings.[7]

Physically, Hampstead Garden Suburb developed much as it had
been intended to do. As a work of art it acquired an international
reputation and influence. Socially, it disappointed the hopes of its
founders.[8] The working class was not attracted, a circumstance not
very surprising when the somewhat rarefied atmosphere in which
it was conceived is considered, and the well-to-do side of the scheme
progressed much more rapidly than the working-class end.[9] Financially the project had promising results at first, then suffered setbacks;
in the long run it achieved a profitable position, but the run, as in
the case of the garden cities, was longer than the commercial investor
cares to contemplate, still less to suffer. Apart from debenture stock
and from loans raised from time to time on first mortgages on parts
of the estate, capital was raised by the issue of 55,000 £1 ordinary
shares. Dividends were limited to 5 per cent and the first payment
of 5 per cent, in respect of the year ended 31st March 1907, was
made in 1910. By 1914 dividends had been paid up to 30th September
1910, but no further payments were possible until 1933. In the next
two years 4½ years' arrears of cumulative dividend were overtaken
so that payments were exactly twenty years in arrear. In 1936 the
Trust was able to issue one additional share for every share held,
instead of paying the same sum as twenty years' dividend, for the

[1] Barnett, *op. cit.*, p. 19.
[2] *Ibid.*, p. 14.   [3] *Ibid.*, p. 19.
[4] *Ibid.*, p. 25.   [5] *Ibid.*, p. 26.
[6] Hampstead Garden Suburb Trust, *op. cit.*, p. 6.
[7] Barnett, *op. cit.*, p. 21.   [8] *Ibid.*, p. 76.
[9] Hampstead Garden Suburb Trust, *op. cit.*, p. 30.

nett revenue had become sufficient to pay 5 per cent on the doubled capital value.[1]

In these circumstances Hampstead Garden Suburb developed gradually, but its publicity was sufficiently thorough, the achievement of its first few years sufficiently comprehensive and clear, for it to exercise considerable influence very quickly. In the years just before the First World War schemes for garden suburbs were being put forward in great profusion. Those who saw in this development the salvation of the industrial town were regularly provided with new examples to report and new causes for rejoicing. The very first issue of *The Town Planning Review*, in April 1910, was able to report signs of progress from many different quarters: a co-partnership society had decided to buy 38 acres for a housing estate at Penkull, one mile from Stoke; Blackburn Small Holdings Society had been reconstituted as the Blackburn Rural City Society and intended to build a new suburb; Pepler and Allen were laying out a residential estate of 100 cottages on just over eight acres at Fforest-fach, near Swansea; Liverpool Garden City Association was proposing to develop, through a co-partnership society, an estate of 28 acres, one mile from the Birkenhead boundary.[2] And so it went on. *Garden Cities and Town Planning* in 1913 was describing, under the heading 'A Picturesque Garden Village', the lavish provision at Cuffley where a quarter of a 542-acre estate was to be occupied by open space, including a golf-course, and no house was to have less than half an acre of garden.[3] In the same year it held up to admiration the new garden suburb at Gidea Park as 'an instructive example of what commercial enterprise on good lines can effect when the teaching of Town Planning is put into practice'.[4] By 1914, apart from Letchworth Garden City and early schemes such as Bournville and Port Sunlight, at least 52 schemes for garden suburbs were completed or in progress.[5]

By this time, the suburbanization, which had developed as an almost blind reaction against the state of towns and as a piece of social opportunism, had acquired a character of its own and the kind of prestige that leads to repeated imitation. It was perhaps just as well that it had achieved some distinctiveness, for H. G. Wells was

[1] *Ibid.*, pp.14–17.
[2] *The Town Planning Review*, vol. I, pp. 75–80.
[3] *Garden Cities and Town Planning*, New Series, vol. III, p. 134.
[4] *Ibid.*, New Series, vol. III, p. 54.
[5] Culpin, *op. cit.*, insertion facing p. 8.

already looking forward to such an increase in the diffusion of cities that the equivalent of the season-ticket holder would be able to choose his residence anywhere within a hundred-mile radius of the city,[1] and contemplated the day when all Great Britain south of the Highlands would be one vast diffused urban area.[2] If the country was largely to consist of suburbs it was desirable that these suburbs should be of good quality. In the eighteen-seventies and eighties no one dared have suggested that there was any strong probability of that. But before 1914 there were many who believed that the situation had fundamentally changed. Town Planning had been recognized as a practical possibility and, for the time being, town planning was regarded as virtually synonymous with 'suburban layout on garden city lines'.

Certain questions therefore immediately arise. Why was there this new element in the situation? Was the new practice of town planning a controlling principle as its supporters claimed? Was the control it implied effective in practice in contributing to a fundamental improvement in living conditions? These are questions that must be considered in approaching any conclusions on the rise and nature of a town-planning movement.

[1] H. G. Wells, *Anticipations of the reaction of mechanical and scientific progress upon human life and thought* (revised edn.), p. 46.
[2] *Ibid.*, p. 61.

PART THREE

A TOWN
PLANNING MOVEMENT

M

CHAPTER VII

The First Town Planning Act and its Origins

Town planning first received statutory encouragement in Great Britain in the Housing, Town Planning, etc., Act of 1909.[1] The town-planning part of that Act was acknowledged at the time to represent the acceptance of something new in the control of the further development of towns. The severe limitations of what it was found possible to achieve under the provisions then enacted have not unnaturally caused the importance of the measure to be belittled, but the importance of a first step often derives from its priority rather than its magnitude, and it may well be judged that this was so in the present instance. Few would be disposed to claim more for the town-planning measure of 1909 than that it was a symptom of change in the orientation of policy and outlook in matters of urban improvement. Its significance depends upon the nature of that change, which can be diagnosed only by an examination of the origin and content of the new measure.

However great the novelty of statutory town planning, it was not concerned primarily with a problem that was either new in itself or newly-recognized. It was an extension of the attempts, discussed in Part II of this book, to remedy the unhealthy condition of towns. Town-planning legislation was stimulated by those attempts in two ways. In the first place, though their achievements were considerable, they were obviously incomplete, and for that reason a demand gradually developed for some more comprehensive treatment. Secondly, the nature of some of the remedial measures that were adopted familiarized reformers with some of the problems and opportunities of a thorough plan for laying-out a considerable estate.

Probably the South African War did more than anything else to increase the urgency of the demand for further improvement of the

[1] 9 Edw. VII, c. 44.

health of towns, because of the high proportion of prospective recruits for the army who were found to be physically unfit. The sequel to this discovery was the appointment of an Inter-Departmental Committee on Physical Deterioration, which reported in 1904. This Committee found that there were not sufficient data for a comparative estimate of the health and physique of the people at different times, but the impression it derived from most witnesses was that there had been no general physical deterioration.[1] There was, however, plenty of evidence of a low physical standard in some classes and the Committee attributed much of this to the effects of urbanization, especially overcrowding and atmospheric pollution.[2] One point in particular it made which was specially relevant to the adoption of town planning. This was that urban conditions which had already proved inimical to health were being continually repeated without improvement:

'In England no intelligent anticipation of a town's growth is allowed to dictate municipal policy in regard to the extension of borough boundaries, with the result that when these are extended the areas taken in have already been covered with the normal type of cheap and squalid dwelling houses, which rapidly reproduce on the outskirts of a city the slum characteristics which are the despair of the civic reformer in its heart. . . . In this connection it would be expedient to secure the co-operation of Local Authorities in contiguous areas that are becoming rapidly urbanized.'[3]

In effect, this was a plea, on grounds of public health, for more positive control over the suburban expansion which had come to be accepted as normal.

Although the likelihood of general physical deterioration was not confirmed by the Committee, its possibility continued to be used by advocates of town planning to buttress their arguments. Indeed, as propagandists will, some of them treated the possibility as an

[1] *Inter-Departmental Committee on Physical Deterioration, Report*, vol. I, p. 13. A generation earlier the same question had been considered by Dr. Rumsey, who also was very uncertain about his conclusion, though he thought that physical infirmity was increasing. The only evidence he appears to have used was the proportion of rejections among army recruits, which he recognized was complicated by variations in the required standard. (H. W. Rumsey, 'On a Progressive Physical Degeneracy of Race in the Town Populations of Great Britain', in *Trans. National Assoc. for Promotion of Soc. Science*, 1871, pp. 466–72.)

[2] *Inter-Departmental Committee on Physical Deterioration, Report*, vol. I, pp. 14–20.

[3] *Ibid.*, vol. I, p. 19.

unquestionable reality. Even in 1912 Henry Vivian, the leading figure in the co-partnership housing movement and a Member of Parliament, pointing out that the influences making it essential to adopt town planning were similar to those which had made it essential in the eighteen-forties to introduce sanitary reform, sought to justify his claim by asserting that 'the time has, in fact, come when, on this question, we have to insist that, in the interest of race-preservation, private gain must harmonize with the public good'.[1] The average modern city was, he maintained, for the most part destructive of the life of its working population,[2] an assertion which might have been justified half a century earlier, but was hardly supported by contemporary facts, except as a recognition that we are all heirs of mortality. In the early twentieth century people were still flocking to the towns, not to step into the shoes of those dead before their time, but simply because urban existence, with all its deficiencies, had become so much more tolerable than rural. A Parliamentary Committee, studying internal migration, had already remarked that 'the contrast between life in the country and in the town is so manifest that it is not to be wondered at that large numbers every year migrate to the latter'.[3]

Still, there were parts of most towns which were in some ways inimical to health and the advocates of town planning made sure that this fact was not overlooked. Some of them carried the argument a stage further back and drew attention to the economic repercussions of unhealthy conditions. One of the most influential, T. C. Horsfall, wrote in 1908:

'Unless we at once begin at least to protect the health of our people by making the towns in which most of them now live, more wholesome for body and mind, we may as well hand over our trade, our colonies, our whole influence in the world, to Germany without undergoing all the trouble of a struggle in which we condemn ourselves beforehand to certain failure.'[4]

That was the kind of argument that had become more forceful as a result of thirty or forty years of keen international competition in industry and trade.

[1] H. Vivian, 'Garden Cities, Housing and Town Planning', in *Quarterly Review*, vol. CCXVI, pp. 493–4.
[2] *Ibid.*, p. 495.
[3] *Select Committee on Housing of the Working Classes Acts Amendment Bill, Report*, p. xxiv.
[4] T. C. Horsfall, *The Relation of Town Planning to the National Life*, pp. 13–14.

Economic lessons were also being drawn from the costly experience of necessary reconstruction in cities. Various guesses were made at the amount of money spent on street widenings. One published in 1915 suggested that it had been £25,000,000 in fifty years.[1] Another in 1910 coupled street widening with the provision of open spaces in built-up areas and placed the joint expenditure at £30,000,000 or more in the previous ten years.[2] No particular weight can be given to such guesses. What was significant was that large figures could be bandied about in discussion and the point made that suitable provision in advance could have prevented the necessity of spending such sums. Anyone with a plausible scheme for saving large amounts of public money can rely on a hearing. Not all the argument was very convincing. No one did or could make clear how, in a period of rapid technical and social change, the volume and type of traffic to which a main thoroughfare would have to be suited in twenty years' time could be estimated, and the thoroughfare constructed accordingly. More reasonable was the argument that, by suitable layout, most residential roads could be segregated from heavy traffic, so that expenditure on their construction could safely be reduced.[3] This was put forward, however, as an example of an incidental economy that could be achieved, rather than a fundamental justification for town planning.

Probably more influential was the growing interest in public amenity. Towns in the late nineteenth century became more healthy and more efficiently managed, but they did not become noticeably more beautiful or more lively. In undistinguished anonymity they crept over and destroyed open spaces, trees, country paths; and gracious rural buildings were removed to make way for them or concealed in an alien setting. Conscious revolt against this condition of things was confined to a few, but it was vehemently expressed and inspired deeds as well as words. Some of the protest was weakened by

---

[1] H. R. Aldridge, *The Case for Town Planning*, p. 133.

[2] J. S. Nettlefold, *Slum Reform and Town Planning. The Garden City Idea applied to existing Cities and their Suburbs*, p. 3. On the basis of incomplete replies to enquiries the Association of Municipal Corporations in 1907 put the total expenditure of local authorities on street improvements and open spaces in the previous ten years at £18,221,004, of which it believed three-quarters could have been saved had there been powers to exercise foresight in development. (*Local Government Chronicle*, 1907, p. 428.)

[3] This argument was often advanced. It was one of the main themes in R. Unwin, *Nothing gained by overcrowding*, and was also produced by, among others, Nettlefold, *loc. cit.*

association with a somewhat precious outlook on art and a failure to take account of the economic and social conditions of the time in suggestions for an alternative. No one denounced the late Victorian town more fiercely than William Morris. In his lecture, on *Art and Socialism* in 1884 he called London a 'spreading sore . . . swallowing up with its loathsomeness field and wood and heath without mercy and without hope, mocking our feeble efforts to deal even with its minor evils of smoke-laden sky and befouled river'.[1] In a slightly earlier lecture he summed up London and the other great commercial cities of Britain as 'mere masses of sordidness, filth and squalor, embroidered with patches of pompous and vulgar hideousness'.[2] The marks of the manufacturing districts were 'black horror and reckless squalor'.[3] Even the domestic gardens and the pine trees of Bournemouth could not save its villas from being 'simply black-guardly'.[1] But Morris had scarcely anything that was immediately practicable to suggest as a remedy. Towns must contain more gardens and they must cease to encroach on the fields,[5] but how this was to happen was not stated. Morris knew that he wanted a completely different society, but he was looking backwards rather than forwards and ignoring the necessity of transition from the present. In his new world the British Isles were to be kept as 'the fair green garden of Northern Europe',[6] a sudden reversal of role for the workshop of the world. The weakness of Morris's treatment of the contemporary urban situation was its complete unpracticality; forgetting six counties overhung with smoke was a delightful pastime, but no cure for the smoke-pall.

Occasionally in his socialistic writings, particularly in contributions to Hyndman's periodical, *Justice*,[7] Morris made some attempt to reconcile his vision of a community of garden cities with the continued existence of factory production. His picture of the organization of communal buildings and services[8] had something in common with the best of Owen, but his utter ignorance of economic realities and his deficient understanding of human nature prevented him from making comprehensive suggestions which were even remotely

[1] W. Morris, *Architecture, Industry and Wealth*, p. 74.
[2] *Ibid.*, p. 103. [3] *Ibid.*, p. 74.
[4] *Ibid.*, p. 52. [5] *Ibid.*, p. 76.
[6] *Ibid.*, p. 61.
[7] The relevant articles are reprinted in May Morris, *William Morris, Artist, Writer, Socialist*, vol. II, pp. 126–39.
[8] *Ibid.*, vol. II, pp. 127–9.

feasible. He held that houses lacked gardens and playgrounds only 'because profit and competition rents forbid it',[1] that factories could stand in large and beautiful gardens because 75 per cent of people would enjoy tending them voluntarily and, if private profit were abolished, workmen need not be kept in the factory more than four hours a day.[2]

With such a cloudy basis, Morris's direct influence on town planning could not be large, but he may have had a greater indirect influence. He helped to strike at the roots of contemporary self-satisfaction, and to convince a few that artistic standards could and should be applied to a much wider range of activities, not least to the condition of towns and the relation between town and countryside.

There were others later who stressed the supreme importance of amenity and pleasing appearance as the fundamental reason why town planning should be adopted. Outstanding among them was Raymond Unwin, the architect of Hampstead Garden Suburb. When he summed up the influences on the town-planning movement he concluded that

'It is the lack of beauty, of the amenities of life, more than anything else which obliges us to admit that our work of town-building in the past century has not been well done. Not even the poor can live by bread alone. . . . In desiring powers for town-planning our town communities are seeking to be able to express their needs, their life and their aspirations in the outward form of their towns.'[3]

To an appreciable extent that attitude was rooted in artistic rather than social considerations, a fact which had an important influence on the content of town planning.

But the general movement for the preservation and increase of amenities was more than that. The broader-minded advocates of town planning linked amenity with public health. Horsfall, for instance, observed that the poor physical and moral quality of so many town dwellers was not attributable to any particular evil such as overcrowding of dwellings, drink or filthy air, but simply to the absence of anything positive to counteract these things, to the deficiency in towns of pleasantness to make people cheerful, hopeful and healthy.[4] He strongly criticized the prevailing British attitude

[1] *Ibid.*, vol. II, p. 129.   [2] *Ibid.*, vol. II, pp. 131-5.
[3] R. Unwin, *Town Planning in Practice* (2nd edn.), pp. 3-4.
[4] T. C. Horsfall, *The Improvement of the Dwellings and Surroundings of the People. The Example of Germany*, p. 21.

that so long as steps were taken to ensure that dwellings were well-planned, well-built, well-drained, well-sewered, and sufficiently surrounded by space not to be cut off from air and light, the inhabitants of the houses had been sufficiently served.[1] To ensure just those conditions was the important, though incomplete, achievement of the public health movement. Horsfall's criticism illustrates both that town planning, the introduction of which he was urging, was derived from the movement for sanitary reform and that its aims and methods were wider in scope than those of the earlier movement.

Although only a small minority of the people was active, more and more voluntary effort was put into attempts to increase public amenities, particularly though not exclusively, for town dwellers. The manifestations of this activity were various. An early one had been the foundation of the Society for the Preservation of the Commons in the Neighbourhood of London in 1865; and the public outcry in the next decade when Epping Forest was threatened with destruction before its rescue by the Corporation of the City of London was a symptom of growing concern about such matters. Towards the turn of the century, interest was obviously growing. The formation of the National Trust in 1895 was one sign of the change and the position of Octavia Hill as one of its three founders links it with the daily work of housing improvement. Though their immediate concerns were different both ultimately sought to make some contribution to the improvement of the physical and spiritual well-being of the people through the influence of their surroundings, by removing or correcting what was degrading and by preserving and enriching what was inspiring and refreshing. Many other small amenity societies for specific purposes were formed about this time and had their own victories, which were those of the public also. Individuals made their contribution with new ideas about what was practicable and desirable, sometimes large, inspiring projects like that for a green girdle round London which Lord Meath published in the *Sphere* in 1901 and which was taken up for discussion elsewhere,[2] sometimes with small proposals of mainly local interest. Public interest in the preservation of amenity even grew strong enough to have a modest influence on the Statute Book with the passage in 1907 of the Advertisements Regulation Act.[3]

[1] *Ibid.*, pp. 160–1.
[2] *The Garden City*, New Series, vol. I, pp. 59–60.
[3] 7 Ed. VII, c. 27.

At the beginning of the twentieth century there were, then, an increasing sensitivity to the condition of the physical environment, increasing awareness of its relation to human experience, increasing doubt as to the possibility of achieving much more on the old lines of public health and housing policy. This was a state of affairs in which the minds of some naturally sought the more comprehensive approach, which they called town planning; a condition, too, which was favourable to the growth of a town-planning movement. Such a movement became apparent to contemporaries in the eighteen-nineties and grew rapidly in the next twenty years.[1]

To be effective the movement needed both its exemplars and its propagandists. Something has been said of the exemplars, for they were the fruits of the various experiments to produce an alternative or a corrective to the earlier course of urban development. The advocates of town planning took as their models the new towns and villages and the garden suburbs of the late nineteenth and twentieth centuries. These were small, few and belated, for until recently it had been almost impossible to secure capital for enterprises of this type, but they were increasing and they were sufficient to demonstrate that the ideas which they embodied could be applied in practice. Letchworth was the greatest influence, not because of its location or its self-contained character, but because of its low-density, its gardens and its tree-lined roads. Within a dozen years of its foundation one writer could remark that its success had compelled every one responsible for town development to think in terms of garden cities and garden suburbs: 'if some estate developers still proceed on the old lines, they apologise and make excuses for it.'[2] Letchworth Garden City and Hampstead Garden Suburb and Brentham were town planning in practice. To some it seemed that all that was necessary for the victory of town planning was to persuade estate developers everywhere to copy their essential features.

Not all propagandists, however, preached so narrow a doctrine. They varied greatly in their interests and influence. Ebenezer Howard was influential through his practical work more than through his writing. It is indeed very doubtful whether most of the enthusiasts for housing on 'garden city lines' had ever read *Tomorrow*, certain that they cannot fully have understood it.

Of other leading figures the one with the most original and comprehensive approach to the subject was Patrick Geddes. He was a

[1] Vivian, *op. cit.*, p. 493. [2] *Ibid.*, p. 497.

biologist who put great stress on the influence of environment and
the extent of the demands which he required a city to fulfil was, at
the turn of the century, most remarkable. A small indication of the
unusual nature of his approach can be gathered from the fact that in
1904 he gave to his first full-scale report on a town the strange sub-
title *A study of parks, gardens and culture-institutes*. He conceived the
city as 'a necessarily unique social personality, a definite regional and
racial development, yet one capable of increasingly conscious evolution'.[1] His problem was to show how this conscious evolution might
be guided. He saw that society was changing in such a way as to
bring questions of a new kind into prominence:

'The world is now rapidly entering upon a new era of civic
development, one in which "progress" is no longer described as in
mere quantity of wealth and increase of population, but is seen to
depend upon the quality of these. The last generation has had to
carry out great works of prime necessity, as of water supply, sanitation and the like; elementary education, too, has been begun; so that
to some, even pioneers in their day, our city development may seem
well-nigh complete. But a new phase of civic development has become urgent—that of ensuring healthier conditions, of providing
happier and nobler ones.'[2]

The way to set about this, he insisted over and over again, was to
survey the social origins, condition and needs of a city or a region
and to relate them to the opportunities and limitations revealed by a
study of the physical nature and resources of the terrain. This approach
was to him a necessity for the well-being of society.

'Starting . . . with the fundamental problem of purifying our
stream and cultivating our garden, we naturally and necessarily progressed towards the idea, first of bettered dwellings of the body, and
then to that of higher palaces of the spirit. The whole scheme,
material and intellectual, domestic and civic, scientific and artistic,
is thus thoroughly one; whereas without such fundamental basis of
natural and industrial reality much of our present-day idealism but
flutters in the void; while our would-be practical world, as yet too
much without this evolutionary idealism, is continually sinking into
material failure or stagnation, moral discouragement, or decay.'[3]

[1] P. Geddes, *City Development. A study of parks, gardens and culture institutes*, p. 221.
[2] *Ibid.*, p. 2.   [3] *Ibid.*, pp. 221-2.

Of all the enthusiasts for town planning Geddes was the one whose attitude was most truly sociological. But because his proposals were more drastic and his lines of reasoning less familiar than those of others his aims were for many, many years less completely realized in practice, although in speech and writing he was forcefully presenting his viewpoint for half a century from the eighteen-eighties. His influence was in inducing people to think about the problems of city development and to do something about them in consequence; but hardly to act as he suggested. His meat was too strong for most of the early town planners. The propagation of his ideas was also hampered by some of his half-baked followers.[1] Yet his influence was a very real one.

There were one or two others who, though they had far less appreciation of the social significance of town planning, were able to exert special influence because of the opportunities and experience which they derived from public work. Chief among them were J. S. Nettlefold and William Thompson. Nettlefold was chairman of the Housing Committee of the Birmingham City Council. He was able to illustrate his arguments from what had been achieved there and besides his own private advocacy of town planning,[2] he also found it possible to use that great municipality to some extent as a mouthpiece for his ideas. For instance, in 1906, when the Housing Committee reported on its first five years of work it emphasized that the creation of new congested districts could be prevented only if the City obtained power to forbid the erection of any new buildings except in accordance with a general plan for developing all uncovered land within the city boundaries; that development would be helped if the Council could obtain power to purchase land without, as then, being obliged to specify the exact purpose for which it was to be used; and that it was desirable for such powers to be conferred by general legislation, not by a local act.[3]

Thompson was an alderman of Richmond in Surrey, and besides playing a leading part in the experiments in municipal housing there, he learned the impossibility of treating the housing question in isolation. He did much to show that town planning involved the synthesis of a number of different activities for the sake of efficiency. His

---

[1] P. Boardman, *Patrick Geddes. Maker of the Future*, p. 250.

[2] Nettlefold published several works relating to town planning. The chief were *Slum Reform and Town Planning* and *Practical Town Planning*.

[3] City of Birmingham, *Report of the Housing Committee presented to the Council on the 3rd July*, 1906, pp. 6–8.

programme was clearly presented to a Parliamentary Committee in 1906. He urged the grant to local authorities of power to purchase and hold land on their outskirts, or alternatively the creation of a Central Commission for land, housing and transit which would purchase rural land on the outskirts of towns and hold it for the nation.[1]

'The traffic and transit questions [he said] will compel us to set up some body of this sort for London and for the large centres; and it seems to me important that the same body should have the power of getting at land outside the districts, before the tramways and other means of locomotion are extended, so that the benefit is reaped by the community. The body which will control the construction of tramways will know first what land is going to be appreciated in value, and will be able to get that land before other people step in. Nowadays a public body spends money on tramways; and then when it wants a hospital or a cemetery outside it has to pay the additional value, which I find is from 25 per cent to 50 per cent in a number of instances . . . I suggest, therefore, that this body which shall be charged with the development of towns shall take action to get the land before the transit scheme is carried out, planning where the means of transit shall be provided.'[2]

In fact all the physical aspects of development were to be considered together, in relation to each other, by a single body, and the inhibiting difficulties of compensation largely avoided.

Of another branch of town planning propaganda the most significant feature was that it made British people aware of what was happening in the same field on the Continent. The most influential writer on this aspect of the subject was T. C. Horsfall, whose work, known from its sub-title as *The Example of Germany*, was published in 1904 and played a leading part in town planning discussion in the next few years. It appeared originally as an appendix to a report on housing conditions in Manchester and Salford and was able to present some striking contrasts in favour of German methods. It included detailed accounts of the housing and town planning legislation and administration of Prussia, Hesse, and Saxony and of municipal work in Düsseldorf, Ulm, Stuttgart, Magdeburg, Frankfurt-am-Main, Cologne, and Mannheim. In particular it drew the

[1] *Select Committee on Housing of the Working Classes Acts Amendment Bill, Report*, p. 65.
[2] *Ibid., loc. cit.*

attention of British readers to German arrangements for the extension of cities: their purchase of land in anticipation of urban growth and their advance preparation of building plans to regulate that growth. Most German towns possessed a considerable amount of land[1] and many of the larger ones had building plans.[2] The emphasis was almost entirely upon the regulation of town-extension. Horsfall's account of Cologne, for instance, had little improvement to record in the older part of the city, but pointed, as to a shining example of municipal management, to the new parts with their well-arranged, wide streets, many of them planted with trees, their many pleasant shrubberies and other open spaces.[3] This direction of emphasis was particularly significant for Britain, where the better regulation of suburban growth had become the leading issue in town development.

Horsfall was not alone in looking to German achievements for guidance. There was increasing realization that in guidance of the growth of towns Britain had lagged behind other countries. Germany was the most telling example, because Germany was the most formidable rival, commercially and militarily, but was not the only one. There had been Town Extension Acts in 1865 in Italy, in 1873 in Sweden, and in 1875 in Austria-Hungary.[4] There were even Town Planning Commissions in some American cities, where the large-scale plan produced for Chicago by Burnham, Bennett and Olmsted was an outstanding influence.[5]

In the early years of the present century new information about what had been achieved in the way of town improvement and new and varied ideas for other steps in the same direction were thus being presented to the British public. Some of this propaganda had additional strength because it was organized. The two most influential bodies were the Garden City Association, founded in 1899, and the National Housing Reform Council, which was established one year later and subsequently renamed itself the National Housing and Town Planning Council.

The Garden City Association has already been mentioned in connexion with the public discussion of Howard's project and the establishment of Letchworth Garden City.[6] It had an almost im-

[1] Horsfall, *op. cit.*, p. 25. [2] *Ibid.*, p. 27.
[3] *Ibid.*, p. 138.
[4] R. H. S. Phillips, *The Political Economy of Town Planning*, typescript, p. 110.
[5] *Ibid.*, *loc. cit.*
[6] Chapter V, *supra*.

mediate influence on practice but did not confine itself to publicity for this scheme alone. It became an instrument for the discussion of town planning generally, especially through its journal, *The Garden City*, which first appeared in October 1904 and which changed its name to *Garden Cities and Town Planning* in 1908. To have current experience and regular publicity combined in one organization was a valuable support for the town-planning movement.

The National Housing Reform Council was important mainly for the clarity of its aims, the wide range of its activities, and the quality of its membership. It was not a large body. In 1908–9 its income reached no more than £2,038, of which only £600 came from British donations and subscriptions.[1] But its members included most of the leaders of housing reform: George Cadbury, W. H. Lever, Joseph Rowntree, T. C. Horsfall, Raymond Unwin, and William Thompson, who became its chairman.[2] It quickly established international contacts[3] and in 1909 began to organize Continental tours to study town planning.[4] At home it tried to stimulate local interest by holding conferences in all parts of the country[5] and by the publication, begun in 1909, of reports of special local inquiries into housing conditions.[6] On the national level it was a body repeatedly urging on the Local Government Board the adoption of a specific policy. This policy included various items relative to the introduction of town planning. It urged that local authorities should be empowered to buy and hold large estates on their outskirts for the future creation of model suburbs; that local authorities, individually or in groups, should have power to prepare town extension plans; that by-laws should be revised to secure more open spaces, lower housing density and cheaper development by encouraging the use of new materials and the avoidance of unnecessary expense in the construction of streets and roadways; and (the item that Alderman Thompson had particularly urged) that a Central Commission should be established to consider the conditions of growth of the various districts of the country, and a Central Fund created for town and village development.[7]

Various other organizations also interested themselves in town planning, and it was in such bodies that the demand for town planning

---

[1] National Housing and Town Planning Council, 1900–1910: *A Record of Ten Years' Work for Housing and Town Planning Reform*, p. 24.

[2] *Ibid.*, p. 2.　　　　　　　　　　　[3] *Ibid.*, p. 4.
[4] *Ibid.*, pp. 10–11.　　　　　　　　[5] *Ibid.*, p. 3.
[6] *Ibid.*, p. 15.　　　　　　　　　　[7] *Ibid.*, pp. 6–10.

was most clearly and strongly stated. The National Housing Reform Council and the Workmen's National Housing Council used to arrange meetings in common, and it was at one such meeting, at Leeds in 1904, that the first resolution in favour of town planning in Great Britain was carried. Other organizations supporting the demand were the Association of Municipal Corporations, the Royal Institute of British Architects, the Surveyors' Institution, and the Association of Municipal and County Engineers.[1] And then in 1906 Birmingham City Council supported the views of its Housing Committee and of Nettlefold by becoming the first local authority to pass a resolution in favour of town planning and municipal land purchase.[2]

The support of many of these bodies was particularly important because it showed that the demand for town planning was arising not simply out of theoretical preoccupations but out of the everyday practical experience of local administration. The demand was coming in part from those who would be responsible for the execution of town planning if it were introduced.

This was in a true tradition of urban reform which had years of solid achievement behind it. Much of the sanitary improvement of the past sixty years had developed from the results of local experience and remedial efforts, often embodied first in private bill legislation and subsequently copied for general use. This process was still in full swing, especially through the intermediary of that Committee of the House of Commons (usually known as the 'Police and Sanitary' Committee) appointed in nearly every session from 1882 onwards to consider local authority bills. The codification of local demands for departures from the general law which this Committee carried out and the pressure for new legislation which, as a result of its experience, it was able to put on the Government led to major improvements in sanitary law.[3]

Yet there were further improvements of the need of which many local authorities had become convinced by experience, but which they felt could be achieved only through immediate general legislation. Town planning was one of these, and the initiative of the Association of Municipal Corporations in seeking powers for its

---

[1] Aldridge, *op. cit.*, p. 151.

[2] Nettlefold, *Practical Town Planning*, p. 435. The voting was 30 to 16.

[3] O. C. Williams, *The Historical Development of Private Bill Procedure and Standing Orders in the House of Commons*, pp. 211-21.

members to carry it out was highly significant. The need to consider what new powers for the planning of suburbs ought to be given to local authorities was raised in a resolution proposed by the Lord Mayor of Manchester at the autumn meeting in 1906 and carried, despite some opposition.[1] In May 1907 a special committee, which had considered the question, reported to the council certain resolutions which the latter thereupon accepted. The most important of them was:

'That power should be given to local authorities to prescribe and regulate the planning of their areas in regard to the laying out of streets in connection with building schemes or otherwise.'

A draft town-planning bill was also prepared[2] and after revision was submitted by a deputation from the Association to the Prime Minister and the President of the Local Government Board.

Pressure from such a source was more likely to induce action than was a mass of propaganda from a minority unless it was able to move the minds of a large part of the public.

There were, however, two conditions which facilitated a general acceptance of town planning in principle. First of all, statutory town planning was approached gradually and, as was pointed out at the beginning of this chapter, some of the remedial measures previously adopted for the unhealthy condition of towns had familiarized people with the work involved in laying out considerable estates. Housing reform had gradually been conceived in terms of larger and larger units. Torrens' Act had made a beginning with individual houses; Cross's Act had introduced an element of town planning by concerning itself with the reconstruction of insanitary areas; the framing of by-laws in accordance with the Public Health Act of 1875 had accustomed local authorities to the imposition of at least a minimum of regulation on new building, and such a measure as the London Building Act of 1894 brought into the scope of public control the formation and widening of streets, the lines of building frontage, the extent of open space around buildings, and the height of buildings. Town planning was therefore not altogether a leap in the dark, but could be represented as a logical extension, in accordance with changing aims and conditions, of earlier legislation concerned with housing and public health.

The second favouring circumstance was that the rapidity of urban

[1] *Local Government Chronicle*, 1906, p. 1048.   [2] *Ibid.*, 1907, p. 428.

change had become much more obvious to everyone as a result of suburbanization. It was evident that the making or marring of a large proportion of the physical environment depended on the immediate course of suburban development. If a means of controlling it could really be found it seemed likely to produce large results. John Burns, the President of the Local Government Board, addressing the first town-planning conference in 1910, pointed out the dominant environmental influence on the subject:

'Most of all [he said] the straggling suburb round the ever-changing city gives a stimulus whose call we ought to have answered years ago; . . . may I bring before you—because it is my duty—the extent of the damage that is being inflicted upon rural England by the indiscriminate unorganized spreading, without control, of straggling suburbs?'[1]

In the fifteen years before 1908 about 500,000 acres of land had passed from agricultural to building use.[2] The manifestations of that change were apparent to anyone with eyes unclosed. And since the recent improvements of private bodies, which fulfilled the prevailing idea of town planning, were all either directly concerned with or, apparently, easily adaptable to the creation of a better sort of suburb, people were ready to acquiesce in the introduction of general legislation on the lines indicated by these private experiments.

The combined effect of all these various influences showed itself in the provisions of the first Town Planning Act and the arguments brought out in Parliament to justify them. There was a double opportunity to consider those arguments, for the bill was originally introduced in 1908 and passed through its earlier stages then, but, although there was little opposition to it, lack of time prevented its passage being completed in that session. A similar bill, with hardly any alteration, was therefore introduced in 1909 and enacted; the debates on it followed much the same lines as those in the previous year.

Above all, the new measure reflected the strength of the prevailing belief that suburbanization was to be the salvation of the town. The spread of suburbs would rid the old city centres of congestion, which would automatically raise their quality; all that was necessary was

---

[1] Quoted in T. Adams, *Recent Advances in Town Planning*, p. 56.
[2] *Parl. Debates*, 4th series, vol. 188, col. 958 (John Burns's speech opening the debate on the 2nd reading of the Housing, Town Planning, etc., Bill in 1908).

to see that the new suburbs were pleasant and healthy: that seems to have been the general idea. The act concerned itself only with the development of new suburbs. A town-planning scheme might be made (it was optional) 'as respects any land which is in course of development or appears likely to be used for building purposes',[1] and this expression covered 'any land likely to be used as, or for the purpose of providing open spaces, roads, streets, parks, pleasure or recreation grounds, or for the purpose of executing any work upon or under the land incidental to a town-planning scheme, whether in the nature of building work or not'.[2] Land already developed or land unlikely to be developed could be included in a town-planning scheme only in special cases where a scheme to deal with land likely to be developed could not otherwise be satisfactorily prepared.[3] Yet a measure covering this limited range of conditions was seriously believed to be an instrument for improving towns in their entirety. When John Burns introduced the first bill in the House of Commons he declared, in a lamentable literary flight, 'The Bill aims in broad outlines at, and hopes to secure, the home healthy, the house beautiful, the town pleasant, the city dignified and the suburb salubrious'.[4] There was, it would appear, both over-confidence in the virtues of suburban expansion and sheer forgetfulness of the limitations of the bill.

Both the provisions of the act and the arguments which had supported it in its passage through Parliament showed how opinion had been affected by private experiments in the creation of improved suburbs. The influence of the Hampstead Garden Suburb Act showed itself in the section which required the insertion of special provisions in every town-planning scheme 'for suspending, so far as necessary for the proper carrying out of the scheme, any statutory enactments, by-laws, regulations, or other provisions, under whatever authority made, which are in operation in the area included in the scheme';[5] and in the provision that, as far as compensation was concerned:

'Property shall not be deemed to be injuriously affected by reason of the making of any provisions inserted in a town-planning scheme, which, with a view to securing the amenity of the area included in the scheme or any part thereof, prescribe the space about buildings or limit the number of buildings to be erected, or prescribe the height or character of buildings, and which the Local Government Board,

---

[1] Section 54(1).   [2] Section 54(7).
[3] Section 54(3).
[4] *Parl. Debates*, 4th series, vol. 188, col. 949.   [5] Section 55(2).

having regard to the nature and situation of the land affected by the provisions, consider reasonable for the purpose.'[1]

From both the Government and Opposition sides the examples of the garden suburbs, lumped indiscriminately with a few detached settlements, were repeatedly cited. In 1908 John Burns, for the Government, drew attention to the enormous advance in town planning made by private effort in the previous ten years, cited as examples Bournville, Port Sunlight, Earswick, Hull Garden Suburb and a garden suburb at Wolverhampton, and declared that the object of the new bill was to enable other people and associations to accomplish similar things.[2] Alfred Lyttelton, the leading spokesman of the Opposition, in the same debate emphasized the educative influence of Bournville, Port Sunlight, Hampstead, Green Street and Ealing, and approved the prescription of a minimum on the lines of the new progress.[3] In the debate on the second bill in the next year Lyttelton simply made the usual general point derived from the practice of garden suburbs: that the old mistake, still being made in suburbs, of placing a great many houses to the acre, ought to be prevented, and that houses should be built with regard to the site, air, and open space for gardening and for the children.[4] C. F. Masterman, the Parliamentary Secretary to the Local Government Board, wound up by remarking that the bill was all the more urgently needed since it was likely to be long before the lessons learned in the garden suburb were universally applied either by local authorities or private owners.[5] Each side echoed the other and both echoed current discussion without either amplifying or clarifying it.

Most of the main arguments of the town-planning movement had been absorbed. It was accepted that the scope of town planning must be wider than that of the old sanitary and housing legislation. The new act stated that the general object of town-planning schemes was to secure 'proper sanitary conditions, amenity, and convenience in connexion with the laying out and use of the land [covered by the scheme], and of any neighbouring lands'.[6] The amenity societies realized that it was a matter affecting their interests, and one member, W. H. Cowan, spoke in the second reading debate on behalf of the Commons Preservation Society, the Metropolitan Parks and Gardens

[1] Section 59(2).
[2] *Parl. Debates*, 4th series, vol. 188, cols. 953–4.
[3] *Ibid.*, cols. 1038–9.   [4] 3 *H.C. Deb.*, 5th series, col. 744.
[5] *Ibid.*, col. 788.   [6] Section 54(1).

Society, and the Society for the Protection of Places of Historic Interest and Natural Beauty. He had no objections to make to the town-planning part of the bill, but protested against the provision in the housing part which apparently gave local authorities power, subject to the consent of the Local Government Board, to acquire commons and open spaces for building purposes.[1]

The significance of foreign examples had also been noted. John Burns declared that 'no one can go to Paris, or Vienna, or Düsseldorf —to Paris especially or even to smaller towns and cities and see the way in which there has been a coherent plan and prescience in town expansion without being struck with the necessity of our being able to do a similar thing here'.[2] His Parliamentary Secretary added:

'We are to follow at a long interval and very slowly, not the example of Germany, but practically the example of the greater part of the civilized world, including Sweden and Norway and countries whose social experiments are not so far advanced as those of large empires. . . . The least we may demand . . . is that we should bring our level of civic development, controlled by the State as a whole, up to the level of other countries of Europe.'[3]

In one respect, however, the claims of town-planning advocates, arguing from foreign experience, were not conceded. British local authorities did not receive powers to acquire land compulsorily for possible future town extension on the German model. Local authorities were merely empowered for the purpose of town planning schemes to purchase land by agreement or compulsorily under the same conditions as for the provision of working-class housing.[4]

[1] 3 *H.C. Deb.*, 5th series, cols. 775-80. He was presumably referring to section 2. A partial concession to the viewpoint which he represented was made in section 45 of the act, which stated: 'Nothing in the Housing Acts shall authorize the acquisition for the purposes of those Acts of any land which is the site of an ancient monument or other object of archaeological interest, or the compulsory acquisition for the purposes of Part III of the Housing of Working Classes Act, 1890 [i.e. for the erection of dwellings for the working classes], of any land . . . which at the date of the order forms part of any work, garden, or pleasure ground, or is otherwise required for the amenity or convenience of any dwelling-house.' Section 73 was inserted to make it necessary to obtain Parliamentary approval for the acquisition of any common or open space for housing or for a town-planning scheme.

[2] *Parl. Debates*, 4th series, vol. 188, col. 958.

[3] *Ibid.*, col. 1041.

[4] Section 60(1). In this act sub-section (3) of section 2 modified the existing provisions of the Housing Acts so that, with the consent of and subject to any conditions imposed by the Local Government Board, local authorities could acquire land *by agreement* even though it was not immediately needed for housing.

Enlarged powers of compulsory purchase might well have brought considerable controversy into what was almost a non-controversial measure. As it was, the only sections of the town-planning part to which appreciable objection was raised were those dealing with compensation and betterment, and an extension of powers to acquire land would have increased the difficulties in that field also.

Although town-extension plans and garden suburbs were the predominant influences, something had also been learned from other aspects of town improvement. It was, for instance, in improvement schemes in built-up areas that the drag imposed on positive action by the nature of compensation provisions and the absence of betterment provisions, had been revealed. Some influence from that experience was probably responsible for the attempt to impose greater stringency in the compensation clauses and for the inclusion of a provision which enabled a town-planning authority to recover from anyone whose property was increased in value by the scheme of that authority, one half of the amount of the increase.[1] This was a striking departure from the practice of the two preceding centuries.

Practical experience in laying out estates inside existing cities was also drawn on to illustrate the possibilities of planning. John Burns took as one of his examples of what was wanted the Millbank estate in Westminster, which was occupied mainly by model dwellings, but also included hospitals and the Tate Gallery.[2] It is interesting to see the influence of the housing trusts thus acknowledged. In fact the new measure was concerned more with the planning of estates than of towns and anything learned from improved estate planning was relevant, whether it was derived from rebuilding in an old town or new building in a suburb or an industrial village. Burns noted some praiseworthy examples in each.

'Let us [he said] take Bournville for the poor and Bournemouth for the rich. Let us take Chelsea for the classes and Tooting for the masses. What do you find? You find in those four instances that your public-spirited corporations and public-spirited landowners have been at work, and I venture to say that if you take Bournville and Bournemouth, Chelsea and Tooting, or towns like Eastbourne, you will find very much done without damage to anybody of what we hope to make universal by this Bill.'[3]

[1] Section 58(3).
[2] *Parl. Debates*, 4th series, vol. 188, col. 954.
[3] *Ibid.*, col. 956.

Bournemouth and Eastbourne were noteworthy examples to choose. Their mention was an acknowledgment, not of what had been achieved by attempts to correct the evils of industrial towns, but of the persistence of a minor tradition of romantic town production, observant of amenity and catering for affluence, side by side with the dominant output of congested and formless industrial towns.[1] There was thus one more element in the passage of the act of 1909: an attempt to copy for general use something which had developed to meet the tastes of a privileged few.

The type of town development which was chosen for emulation was in many ways curious for an urban nation. Emphasis was no longer on the traditional advantages of the town, suitable provision for a wide variety of functions and activities in reasonable proximity, the physical conditions in which the stimulus of diverse and changing contacts are available to every inhabitant; it was on separation, on space rather than on what filled it, on trees, grass and gardens more than on shops, factories and pavements. It was as though people, having seen that nineteenth-century town development had been marked by grievous errors, had decided that they could be reconciled to an unavoidable urban existence only if, in the twentieth century, their towns were made as untownlike as possible. Doubtless the element of imitation was strong. The most recently successful people lived in just such spacious, unvaried surroundings, marked by a certain studied informality; if others could do likewise on a smaller and cheaper scale, they achieved at least the outward appearance of some mundane success, and the possibility of its attendant inner satisfactions. And there was little that was in the truer urban tradition of physical compactness and social variety and yet was sufficiently recent and of sufficiently obvious merit to serve for general imitation.

Yet there was more to it than this. There was a widespread belief that in moulding the physique and character of its inhabitants the town had failed, as the countryside had not failed. Most of the population had to live in towns; therefore the ideal was to graft something of the nature of the countryside on to the towns. The most practical propagandist in the field, Ebenezer Howard, preached that this was readily possible and produced his scheme for an environment of town-country; and others adapted the doctrine to other contexts. They really believed that in planned suburbs the nature of town and country could be combined, to the benefit of all,

[1] Chapter II, *supra*.

and overlooked the strong possibility that the resultant hybrid might display the virtuous characteristics not of both, but of neither. Even those fully aware of the deficiencies of existing suburban life still believed this. When C. F. G. Masterman spoke not as the Parliamentary Secretary jointly responsible for guiding the first town-planning bill through the House of Commons, but as a private social observer, he wrote at length of the superficiality, snobbishness and timidity in the life and outlook of the suburbans; yet he believed that suburban life was likely to improve and that already, together with the life of the artisan class, it was 'the healthiest and the most hopeful promise for the future of modern England'. And the most rapid way in which, he thought, that promise might be fulfilled was by the further sub-urbanization of cities, whereby 'something of the larger sanities of rural existence could be mingled with the quickness and agility of the town'.[1] That this possibility was illusory could be definitely demonstrated or disproved only by experience. Statutory town planning helped to make that experience possible.

The Act of 1909 introduced a change to which all the experience of the preceding three-quarters of a century in town development and town improvement had contributed. This would perhaps appear to constitute a claim that it was a measure of major significance. And in a sense it was, but, as was suggested at the beginning of this chapter, only because it turned activity rather vaguely into a new direction, not because of the distance it sent it along the new road. Though it had many and important antecedents, statutory town planning immediately after 1909 was a mild, uncertain affair. Town planning for all was a novelty which might be gingerly tried, but there was every deterrent to prevent any body from indulging in it to excess. There was now an act which permitted local authorities, if they were so disposed, and if they obtained the consent of the Local Government Board, to prepare town-planning schemes, but only for land about to be developed. What exactly constituted town planning was uncertain. As Alfred Lyttelton pointed out, 'there are few in this country who know much about town planning. . . . If you had twenty schemes to organise, I doubt whether you would be able to get the expert advice necessary before they could be put forward in even the most elementary stage.'[2] The Local Government Board was to make general provisions for certain matters mentioned

[1] C. F. G. Masterman, *The Condition of England*, p. 95.
[2] 3 *H.C. Deb.*, 5th series, col. 749.

in the act, and the most important which related to the actual physical content of town-planning schemes were:

(1) Streets, roads, and other ways, and stopping up, or diversion of existing highways.
(2) Buildings, structures and erections.
(3) Open spaces, private and public.
(4) The preservation of objects of historical interest or natural beauty.
(5) Sewerage, drainage, and sewage disposal.
(6) Lighting.
(7) Water supply.
(8) Ancillary or consequential works.[1]

These were presumably the subjects with which any town plan would be concerned, but what the relation between them was to be was left to be discovered empirically without any guiding principle.

The administrative detail which did much to determine the scope of town planning in practice was settled in 1910 and embodied in regulations made by the Local Government Board under the provisions of the Act.[2] The nature of the regulations appeared to be influenced mainly by a determination to make plain that everyone who might conceivably be affected, however minutely, by a town-planning scheme should have the fullest time and opportunity to make his views known about it. The Local Government Board defended this attitude in a circular to local authorities when the regulations were issued:

'The Board think it desirable that local authorities and others concerned in the making of a town-planning scheme should realize at the outset that a considerable period must of necessity elapse between the time of the inception of a scheme and its final approval. The necessity of giving effect to the clearly expressed intention of the Act in regard to affording persons interested or affected full opportunity of considering the proposals at all stages involves considerable delay, but the Board in settling the regulations have made the periods for notices as short as possible, having due regard to the objects to be attained. So far as administrative action upon the

[1] 4th Schedule.
[2] S.R. & O., 1910, no. 436. *The Town Planning Procedure Regulations* (*England and Wales*) 1910. Regulations for Scotland were made by the Local Government Board for Scotland.

part of the Board is concerned they will endeavour to expedite as much as is practicable the dealing with applications to them in regard to town-planning schemes, but the careful consideration of a case in all its aspects and the arrangements for the holding of the necessary local inquiries must necessarily take a substantial amount of time.'[1]

But delay was carried to quite absurd lengths. Not only had a local authority (in England the council of a borough or urban or rural district) to obtain permission from the Local Government Board before it could even begin to prepare a scheme, let alone take any action to implement it, but it had to give to the owners, lessees and occupiers of all land which it proposed to include in the scheme that it wished to prepare, at least two months' notice of its intention to apply to the Board for permission to prepare the scheme.[2] At every stage further complications were introduced. The result was a labyrinthine procedure in which any scheme might well be lost for ever and which was likely to make town planning appear to all but the most enthusiastic a task involving efforts much more than commensurate with the advantages which it might procure.

Altogether, statutory town planning was marked by the most drastic limitations. Its application was an option exercisable only in the face of deterrents; it applied in any case only to a small proportion of land and a narrow range of conditions; and it was concerned only with the physical layout of land and buildings; the social considerations which might guide that layout were left either to be disregarded or to be sought empirically for every separate scheme. Statutory town planning was no more than a halting advance, not a conclusive victory.

[1] L.G.B., *Circular to L.C.C., Town Councils and Urban and Rural District Councils, order no.* 55373, dated 3rd May, 1910. This circular was reprinted in Nettlefold, *op. cit.,* pp. 392–6.

[2] S.R. & O., 1910, no. 436, article I(a).

CHAPTER VIII

Approaches to Town Planning 1909—1947

IT was one thing to have a Town Planning Act and rather a different one to have town planning, but the distinction seems to have been realized by very few in the years just after 1909. As Professor Adshead pointed out reminiscently many years later, it was a time of exuberance among town planners, which lasted until just after the First World War.[1] First steps towards the implementation of the Act were taken in a number of places, at the same time as more and more estates were being laid out privately on lines approved by town planners. By the end of 1912 two schemes had actually been prepared and submitted to the Local Government Board, both by Birmingham Corporation, and the Board had approved the preparation of seventeen other schemes, at Bournemouth (two), Ruislip-Northwood, North Bromsgrove, Chesterfield, Oldbury, Liverpool, Hanwell, Halifax (two), Sheffield (three), Newcastle-upon-Tyne, Southport, Stoke-on-Trent, and Walthamstow.[2] Such activity was well maintained and by 1915 74 local authorities had been authorized to prepare 105 schemes, covering 167,571 acres.[3] It caused much gratification and in 1913 the *Town Planning Review* declared that it was undeniable that the Town Planning Act had been an extraordinary success: 'few Acts of Parliament have created such universal appreciative interest and been launched with such promises of success.'[4]

It was, perhaps, early to be looking for positive results. The first thing needed was practical work in the preparation of schemes and valuable experience in a variety of circumstances was undoubtedly

---

[1] *Journal of the Town Planning Institute,* vol. XXIV, p. 191.
[2] *Town Planning Review,* vol. III, p. 280.
[3] T. Adams, *Recent Advances in Town Planning,* p. 53.
[4] *Town Planning Review,* vol. IV, p. 1.

obtained. The first scheme to be finally approved (in 1913), that for Edgbaston, Quinton and Harborne, covering 2,320 acres in Birmingham, was for purely residential development; the second, for East Birmingham, was designed to create a predominantly industrial area;[1] the third, at Ruislip-Northwood, provided for the association of private plans with the town-planning scheme, which was mainly concerned with the orderly development of a rural district as the residential suburb into which economic factors were converting it. The two Birmingham schemes received some severe criticism on the ground that they adopted unnecessarily expensive methods of development, made too little use of the economical land purchase which the act permitted, and made quite inadequate provision for open spaces.[2] The Ruislip-Northwood scheme became the shining example of the possibilities under the 1909 Act. The heart of this scheme was really the private plan of the largest landowner, King's College, Cambridge, to develop its 1,300-acre estate at Ruislip Manor as a garden suburb.[3] The extension of the scheme by the local authority to cover some 6,000 acres made it possible to develop economically a substantial area on the lines approved as the best by contemporaries and exemplified by private experiments. But Ruislip-Northwood was an exceptional case, because of the coincidence that it was a suburban residential area just being opened up by improved communications, that it had some unusually vigorous councillors and that its largest landowner was independently interested in model estate development. The Act was not likely to be working very often in such a favourable combination of circumstances.

In all these schemes it was necessary to decide whether certain things should be done in one way or another, which meant considering why one method would achieve certain ends better than another. But this involved questions of the whole scope and aims of town planning. This matter was a source of much discussion in this period, quite apart from the preparation of specific schemes. In addition to private discussion, various public conferences on town planning, the formation of new institutions connected with the subject and the suggestions of bodies already in existence all contributed to the establishment of town planning as a subject and to the attempt to

---

[1] G. Cadbury, junr., *Town Planning with special reference to the Birmingham Schemes,* p. 89; C. Gill and A. Briggs, *History of Birmingham,* vol. II, p. 162.

[2] J. S. Nettlefold, *Practical Town Planning,* pp. 105–24.

[3] W. Thompson (ed.), *Town Planning in Practice. With an Account of the Ruislip (Middlesex) Town Planning Scheme,* pp. 3–9.

determine what was its content. The foundation of the School of Civic Design at Liverpool University in 1909 and the formation of the Town Planning Institute, which held its inaugural meeting in November 1913 and drew its members mainly from the Royal Institute of British Architects, the Institution of Civil Engineers and the Surveyors' Institution,[1] provided new media for the stimulation and dissemination of ideas.

The Royal Institute of British Architects was particularly influential. In 1910 it called the first town-planning conference to be held in Great Britain and it had its own town-planning committee, which in 1911 published some interesting notes on the content of town planning. It declared positively that a successful scheme must be based on a thorough civic survey, recording the physical state of the site, the social and economic condition of the people, and the historical and archeological interest of the locality and its buildings.[2] This preparation of data was to be the work of a surveyor, aided by the engineer, the valuer, the economist, the sociologist and the antiquarian.[3] The plan for future development should begin with provision for adequate traffic facilities, then arrange to provide main centres for various functions, such as administration, education and commerce.[4] The committee also noted the desirability of zoning land according to its most suitable future use: land close to railways, waterways and docks was to be reserved for industry, the healthiest spots on high ground and sunny slopes for residence.[5] There was much in these recommendations that was admirable and clear-sighted. Far more questionable was the supreme role allotted to the architect. To others he might leave the task of discovering what existing conditions were and, in general terms, what future requirements they indicated. But the work of deciding how those requirements could best be satisfied was to be left solely to the architect:

'For the design of the town plan, the architecturally trained mind is as essential as for the design of a single building; for the work consists in applying upon a wider field and with greater scope the same principles which govern the designing of individual buildings. The appreciation of masses and voids, the apprehension of the right

[1] *Town Planning Review*, vol. IV, p. 329.
[2] Town Planning Committee, R.I.B.A., 'Suggestions to Promoters of Town Planning Schemes', in *Journal of the R.I.B.A.*, 3rd series, vol. XVIII, p. 662.
[3] *Ibid.*, p. 668.   [4] *Ibid.*, pp. 663–6.
[5] *Ibid.*, p. 667.

points for emphasis and the power to combine into one creation many differing parts by bringing them into harmonious proportion are equally required in the field of town planning, if there is to be produced that rhythm in the plan, and that spacious breadth of ordered elevation in the groups of buildings, which so largely constitute the beauty and grandeur of cities.'[1]

That was a significant dictum and it was shared by others. Raymond Unwin, for instance, was pointing out that the grant of town planning powers to municipalities was of particular appeal to architects, who realized that efforts to improve the design of individual buildings would be of comparatively little value without a renewed opportunity of bringing them into true relationship with one another.[2] Whether its sponsors realized it or not, this outlook, which treated town planning as a predominantly architectural function, was bound to result in concentration on the outward appearance of things, not on the satisfaction of social needs, although it was growing awareness of social shortcomings that had created a demand for statutory town planning. Experts from fields outside architecture were allotted a place in town-planning enterprise only as assistants rather than partners. There was little point in stressing the need for a thorough civic survey if the changes of which it showed the desirability were to be subordinated to extraneous considerations. The survey then might achieve no more than to save one or two things from destruction. At its worst the architectural approach to town planning could fall into an utterly negative attitude. To save some fragments from the rural holocaust and see at least reasonably pretty buildings in reasonably pretty gardens was all that some people required of town planning. In 1911, for instance, the Sheffield Society of Architects and Surveyors was told, about a proposed plan for the suburbs of the city:

'the scheme is . . . only for the immediate and effective control of the extensions to suburbs, to prevent them being injured more than is necessary by the construction of roads and erection of buildings. Whatever is done must to a great extent destroy their natural beauty, and it is incumbent upon us all to preserve those beauties as far as is consistent with the provision of houses for the people.'[3]

[1] *Ibid.*, p. 668.
[2] R. Unwin, *Town Planning in Practice*, p. 375.
[3] E. M. Gibbs, *The Future Extension of the Suburbs of Sheffield*, p. 23.

Town planning apparently was the preference among a choice of evils. Another advocate of town planning told the University of Manchester that in this field the ideal would be to do nothing,[1] but the deplorable state of towns made it necessary to attempt the rash game of town planning.[2] His suggestions were concerned only with the improvement of the street plan, the provision of open spaces within a town and the preservation of a green girdle round it.[3]

So much of the impetus behind town planning at that time seems to have been derived merely from a wish to minimize inevitable disaster. Yet the belief of those who looked on town planning as an extension of architecture was that a vast spread of new building was inevitable and that they could so design it that the outcome would be a positive triumph of human creation. They had one over-riding principle of layout, the principle of low density. Only about one-sixth of a residential site should be occupied by buildings, said Raymond Unwin, and it was preferable not to have more than 10 to 12 cottages per acre of net building land (exclusive of roads).[4] All problems of town planning would be simplified, he maintained, by the application of Howard's Garden City idea, but the form of application which he proposed was the creation of groups of suburbs round a central nucleus, not of economically associated but distinct towns.[5]

It was town planning of the kind advocated by Unwin which established itself as town planning in practice. Indeed, its influence went far beyond the field formally designated as town planning. Low-density housing with ample gardens before and behind and often with tree-lined streets became normal for new suburban estates whether they were developed under town-planning control or not. Town planning on these lines captured official favour. In the First World War the recommendations of the Tudor Walters Committee about the construction and layout of working class houses (recommendations which greatly influenced the nature of municipal building in the next twenty years) conformed very closely to what had been adopted under town-planning schemes. The Committee in fact recommended that future house building should be regulated

[1] P. Waterhouse, 'Old Towns and New Needs', in P. Waterhouse and R. Unwin, *Old Towns and New Needs; also the Town Extension plan; being the Warburton lectures for* 1912, p. 30.
[2] *Ibid.*, p. 14.
[3] *Ibid.*, pp. 16–25.
[4] Unwin, *Town Planning in Practice*, pp. 319–21.
[5] Unwin in Waterhouse and Unwin, *op. cit.*, pp. 47–8.

by town-planning schemes instead of by rigid by-laws.[1] Within this framework it proposed the construction of large numbers of two-story houses with not less than three bedrooms each[2] and thus prepared the way for one of the standard visual symbols of twentieth-century Britain, the low-density council housing estate.

To those who regarded town planning from the point of view just described the deficiencies of the Act of 1909 were superficial, not fundamental. When it was applied it suited their purpose fairly well. They were frustrated by the delays in procedure which, with the support of the Tudor Walters Committee,[3] they sought to have amended; by the occasional inconvenience of having to plan for a single local government authority; and by the disinclination of most authorities to use their town-planning powers. They were satisfied with the type of thing that was being done in the name of town planning but they wanted more of it and more quickly.

There were some, however, who were doubtful whether this kind of thing was what they understood by town planning at all. The most clear-sighted of those who had supported the Garden City realized that one of its essential characteristics was its completeness; it was designed from the beginning as a self-contained whole, providing its own social resources. To them, planning which was concerned only with tacking additional suburbs on to existing towns was not *town* planning; a garden suburb was not a garden city. Mr. C. B. Purdom came to the attack in 1914 with a declaration that the Garden City Association ought not to support the extension of large towns and the multiplication of suburbs. He wrote:

'I have very slight interest in town planning that owes its origin to the Act of 1909, and frankly, I see very little that is good in the Garden Suburb, or "town planning on Garden City lines" . . . I always regretted the day that the Garden City Association weakened its good wine with the water of town planning. Time will show, I believe time has already shown, that it was a mistake. The Garden City is too good an idea to be confused with inferior practices.'[4]

But he had to admit that there was unfortunately hardly anyone in

---

[1] Local Government Board, *Report of Committee on Building Construction in connection with the Provision of Dwellings for the Working Classes in England and Wales, and Scotland*, p. 78.

[2] *Ibid.*, pp. 79–80. [3] *Ibid.*, p. 78.

[4] C. B. Purdom, 'A Criticism', in *Garden Cities and Town Planning*, new series, vol. IV, pp. 124–5.

the Garden City movement able to keep his head and repudiate the
Garden Suburb movement.[1]

Another line of attack was directed against the uncritical adoption
of low density, whether in suburbs or in cities, which was characteristic of statutory town planning and of private activity in improved
estate development. Mr. Trystan Edwards pointed out in 1913 that
low-density housing was spoiling too much of the countryside and
that the area allotted to housing ought to be limited. He denounced
the garden suburb as possessing neither the crowded interest of the
town nor the quiet charm of the country and as involving much
inconvenient and unwanted travelling.[2] He strongly criticized the
prevalent attitude to town development, embodied in the movement
for garden suburbs and garden cities, because it was based on a
misunderstanding of the nature of towns and because it promised
the impossible:

'The promoters of garden cities promise to their clients a rustic
environment which cannot be had under the circumstances and the
attempt to maintain the fiction of rusticity, when the conditions of
rusticity are absent, is responsible for a type of development which
does not deserve to be called modern or advanced but is, in effect,
rank retrogression.'[3]

As he pointed out, the fact that slums grew in towns was no reason
for abandoning the whole urban tradition.[4] There was an alternative
to the type of development proceeding under the names of town
planning and garden city housing:

'A well-arranged town, smokeless and quiet, with its traffic under
good control, having houses and streets in close formation; a town
which has a sufficiency of parks, squares, and other public places,
but yet contains a considerable population in a relatively small area;
a compact town with a limited number of fairly large detached houses
just outside it, immediately beyond which there is nature undefiled:
this is an ideal which seems more attractive than the monotonous
diffuseness of Garden Cities.'[5]

[1] *Ibid.*, p. 125.
[2] A. T. Edwards, 'A Criticism of the Garden City Movement'. in *Town Planning Review*, vol. IV, p. 155.
[3] A. T. Edwards, 'A Further Criticism of the Garden City Movement' in *ibid.*, vol. IV, pp. 316–17.
[4] Edwards, 'A Criticism of the Garden City Movement' in *ibid.*, vol. IV, p. 157.
[5] Edwards, 'A Further Criticism of the Garden City Movement' in *ibid.*, vol. IV, p. 318

But this was a lone voice, preaching what then seemed barbarous heresy.

There was still Geddes, however, to try to cure town planning of its current over-simplification. The architectural approach was not his. For him, town planning was to be regulative of architecture, and the study of civics was to be regulative and educative for town planning.[1] He took a very active part in discussion of town planning. When the first town-planning conference was held in London in 1910 an exhibition was held in connexion with it at the Royal Academy. Geddes prepared one exhibit dealing with Edinburgh, its geology, history, economic life, architecture and housing conditions, something far more comprehensive than anything else in the exhibition.[2] In 1911 he enlarged it to form a general 'Cities and Town Planning Exhibition' which was opened at Chelsea by John Burns, and afterwards went on tour to Edinburgh, Dublin, and Belfast.[3] Two years later this exhibition was shown at the Ghent Exposition Internationale, where it won the Grand Prix for the best collection on civic development and planning.[4]

The real point about Geddes's exhibitions and discussions was that he took it for granted that town planning was concerned with the whole range of life and activity in a town, whereas current town-planning practice was based on an outlook so much more restricted that, by Geddes's criteria, it is doubtful whether it can be classed as town planning at all. Sir Patrick Abercrombie has remarked that it once seemed possible to combine the German town extension plan, the Parisian boulevard, the English garden village and the American civic centre and park system into a mixture that could be applied indiscriminately and beneficially to every town and village in the country, and that this pleasing dream was first shattered by Geddes's Edinburgh exhibit in 1910.[5] But, to judge from subsequent discussion and practice, the dream was not shattered then; it was troubled a little perhaps, but no more. Geddes's teaching only began to command assent, indeed perhaps only to be understood, when those who received it had been chastened by a longer experience of the inadequacies of statutory town planning in practice.

---

[1] P. Geddes, *Cities in Evolution. An introduction to the town planning movement and the study of civics*, p. 298.
[2] P. Boardman, *Patrick Geddes. Maker of the Future*, p. 244.
[3] *Ibid.*, pp. 253–4.   [4] *Ibid.*, p. 264.
[5] Quoted in *ibid.*, p. 244.

No other critic had so comprehensive a view of town planning as Geddes, but there were one or two others who quickly realized that the concept expressed in current statutory town planning was altogether too limited. By 1914, J. S. Nettlefold, for instance, was complaining of the futility of the Local Government Board as a central authority for town planning and was advocating the formation of a new Department to deal with all aspects of the subject.[1] He had observed that one essential part of town planning, the design of new main roads, came generally under the Road Board, which, under the Development and Road Improvement Act, 1909,[2] had been given power to acquire land on either side of any proposed new road, up to 220 yards from the middle, a power which could be very useful in town planning.[3] And there were restrictions in both town-planning law and practice which he found quite indefensible. The restriction of town planning to suburbs, instead of towns being treated as a whole, was one. Nettlefold's policy was to prepare a skeleton plan of the whole district, providing for improved communications between the centre and its suburbs, proper communication as far as possible with other towns by road, rail or water, and the protection of new districts against overcrowding.[4] He also pleaded for the co-operation of all the arts and sciences in town planning instead of reliance being placed on the borough surveyor to deal with every aspect.[5]

When, however, in 1919 the statutory basis of town planning was first revised,[6] little attention was paid to the most fundamental criticisms. The points which were met had been sources of difficulty even to those who whole-heartedly acquiesced in the existing nature of town-planning schemes.

First of all, the official procedure was made a good deal less deterrent. In nearly all cases local authorities were empowered to prepare town-planning schemes without seeking the prior approval of the Ministry of Health, which had succeeded the Local Government Board. Secondly, in order to make planning powers effective,

---

[1] Nettlefold, *op. cit.*, pp. 179–82.
[2] 9 Edw. VII, c. 47.
[3] Nettlefold, *op. cit.*, pp. 182–3.
[4] *Ibid.*, p. 188.   [5] *Ibid.*, p. 201.
[6] By the Housing, Town Planning, etc., Act (9 & 10 Geo. V, c. 35). The chief provisions of this measure were summarized in a Ministry of Health circular, which can be found reprinted in A.D. Sanderson Furniss and M. Phillips, *The Working Woman's House*, pp. 78–84.

it was made obligatory for every borough and urban district with a population of more than 20,000 to prepare a town-planning scheme by 1st January 1926, and the Ministry of Health was empowered to act in case of default. This might appear to have been a big step forward, but a glance at what happened in practice dispels that illusion. By the Housing Act of 1923[1] the period allowed for the preparation of schemes was extended to 1st January 1929. Many authorities failed to prepare a scheme, no action was taken, and in 1932 compulsion again disappeared from town-planning law.

Two other changes made in 1919 met difficulties which had occasionally arisen in the earlier practice of statutory town planning and were also in the direction desired by those who wanted to increase the practical scope of town planning, but they were so restricted as to be of little benefit. Greater opportunity was given for land already occupied by buildings to be included in the area of a town-planning scheme, but the main subject of schemes was still the regulation of the layout of land which was being newly developed. There was no question of planning a town as a whole, and unhealthy and decrepit districts could still be treated only under the housing acts. Provision was also made for the formation of joint town-planning committees of several neighbouring local authorities, if they so decided among themselves. But these joint committees had usually no executive power, only an advisory function. They could prepare a plan dealing with the whole region administered by the constituent authorities but they could do nothing to ensure that all or any part of it was carried out, unless the local authorities delegated their planning functions to the joint committee, in which case the regional plan must be as detailed as any individual town plan.

On the whole the changes made after the First World War in the basis of statutory town planning were useful but slight. The conception of the subject among those concerned with it showed more improvement. Much thought about town planning remained very conventional, much was confused, but the clearest thinkers were concentrating on new aspects. For the most part they concerned themselves less with the decorative layout of estates, which had been and continued to be the mode in practice, and more with the nature and functions of whole towns; and not merely with towns as complete individual units, but with towns in relation to other towns, to the whole surrounding region, and sometimes to the national life.

[1] 13 & 14 Geo. V, c. 24.

An interesting development was the formation in 1918 of the New Towns Group by Ebenezer Howard, C. B. Purdom, F. J. Osborn, and W. G. Taylor.[1] This group advocated that the building of new towns in every region of Britain should be taken up as a national policy, to be carried out by the government and municipal bodies. Howard himself had no hope that this campaign would have any practical results and instead proceeded on his own account to buy a site for a new town at Welwyn.[2] So instead of being engaged in a prolonged propaganda campaign for a national policy of new towns, this group was absorbed into the task of actually creating one new town.

It had always been part of Howard's idea of the garden city that the small new cities might act as satellites to large established centres of population with which they would have certain social links. Not much attention had hitherto been paid to this suggestion, but it began to attract a little support. In 1920, for instance, a committee appointed by the Ministry of Health suggested that one contribution to the relief of overcrowding in London should be the development of self-contained garden cities; either round an existing nucleus or on new sites, with state assistance to encourage and hasten them in their early stages.[3] The suggestion was not adopted and the satellite town remained only a very slowly spreading idea.

Spread it did, however, and fused with other ideas. It was in the nineteen-twenties that the concept of controlled, large-scale decentralization of industry and population was first clarified. By 1930 it received sufficient attention for a group of British planners to produce a symposium about it.[4] The view was gaining increasing influence that individual towns could not be planned in isolation and the principle of decentralization was studied in relation not only to the diffusion of the town among suburbs, but also to regional and even national planning. Mr. Davidge was urging that a planned decentralization policy must be preceded by a national survey of natural resources, food supplies, transport resources, the growth of urban centres, and existing industries and their relative needs of

[1] F. J. Osborn, *New Towns after the War* (2nd edn.), p. 7. This book was originally written in 1918 as part of the propaganda of the New Towns Group.

[2] *Ibid.*, pp. 8–9.

[3] Ministry of Health, *Interim Report of the committee to consider and advise on the principle to be followed in dealing with unhealthy areas*, p. 6.

[4] H. Warren and W. R. Davidge (eds.), *Decentralisation of Population and Industry. A new principle in town planning.*

expansion.[1] He put forward a list of the major items that ought to be considered in a national plan:

(*a*) The conservation of land by drainage schemes, reclamation and the prevention of erosion; the encouragement of all forms of agriculture.

(*b*) The distribution of minerals and the requirements of the major industries.

(*c*) Commercial development, marketing of produce, and the unification of methods of transport.

(*d*) The location and extension of urban development and the promotion of rural development.

(*e*) The extension of all public services and their anticipated effect on land utilization.

(*f*) The progressive improvement of all transport facilities of national importance.

(*g*) The essential reservation of areas of land conspicuous from the point of view of national health and revenue.[2]

All this was a very far cry from the accepted current practice of planning. A changing attitude was developing also to the question of decentralization within the town itself. Thomas Adams was arguing that the diffusion of towns along lines of communication was not wrong in itself. The necessary improvement was so to control it as to secure a well-balanced distribution and arrangement of industrial business, residential and agricultural uses.[3]

Thus there were signs that among a few people a changed concept of the scope and nature of town planning was gaining acceptance. Emphasis was passing from the design of residential estates to the more general problem of the allocation of land among various uses. Planning was beginning to be seen less in terms merely of visual appearance, health and amenity, and more in terms of social and economic function. It is this change of viewpoint which gives to some (though not all) of the contributions to Warren and Davidge's book the appearance of being, in England at least, some ten or fifteen years ahead of their time. In 1930 these changed views were those only of a minority and their subsequent spread through the town-planning profession and their achievement of some influence on public opinion is of major significance in the development of a recognizable national town-planning policy.

[1] *Ibid.*, pp. 88–90.   [2] *Ibid.*, p. 94.   [3] *Ibid.*, p. 149.

It is not unreasonable to look for one source of this change in attitude to the experience gained in preparing plans for the joint town-planning authorities first permitted in the 1919 Act. By 1930 eighty joint committees had been established, representing over 1,000 local authorities with a population of more than 30,000,000 and an area of 21,000 square miles.[1] A few of these dealt with a very wide area. The Manchester Regional Committee, for instance, represented nearly eighty local authorities and acted for an area of 750 square miles.[2] Although these committees were only advisory, they gained valuable experience of new problems. It was where they were confronted by the prospect of unavoidable rapid economic change that the consultants employed by joint committees found their imaginations most stimulated, and most widened the scope of their plans. An interesting example was the plan prepared between 1925 and 1928 for east Kent, where the exploitation of a new coal-field caused anticipations of a large influx of other industries and of population. The authors acted on the general view that 'during the nineteenth century the mistake was made of providing for a wholly insufficient amount of growth—the danger of preparing on too lavish a scale does not appear as yet to have shown itself'.[3] So they planned on the assumption that the region's existing population of 300,000 would be increased by 278,000 by immigration and 99,300 by natural increase in thirty years.[4] This illustrated some of the pitfalls of planning, for neither industry nor population increased on anything like the scale anticipated.[5] But it also turned attention to the problem of locating and siting new settlements in relation to economic needs and activities, a problem with which British town planning had hitherto scarcely concerned itself. And this was not all wasted effort, for coal-mining itself expanded in the region and one of the small

---

[1] *Ibid.*, p. 70.
[2] International Garden Cities and Town Planning Federation, *Report of Conference at Gothenburg*, 1923, p. 11.
[3] P. Abercrombie and J. Archibald, *East Kent Regional Planning Scheme. Preliminary Survey*, p. 69.
[4] *Ibid.*, p. 71.
[5] It has been one of the besetting sins of town planners that they have founded proposals on estimates of population based on the most cursory examination of past and present figures. To many of them changes in the age composition have seemed to have had no significance at all for future trends, and they have been prepared to work on the assumption of flat rates of increase projected forward indefinitely. For a glaring example *vide* Gibbs, *op. cit.*, p. 6.

new mining towns proposed, Aylesham, was located and under construction before the final report was published.[1]

But it would be easy to exaggerate the importance of attempts at regional planning in the inter-war period. One later writer suggested that the publication of each report meant that a number of the most intelligent people in each area had been convinced, by local demonstration, of the degree to which current planning powers were incapable of achieving the aims desired of them, and that sixteen years of such demonstrations may have largely accounted for the rapid progress of the idea of planning during the Second World War.[2] There is, however, little evidence of such public conviction in the twenties and thirties, and it seems more probable that few people not professionally concerned took any interest in regional planning reports, and that, of the small number who came across them, a substantial proportion only saw evidence that planners were spending money on the discovery of information of which they made no effective use.

For in fact, where the stimulus of rapid economic change was not present, regional plans showed no great advance in scope beyond the town plans of 1909–19. Many of their positive proposals were not concerned with questions affecting the region as a region, but were merely suggestions for the uniform treatment of the same problem that came up in different localities within the region. For instance, in south-east Sussex, a common problem was noted for remedy at Pett, Fairlight, Rye and Winchelsea, which were all troubled by the erection of huts and disused tramcars.[3] And so with many other things. The one invariable proposal of regional significance was for some lengths of new main road, usually located more or less arbitrarily. But in many cases there was little more than that. It was noticeable, too, that, though the attempt to plan on a regional scale occasionally forced planners to think of the economic functions which their work had to serve, they always took the economic setting as given and never considered including in their plans elements which might deliberately modify it. This assumption was well illustrated by the authors of the Cumbrian Regional Planning Report in 1932, when they remarked on the excellent quality of Maryport

---

[1] Abercrombie and Archibald, *East Kent Regional Planning Scheme. Final Report*, p. 50.

[2] Astragal, 'History', in I. R. M. McCallum (ed.), *Physical Planning. The groundwork of a new technique*, p. 6.

[3] Adams, Thompson and Fry, *South-East Sussex Regional Planning Scheme*, p. 19.

and declared that 'what it lacks is trade; if general trade revives, Maryport can revive',[1] yet related none of their proposals directly to the strengthening of industry in the district.

Regional planning remained in Britain so unpractised a subject, so seldom fertilized by the necessity of translating paper propositions into action, that its influence on the progress of opinion, both professional and lay, was bound to be limited. True, the early surveys of advisory joint committees had shown that, given suitable powers and the will to exercise them, they might make a unique and useful contribution; and in the Local Government Act, 1929,[2] the possibility of actually carrying out plans on a regional instead of a local basis was increased by associating county councils with regional schemes and by giving the Ministry of Health powers to overcome the reluctance of local authorities to delegate their functions to joint committees.[3] These powers were incorporated in and strengthened by the Town and Country Planning Act, 1932,[4] but the difference which they made in practice was small. The treatment of the Greater London region may serve as an example of the small support which regional planning actually received. Nowhere was it more obvious that problems existed which demanded treatment on a regional basis. In 1920 the Unhealthy Areas Committee recommended the immediate preparation of a plan broadly assigning to each district in and around London its future functions. In 1923 the majority report of the Royal Commission on London Government recommended the appointment of a statutory advisory committee for a London area with a radius of 25 miles, while the minority report proposed a body with positive powers. In 1926 various bodies presented to the Ministry of Health a memorandum advocating the creation of a joint board for which experts should prepare a statutory outline plan for Greater London. Finally, in 1927, the Greater London Regional Planning Committee, which had only an advisory function, was set up.[5] This body in its first report in 1929 drew attention to the need to establish a regional planning authority for Greater London with power to prepare a master plan to which the schemes of local

---

[1] P. Abercrombie and S. A. Kelly, *Cumbrian Regional Planning Scheme*, p. 158.

[2] 19 & 20 Geo. V, c. 17.

[3] W. I. Jennings, *The Law Relating to Town and Country Planning* (2nd edn. by J. R. Howard Roberts), p. 6.

[4] 22 & 23 Geo. V, c. 48.

[5] P. Abercrombie, 'Plan for London' in National Housing and Town Planning Council, *Annual Report* 1936-7, p. 44.

authorities should conform.[1] Four years later it decided that it was unsuitable to keep itself in being from year to year and passed a resolution recommending the formation of a more permanent joint committee, which would be mainly advisory but would be made competent to exercise any planning powers which might from time to time be expressly delegated to it by any one or more of the town-planning authorities within the region.[2] But this proposal was never carried out and eventually, after ten years' existence, the Greater London Regional Planning Committee was dissolved[3] and the region was left without any body which was concerned with its planning as a whole.

Regional planning in general received little public support. The Ministry of Health went so far in 1931 as to appoint a Departmental Committee on the subject but gave it only very limited terms of reference. It was restricted to the consideration of the thirty-two regional reports already made[4] and was instructed to discover what useful proposals they contained which could immediately be carried out. 'What the Government are looking for', it was told by the Minister of Health, 'are schemes of public advantage which can be put in hand at an early date,'[5] in fact anything to mitigate unemployment. The Committee produced an interim report in which, while it commended the idea of regional planning and suggested that it should be encouraged throughout the country so as to enable a national survey of future development, it stated that the existing regional schemes could provide no great volume of additional work.[6] With that, the question was dropped and regional planning resumed its previous obscurity.

If some town planners were beginning to think in terms of regional and national development and to pay more attention to the social and economic purposes of their subject, it was less because of any positive achievements which they had experienced than because of the increasingly obvious shortcomings of the rapid contemporary urban development and because they were in touch with what was being done in other countries. From the United States, in particular, came a strong influence. Planners were able to observe the work that had been done there in the preparation of master plans

---

[1] Greater London Regional Planning Committee, *First Report*, p. 6.

[2] *Ibid., Second Report*, p. 10.   [3] Abercrombie, *op. cit.*, p. 45.

[4] Ministry of Health, *Report of Departmental Committee on Regional Development*, pp. 3 and 11.

[5] *Ibid.*, p. 12.   [6] *Ibid.*, p. 10.

for various regions, and the far weightier attention given in that country to the study of sociology had reactions on the concept of town planning which could hardly have originated elsewhere. It was, for instance, from the U.S.A. in the nineteen-twenties that there came the curious social concept of the neighbourhood unit,[1] which in British town planning in the nineteen-forties achieved so general and so uncritical a vogue.

The nature of British urban development in the period between the two World Wars is striking evidence of the unchallenged maintenance and powerful reinforcement of the trend which had established itself before 1914, and it also became eventually one of the strongest factors promoting a demand for a change in the nature of town planning. Whatever changes took place after 1918 in the statutory basis and in the concept of town planning, there was very little change in its practice. Almost everywhere the period saw an enormous multiplication of the low-density residential suburbs which had been the admired symbol of statutory town planning in its original form, and this happened whether the districts concerned were subject to town-planning control or not. And since the greatest cities had the greatest numbers of people to diffuse, there was a marked incease in the physical (as well as numerical) dominance of those great agglomerations of population which Geddes had earlier recognized and had dubbed conurbations.[2] The movement reached its greatest intensity in the nineteen-thirties, when suburban housing was facilitated by a national policy of cheap money, and its most spectacular spread in Greater London, where the administrative county of Middlesex was transformed into a social and governmental creation that would have seemed fantastic in all previous ages. But it was strongly marked earlier and elsewhere. Even in 1921 35 per cent of the occupied population of Wallasey, 30·3 per cent of that of Waterloo and Seaforth, 29 per cent of that of Great Crosby, 25 per cent of that of Little Crosby, and 24 per cent of that of Hoylake all travelled daily to work in Liverpool.[3]

---

[1] For an account of the development of this concept and some of the data on which it was based *vide* C. A. Perry, *Housing for the Machine Age, passim.*

[2] In *Cities in Evolution* (1915), pp. 34–40.

[3] South-West Lancashire Joint Town Planning Advisory Committee, *The Future Development of South-West Lancashire*, p. 19. The figures were taken from the survey made in the course of the 1921 Census, which showed clearly that appreciable separation of places of work and residence had become an important feature in the life of most large provincial cities, as well as London.

The taste and the income position of the growing middle and lower middle classes were a strong influence. Their exceptionally high representation in the population of some residential suburban districts was sometimes remarked. In 1921, for instance, of the adult male population of Beckenham 4·4 per cent were engaged in professional, 10·6 per cent in commercial occupations, and 9·7 per cent were commercial clerks.[1] On the whole, too, the new suburbs continued to be characterized by relatively high figures of rateable value per head of population. For instance, the figure in 1938 for every one of the urban authorities in Surrey, except Mitcham, was above the national average, in most cases considerably above;[2] of the twenty-six local government areas in Middlesex, only four had ·a figure below the average,[3] and two of these, Edmonton and Tottenham, were largely built in the nineteenth century, and another, Yiewsley and West Drayton, was one of the few districts of the county which had undergone only a modest suburban development and still retained an appreciable interest in agriculture.[4] Similarly most of the newer Cheshire suburbs of the Manchester and Stockport area had much higher rateable values per head of population than the provincial average, while older districts such as Salford, Irlam, Swinton and Pendlebury, and Middleton returned figures well below the average.[5]

But suburban spread was no longer merely the result of catering for a growing class in comfortable financial circumstances. After the First World War many of the largest local authorities adopted a policy of building low-density residential estates in suburbs with subsidized rents for their working classes, and later, though not on a large scale until the nineteen-thirties, private enterprise joined in the provision of fairly cheap suburban houses.[6] In the nineteen-twenties South Essex was an outstanding example of a region which

[1] W. R. Davidge, *Report on the Regional Planning of West Kent*, p. 60.

[2] Ministry of Health, *Rates and Rateable Values in England and Wales* 1938–39, pp. 10 and 30.

[3] *Ibid.*, pp. 24–5.

[4] The exception to the general pattern was Hayes and Harlington, which was mostly a new working-class and manufacturing area, but also retained a certain amount of agriculture.

[5] Ministry of Health, *op. cit.*, pp. 10–13 and pp. 21–2.

[6] Of the houses with a rateable value of not more than £13 (£20 in the Metropolitan Police Area) local authorities built 585,000 against 14,000 by private enterprise between January 1919 and March 1931. But from April 1931 to March 1939 local authorities built only 162,000 and private enterprise 688,000. (M. Bowley, *Housing and the State* 1919–1944, p. 272.)

was occupied by large numbers of residents of small means, as a result of the presence of cheap land and convenient (though increasingly overcrowded) travel to London, the building of large housing estates by the London County Council, and the rapid industrialization of the river front.[1]

In the welter of development any idea of town planning was usually either ignored or misapplied. In South Essex it was remarked that nearly every station on the two main railway lines to London had become the centre of a dormitory town for London workers, but the manner of growth was haphazard and the estate development stereotyped. Every house had a wide frontage and a considerable curtilage of land, and many were built of insubstantial materials. The result of such development was that local authorities often found it too expensive to carry out thorough sewerage schemes or to make up roads.[2]

Even where some sort of plan was prepared for development on a large scale it was often marked by sorry deficiencies. The incursions of the London County Council into Essex can hardly be regarded as models of judicious planning. Quite early, it was pointed out that the new L.C.C. housing estates were not what they professed to be. When in 1919 the L.C.C. had bought 3,000 acres and proclaimed its intention of accommodating 120,000 people there, the scheme had been called a garden city and satellite town. But in fact the estate was developed piecemeal as a working class suburb. The earliest building adjoined the built-up area of Ilford, without any attempt to separate the new settlement from it, the building was unrelated to industrial development, and, for dormitory purposes, the site was unsuitable because of inadequate roads and congested railways.[3] The whole course of development of the Becontree estate continued to be extremely unbalanced, partly, perhaps, because the L.C.C., which designed it, was not the authority responsible for its social services. For instance, it went on building houses even when it was obvious that there would be no schools for the children of the tenants.[4] Nearly all the estate suffered from serious school overcrowding until 1929 and for considerable periods the northern part of it had no infant schools.[5] Not until 1935 was a start made in the building

[1] S. D. Adshead, *The South Essex Regional Planning Scheme* 1931, pp. 75–6.
[2] *Ibid.*, p. 16.
[3] C. B. Purdom, *The Building of Satellite Towns*, pp. 35–7.
[4] T. Young, *Becontree and Dagenham*, p. 27.
[5] *Ibid.*, p. 80.

of the first secondary school within Dagenham Urban District.[1] At first there were no shops, churches or public-houses near the houses, and public-house facilities scarcely existed at all before 1928.[2] Little was done to attract means of employment to the locality, although industrial development had been anticipated. There was in fact scarcely any increase in local industry until the estate had been in existence for ten years,[3] when the transfer of the Ford Motor Works to Dagenham brought a huge addition. There was doubtless a good deal to be said for Becontree when it was complete, but surely this was not the way to go about the process of development.

Private estate development which paid lip-service to both social and architectural planning was prone to be no better and was frequently worse. It concerned itself only with residence and amenity, since the residents could safely be assumed to be content to earn their living elsewhere. Despite the garish search for the expression of individuality in house-design, whose outcome was usually a seemingly endless succession of incongruities, the same sort of suburb, without any real distinctiveness, was repeated in every heavily-populated part of Britain. From 'town planning' the one element of low-density in housing had been taken over and applied indiscriminately. But was there anything more to take over from what had hitherto been practised in the name of town planning?

In the inter-war period, though the sprawl of suburbs was due mainly to a vast spread of residential estates, it was not entirely so. For there was some movement of industry also to peripheral urban locations. A survey, completed in 1933, of the industrialization of the north and west of outer London revealed that between 70 and 75 per cent of the factories there had appeared since 1918.[4] Much of this development was due to direct decentralization from the heart of London, for, of 627 factories studied, 243 represented migrations from London, while 232 of the remainder belonged to newly-established firms.[5] One feature of the outward movement of industry was the growing importance of trading estates, which were in a few cases developed by public authorities but usually by private enterprise. Many of the estate companies were at first mainly financial and confined themselves to the purchase and preparation of factory

[1] J. G. O'Leary (ed.), *Public Services in Dagenham*, p. 17.
[2] Young, *op. cit.*, pp. 79–81. [3] *Ibid.*, p. 27.
[4] D. H. Smith, *The Industries of Greater London, being a survey of the recent industrialisation of the northern and western sectors of Greater London*, p. 170.
[5] *Ibid.*, p. 171.

sites for building, which they then leased or sold to manufacturers, to whom sometimes they also advanced loans for the construction of the factory. But in the nineteen-thirties it became much more common for the estate companies themselves to build factory units of a standard type for letting, in which case they normally arranged for the provision of all public services.[1] This was the practice which had for some time been adopted by one of the earliest,[2] largest and most successful trading estate companies, that at Slough, which by 1938 had 210 tenant firms employing 28,500 workpeople.[3]

In the layout of individual trading estates there was often much that was admirable. Convenience and economy were carefully studied and some of the social aspects of industrial employment sometimes received considerable attention. Slough Estates Ltd., the proprietor of the local trading estate, (to quote one example) co-operated with the Buckinghamshire County Council and some of the manufacturers in the district to provide funds to build at Slough a large social centre, including a nursery and infant welfare centre, instructional rooms, gymnasia, badminton and tennis courts, billiards and games rooms, a swimming pool, two large halls and canteens. Membership was open to workers in the district and their families at three shillings per year if their employer subscribed to the centre or ten shillings per year if he did not.[4]

But however admirable the *internal* arrangements of individual estates, *externally* they seldom did much to lessen the confusion in the arrangement of cities. In some places and in some respects the spread of industry to the suburbs only created fresh difficulties and nullified recent improvements, precisely because of its location. For instance, relief from increasing congestion of traffic was sought by the construction of new arterial and by-pass roads, but it became normal for a large proportion of the frontage of these roads to be occupied within a few years by factories. The principal commercial firm constructing trading estates in the London area located every one of its estates beside an arterial road.[5] Further difficulties were

---

[1] D. G. Wolton (ed.), *Trading Estates. The Growth and Development of the Modern Factory Unit*, p. 55.

[2] The estate was used by the Government as a motor transport depot in the First World War. It was acquired in 1920 by Slough Estates Ltd., which began to develop it as a trading estate in 1924.

[3] *Royal Commission on the Distribution of the Industrial Population, Report*, p. 285.

[4] *Ibid.*, p. 284.

[5] Wolton, *op. cit.*, p. 89.

caused because suburban factories were located with little consideration of where their labour was or could be resident, so that daily
travel was extended and multiplied. Trading estate companies sometimes undertook housing development in the neighbourhood, as
was done at Queensbury,[1] but that was exceptional. It was sometimes claimed that voluntary choice had resulted in fairly satisfactory
relative location of factories and houses. Mr. D. H. Smith pointed
out that in Greater London the population increased most rapidly
in that sector, the western, where industry grew fastest. But that
was a large area, and he admitted that whereas in such districts as
Park Royal, Southall and Hayes factory growth was much faster
than that of local labour supply, the reverse was true of Wembley,
Hendon and Kingsbury.[2]

The general picture of urban development between the wars is
one of confusion, of the predominance of the haphazard, which the
existence of statutory town planning did very little to relieve. It is,
in fact, the most significant commentary on the nature and position
of statutory town planning in this period that there is scarcely any
point in inquiring to what extent it was adopted, for there was
usually little recognizable difference between the outcome of development under town-planning schemes and development outside them.
Small wonder that Professor Adshead looked back on most of this
period as one of depression among town planners, when it seemed
that all was being lost in a tangle of regulations.[3] In fact, although
between 1919 and 1932 town planning was nominally a compulsory
function of the larger urban authorities, and though since 1920 it
had been supervised by a special department of the Ministry of
Health, it was exercised on only a small scale. On the whole, schemes
were forthcoming more readily from authorities which were not
obliged by statute to prepare them than from those which were. By
30th September 1931, 1,002 resolutions to prepare schemes had been
passed by local authorities in England and Wales, but only 229
preliminary statements had been submitted to the Ministry of Health,
and only 29 schemes had reached the stage of approval by the
Ministry. This was not an impressive record when there were 267
local authorities which were obliged by statute to prepare a scheme.
In the whole period from the passage of the Act of 1909 to 1st April

---

[1] *Ibid., loc. cit.*

[2] Smith, *op. cit.*, p. 183.

[3] *Journal of the Town Planning Institute*, vol. XXIV, p. 191.

1932 only 75,020 acres in all Great Britain were included in approved town-planning schemes.[1]

The slow progress up to that time in carrying out the provisions of the Town Planning Act did not, in one sense, matter much. Had the provisions or the ideas of those responsible for their application been different, it might have mattered a great deal. But statutory town planning in practice was merely suburban estate planning and left most of the fundamental problems of town life practically untouched.

Such positive contributions as there were to the creation of a better sort of town, duly related to its environment, social and economic as well as physical, came mostly from outside statutory town planning. Just as, at the beginning of the century, the establishment of the first garden city had been the most influential of all examples for British town planning, so after the First World War the making of the second garden city, at Welwyn, again under the leadership of Ebenezer Howard, was similarly distinguished, for it was almost the only instance where there was a real attempt to shape a town in accordance with some view of the *whole* needs of living and working. And even if there were great errors and deficiencies in the conception, such an attempt was what was most necessary for town planning. Some of the statements in one of its early prospectuses show that Welwyn Garden City was begun with fundamental questions in view. Among the claims were: that it showed the way to reduce the cost and congestion of suburban traffic and to add two or three hours daily to the effective leisure of workers;[2] that 'manufactures carried on, as they are increasingly carried on, in makeshift premises in Central London, and other great cities, cannot hope to be efficient or to meet either the legitimate demands of labour or the renewal of international competition';[3] that it was 'urgently necessary that a convincing demonstration should be given of some more scientific method than has hitherto prevailed of providing for the expansion of the industries and population of Greater London and other great urban centres'.[4] The new town was intended from the beginning to be not only a garden city but also a satellite town for London;[5] not a dormitory for daily travellers, but a place with

[1] *Royal Commission on the Distribution of the Industrial Population, Report*, p. 109.
[2] Welwyn Garden City Ltd., *Welwyn Garden City. A New Town of National Importance*, p. 1.
[3] *Ibid.*, p. 3.   [4] *Ibid.*, p. 2.
[5] Purdom, *op. cit.*, p. 172.

its own economic life. It was a place of residence that sought to attract industry and provide it with ideal conditions. Of the 2,378 acres of the estate, 170 were originally reserved for industry,[1] but this had subsequently to be increased.[2]

It is not necessary here to discuss in detail the development of Welwyn Garden City. It is sufficient to observe that it overcame its difficulties and was an ever-present example of improvements in town development that had been proved to be possible. Welwyn was able to take advantage of lessons derived from the establishment of Letchworth; it grew more quickly and it became a reasonably successful business enterprise more quickly though it was financed for the most part at an excessively high rate of interest and had to undergo a financial reconstruction in 1934.[3]

The main concern here is the influence of the garden cities[4] on opinion and practice in the town-planning movement. The most significant symptoms were attempts to copy them and attempts to persuade others to go and do likewise. Probably the most important piece of emulation was the decision of a local authority to build its own garden city. The idea of acquiring an estate at Wythenshawe and building a garden city on it arose in the Housing Committee of the Manchester City Council soon after the First World War,[5] but, partly because the project at first obtained little positive support in the quarters that could have assisted it most, it was slow in being executed. Development of the original estate was delayed because until 1930 Parliament refused to allow it to be brought within the city boundary. The Ministry of Health refused powers to purchase additional land compulsorily and the ratepayers refused to support a private bill containing a clause enabling the compulsory purchase of 100 acres which were needed with particular urgency.[6] Nevertheless, the required land was eventually obtained and the laying out of the estate proceeded in the nineteen-thirties.[7] Wythenshawe was too

---

[1] *Ibid.*, p. 241.

[2] F. J. Osborn, *Green-belt Cities: the British Contribution*, p. 76.

[3] *Ibid.*, pp. 106–8.

[4] It should be remembered that while Welwyn was being built, Letchworth was still being gradually expanded.

[5] E. D. Simon and J. Inman, *The Rebuilding of Manchester*, p. 37.

[6] *Ibid.*, pp. 39–41.

[7] Building began in 1929 with the construction of 142 houses on a small part of the estate where main services were already available. Development of the rest of the estate was impossible until it was brought within the City of Manchester on 1st April 1931, because Manchester Corporation was unable to arrange with the District Council for the provision of main services.

close to Manchester, both physically and administratively, for it to be clearly distinguished as a satellite town rather than a garden suburb. Only half a mile of open space was ever intended to be kept to separate it from the city; and the proportion of industry to housing on the estate was too low for a self-contained community. Only ten per cent of the area was set aside for non-residential buildings of all kinds, against 54 per cent for housing.[1] A few small industrial undertakings were attracted, but not enough. In 1938 Sir Gwilym Gibbon declared that trading in Wythenshawe was 'not much more than a kindergarten'.[2] Nevertheless, despite its imperfections, the execution by a public authority of such an experiment in decentralization was important both as a symptom of changing ideas about town planning and as a further example of what could be done. It was reinforced when Liverpool Corporation embarked on a comparable project at Speke, where greater attention was paid to the needs of industry and industrial settlement was more rapid.[3]

These isolated examples of attempts to create complete and balanced urban settlements were very little to set against the vast flood of development of a different kind, much of which was not contrary to what had been officially encouraged in the name of town planning. But they had a reasonable chance of not being dismissed merely as interesting experiments of no appreciable significance for the treatment of contemporary problems. This was because certain social and economic difficulties, bound up with the nature of the urban environment, were making themselves more and more apparent. They were difficulties which statutory town planning, as hitherto exercised, had usually failed to touch, or in some cases even aggravated, but which a more comprehensive form of planning control might do something to relieve. The most important of them were growing traffic congestion and the increasing localization of heavy and protracted unemployment.

Traffic difficulties were not new. They had been a factor influencing the demand for statutory town planning at the beginning of the twentieth century. But since then they had been greatly intensified. One estimate suggested that between 1903 and 1933 the number of passenger-miles travelled annually in Great Britain increased by

---

[1] Ministry of Health, *Report of the Departmental Committee on Garden Cities and Satellite Towns*, p. 31.
[2] *Journal of the Town Planning Institute*, vol. XXV, p. 164.
[3] W. G. Holford, 'Trading Estates', in *ibid.*, vol. XXV, p. 156.

181 per cent,[1] and most of this represented an increased burden for the roads. The number of motor-cars rose in this period from 8,465 to 1,195,882[2] whereas the number of horse-drawn carriages licensed fell by a smaller amount, from 437,000 to 23,013.[3] The number of tramway passenger journeys had risen from 1,712,000,000 to 4,032,000,000,[4] while the number of passenger journeys by bus, for which there were no available figures in 1903, had reached 5,418,000,000 in 1933.[5] In addition there were substantial increases in goods traffic.

All this was reflected in increasing congestion of city streets and main roads, despite a considerable amount of road improvement. People became steadily more conscious of the difficulties thus created, although it was impossible to express them quantitatively with any precision. Part of the toll was in death and injury, part in increased commercial costs. Some illustrations of the latter were attempted. In 1927 the operating manager of the London General Omnibus Co. estimated that if the average speed of his firm's buses could be raised from eight to ten miles per hour (not a very formidable speed) it would save £300,000 a year.[6] The President of the Commercial Motor Users' Association estimated that within a three-mile radius of Charing Cross, congestion caused an average loss of one-eighth of working time, which he very roughly translated into money terms as an annual loss of £11,250,000.[7]

Obviously this was one field in which there was great scope for improvement in the physical design of towns. But town planning had paid little attention to the problems of road traffic.[8] The worst congestion was in districts long built up and, in most circumstances, town planning could not be applied to them before 1932. Many of the most urgently needed road improvements were outside both towns and their suburbs. Every regional plan made proposals for some additional main roads and road improvements, but, as has been seen, regional plans seldom had any executive force behind them. Planning of suburban estates, even when it was well done,

[1] E. J. Broster, *An Economic Study of the Growth of Travel in Great Britain*, 1903–33 (*unpublished typescript*), p. 57.

[2] *Ibid.*, table XI.   [3] *Ibid.*, p. 48.
[4] *Ibid.*, table IV.   [5] *Ibid.*, table VI.
[6] *Royal Commission on Transport, Report*, p. 192.
[7] G. L. Pepler, 'What traffic congestion costs', in Warren and Davidge, *op. cit.*, p. 36.
[8] When Sir Alker Tripp wrote his book *Road Traffic and its Control* in 1938, he could find no previous comprehensive treatment of the subject, either in town planning literature or anywhere else. (H. Alker Tripp, *Town Planning and Road Traffic*, p. 9.)

could not contribute much to traffic improvement, because it dealt with such small areas. A short stretch of excellent main road that merely connected long stretches at either end which were congested, twisted and constantly interrupted by cross-roads was of very little use. And the haphazard way in which suburban expansion *as a whole* went on was a very mixed blessing to transport undertakings. They wanted the movement to continue because their revenue depended on it. When the London Passenger Transport Board in 1935 announced a programme of new works it stated that they would be remunerative only if the population in the districts to be served rose by 600,000.[1] But they wanted the movement to continue in a better-regulated manner, so as to avoid repeating the problem of the peak in new localities and so adding to their costs. The London Passenger Transport Board complained that there was little co-ordination of housing and factory development, with the result that there was a demand for additional short-distance bus services in outer areas at peak hours. Park Royal was cited as an outstanding example of this unsatisfactory state of affairs. Between 1918 and 1937 the number of factories there rose from 18 to about 230, most of whose workers had to use public transport. But for most of the day Park Royal produced very little traffic. No one ever went there to shop or for pleasure.[2]

Such improvement as was made in roads was effected outside formal town planning. Central responsibility belonged to a different government department, the Ministry of Transport, which constructed many new roads. For instance, in twenty years after the First World War it executed most of the programme of new arterial roads for London which had been prepared by the Arterial Roads Conference of 1913. But it permitted their advantages to be enormously reduced by failing to exercise its powers, under the Development and Road Improvement Funds Act of 1909, to acquire the land on either side of the new roads.[3] So the frontage was rapidly built up and the free flow of traffic impeded. This was essentially a deficiency in the exercise of town-planning powers, even though they were not formally designated as such.

Out of all these difficulties and failures came some increase of interest in securing a better relation of traffic questions to the practice

[1] L.P.T.B., *Annual Report and Accounts*, 1935-6, p. 11.
[2] *Ibid.*, 1936-7, pp. 25-6.
[3] Abercrombie, *op. cit.*, p. 44.

of town planning, and this sometimes led to the formulation of positive proposals. A notable example was provided by Major Crawfurd, a member of the Royal Commission on Transport, who prepared a long memorandum which was published with the Commission's Report in 1930. His proposed remedies for existing congestion included the following significant items:

(1) A statutory duty should be imposed on the appropriate authority to prepare a reconstruction plan for each built-up area above a defined limit of population.

(2) The statutory authority should be the borough or urban district council except in London, where it should be the London County Council.

(3) The new Advisory Council to the Ministry of Transport should undertake the work of help and supervision in the re-planning of all built-up areas, including the provision of information and expert assistance.

(4) The principle of recoupment of betterment should be embodied in legislation; its application should be elastic so as to suit the circumstances of any particular case.[1]

(5) Town-planning procedure should be overhauled in order to remove all unnecessary causes of delay in carrying out schemes.[2]

The other major difficulty, which impinged increasingly on public attention, the appearance and apparent permanence of heavy unemployment as a characteristic of certain localities, was more novel. It was during the post-1929 slump and its aftermath that this situation became obvious to all, but there were signs of its development even during the preceding years of moderately high economic activity. The Registrar-General estimated the migration from County Durham to be only 19,000 between 1921 and 1926, but 129,000 between 1926 and 1931,[3] and attributed this increase entirely to the decline in opportunities of employment in the area. As the employment situation steadily became worse in some districts, Government schemes

---

[1] Land values continued to be perhaps the most formidable of all obstacles to improvements: 'One of the greatest bugbears of pre-war days, when, the moment any road improvement was officially mooted, there was a rocketing upwards of the values of the lands or buildings affected.' (Tripp, *op. cit.*, p. 39.)

[2] *Royal Commission on Transport, Report*, pp. 207–14.

[3] Ministry of Labour, *Reports of Investigations into the Industrial Conditions in Certain Depressed Areas*, p. 75.

were instituted to assist unemployed people to remove to other areas,[1] but these were mere palliatives, which hardly nibbled at the edge of the problem. Some considerable districts came to be recognized as 'depressed areas', notably West Cumberland, Durham and Tyneside, South Wales and Monmouthshire, and Scotland. In 1933 special investigations were made for the Ministry of Labour into industrial conditions in all these areas. Each of the reports drew attention to the large surplus of labour in the area with which it was concerned, and to the need to attract new industries. But as to how this attraction might be performed they were for the most part very mild and very vague. The report on Scotland stated that new industries should be attracted but should not be compelled by the Government to settle in any particular area. The depressed part of Scotland[2] might, however, be given priority in the allocation of Government orders.[3] The report on Durham and Tyneside was much the clearest. It pointed out that the new industries which the district required were those which employed a high proportion of labour to capital;[4] that the deterrents to their settlement included high rates, which ought to be removed, and the accumulation of rubbish heaps and derelict buildings, which ought to be cleared.[5] It suggested tentatively that the Government might acquire sites for development as trading estates[6] and it emphasized that there was a clear issue of national policy. The treatment of depressed areas depended on the Government's attitude to industrial location within the country as a whole. 'Any large-scale movement of population', it declared, 'involves an immense waste of social capital. Not only have houses, schools, roads, sewers, hospitals, etc., to be built in the newly settled area, but there must always remain a residue of persons who cannot be transplanted and must therefore become a charge upon public funds.' Consequently it suggested that the Government should undertake some form of national planning of industry.[7]

The suggestion was not adopted, but the question could not indefinitely be ignored. For the structure and location of industry

[1] *Vide*, e.g., Ministry of Labour, *Industrial Transference. Household Removal Scheme.*
[2] This was stated to cover all Lanarkshire (except Glasgow), the West Lothian coal and shale field, the Ayrshire coalfield, the Cowdenbeath and Lochgelly district, and the districts around Falkirk, Port Glasgow, and Alexandria. (Ministry of Labour, *Reports of Investigations into the Industrial Conditions in Certain Depressed Areas*, p. 195.)
[3] *Ibid.*, pp. 223–5.   [4] *Ibid.*, p. 82.
[5] *Ibid.*, p. 84.   [6] *Ibid.*, p. 85.
[7] *Ibid.*, p. 107.

were constantly changing and it was clear that, left uncontrolled as they were, they were doing very little to relieve the local concentrations of unemployment. The following figures show the excess of the number of factories opened over the number closed each year in the various regions of Great Britain:[1]

Region	1932	1933	1934	1935	Total 1932–5
S. and S.-W. England	35	12	13	4	64
Greater London	167	111	71	29	378
Wales	5	–	1	–1	5
Midlands	21	–26	3	–2	–4
Eastern Counties	18	4	13	15	50
N.-W. England	– 9	–17	–55	–18	–99
N.-E. England	– 2	–17	–25	–10	–54
Scotland	–17	–16	– 3	7	–29
TOTAL	218	51	18	24	311

New factories were being established chiefly in the most prosperous areas. And though, from 1933, economic activity was steadily reviving, the recovery was much less marked in Scotland, Wales, north-east England and north-west England than in the rest of England. The position was, in fact, that some areas reached extreme boom conditions while others were truly derelict.[2]

The emergence and persistence of localities marked by an unbroken high level of unemployment did more than anything else to turn attention to the possibility of supplementing local plans by provisions deliberately designed to stimulate industry, and of relating them to some wider scheme for the distribution of population. The depressed areas found themselves transformed, by a change of nomenclature, into 'special areas', with two commissioners to take charge of their economic improvement with the aid of grants from Government funds. Necessity soon drove the Government to countenance small positive measures to influence the location of industry as far as these areas were concerned. In his second report the Commissioner for Special Areas (England and Wales), Sir Malcolm Stewart, recommended the provision of trading estates to attract new industries and small industrialists.[3] Companies were therefore formed for this purpose, and were financed from the Special Areas Fund,

---

[1] This table has been compiled from the figures given in Table I of the Board of Trade's successive annual *Surveys of Industrial Development*.

[2] British Association, *Britain in Recovery*, pp. 108–9.

[3] *Royal Commission on Distribution of the Industrial Population, Report*, p. 285.

and a start was made in 1936 with the first of these estates at Team Valley in Durham.[1] Other government-sponsored trading estates soon followed, the largest being at Treforest in South Wales and Hillington near Glasgow.[2]

In 1936, in his third report, Sir Malcolm Stewart made another, more general remark, which proved very fruitful. He suggested that the haphazard growth of London was dangerous and that an embargo might be placed on further factory construction in Greater London. The sequel to this suggestion was the appointment of a Royal Commission on the Distribution of the Industrial Population, the famous Barlow Commission.[3] This was the first clear official recognition that the location of settlements of population for the nation as a whole was a matter worthy of investigation and, possibly, regulation. There had been tentative moves in that direction earlier. In 1935 the Ministry of Health had received the report of a Departmental Committee on Garden Cities and Satellite Towns, among whose recommendations had been that the distribution and location of industry and population should be planned and co-ordinated in the public interest; and that the distribution and location of industry and residence should be dealt with as a national, not a local problem.[4] The Committee had added that it was not feasible arbitrarily to locate industry, but the attractions which could be offered to industry and the general influence exertable by a central Planning Board (whose creation it advocated) and by local authorities, through town and regional planning and other powers, should suffice to ensure that industry would secure the locations desired for it.[5]

But nothing came of that. The appointment of the Barlow Commission was indicative of the effect of a rather longer pressure of experience and of a change in the nature of the experience itself. For in the late nineteen-thirties the economic difficulty indicated by the continued existence of depressed areas was supplemented by realization of a possible significant military weakness in the vulnerability of spreading conurbations to aerial bombardment. It was at least possible that industrial and residential location was a matter not merely of prosperity or depression, but perhaps of life or death, and,

---

[1] Wolton, *op. cit.*, p. 105.

[2] *Royal Commission on Distribution of the Industrial Population, Report*, pp. 286–7.

[3] *Ibid.*, pp. 3–5.

[4] Ministry of Health, *Report of Departmental Committee on Garden Cities and Satellite Towns*, pp. 25–6.

[5] *Ibid.*, p. 27.

as such, not to be left to the unobserved winds of self-interest and whim. Official interest was, therefore, drawn in a direction which a small number of private persons had for several years been indicating with growing forcefulness.

Some members of the town-planning movement had been proclaiming that the distribution of population over the country as a whole was the core of their subject. Mr. F. J. Osborn in 1934 declared that business location was the real key to planning, although official town and country planning was then unable to guide in any way the general movement or growth of industry.[1] He considered that the most urgent administrative need was the creation of a National Industrial and Commercial Siting Board, under the control of a Minister of Planning. This body would have power to decide in which districts industrial development should be encouraged, in which merely permitted, and in which prohibited save with special permits; to decide on the sites for new towns and to schedule the land necessary for them, after which they would be developed by an appointed *ad hoc* body; and to co-operate with all other planning agencies. It would have no constructional functions, but municipal authorities would be empowered to lay out industrial estates. Town planning, declared Mr. Osborn, would then become possible;[2] which was an illuminating comment on twenty-five years of statutory town planning.

A little earlier, in 1933, Mr. Trystan Edwards launched the movement for the building of 100 new towns, which was commended to the public in a letter to *The Times*, signed by a number of men drawn from very varied backgrounds. This scheme also called for the guiding of factory migration to the new towns[3] and the creation of an administrative commission, which would not only choose the sites of the new towns but would also supervise the initial stages of their planning.[4] This project likewise reflected disillusionment with past and present attempts at town improvement. Its author remarked that tinkering with existing towns could not solve the slum problem: the dormitory suburb had been almost a complete failure in this respect, because slum-dwellers could not afford the travelling costs; and re-housing in tenements had failed because the increased cost of

[1] F. J. Osborn, *Transport, Town Development and Territorial Planning of Industry*, p. 23.
[2] *Ibid.*, pp. 27–33.
[3] J 47485, *One Hundred New Towns for Britain* (3rd edn.), p. 70.
[4] *Ibid.*, p. 71.

construction raised rents and because this type of dwelling deprived children of fresh air and exercise.[1]

It would be too much to claim that private movements of this kind directly roused authority to reconsider some of the fundamental conditions affecting town and country planning. But they were both indirect influences and symptoms of a changing background and new requirements in the field of town planning. In this way they are related to the appointment of the Barlow Commission.

In the nineteen-thirties, before that event, although the new influences that have just been discussed were becoming steadily more noticeable, their effect on the actual practice of town planning was comparatively slight. One thing all experience served to show: the severe limitation on the effectiveness of town planning as a result of its virtual restriction to peripheral areas of new development. The principal new measures of the period, the Town and Country Planning Act, 1932, and the Town and Country Planning (Scotland) Act, 1932,[2] removed that restriction by giving local authorities power to prepare planning scheme for any land. Yet that made less difference than might have been expected. It made little difference, for instance, to the relief of congestion, whether of traffic or residence, in built-up areas. A great deal was done in these years to relieve congestion, mostly by slum clearance, but it was in the form of surgical operations under the Housing Acts, rather than as part of considered schemes for the re-design of towns. The extension of planning powers to country districts might perhaps have been expected to facilitate provisions of regional significance, such as the improvement and preservation of road links. But roads continued to be dealt with mainly outside planning schemes, and even the attempt to keep them clear for their proper purpose instead of being rapidly hemmed in by buildings was made as an independent function, quite separate from town and country planning. The growing traffic difficulties and the continued expansion of suburbs, which have been mentioned, led to a strengthening of powers for this purpose, by the Restriction of Ribbon Development Act, 1935,[3] but that also did not make very much difference to the form which development took.

The extension of planning powers to all types of land did make a considerable difference to the area over which town-planning control was exercised. Whereas at 1st April 1932 only 75,020 acres of Great Britain were included in approved town-planning schemes, the area

[1] *Ibid.*, p. 10. [2] 22 & 23 Geo. V, c. 49. [3] 25 & 26 Geo. V, c. 47.

had risen seven years later to 1,093,785 acres,[1] which was at least a sign of increased interest (for planning was once again an entirely optional function), even if the appearance of the country leads to doubts about the effectiveness of the control which was exercised. The greatest quantitative change brought about by the Act of 1932 came from its creation of a sort of quarter-way stage towards town planning: interim development control. When a local authority made a resolution to prepare or adopt a town-planning scheme it received powers of interim development control, whereby any person seeking to build in the area covered by the resolution must obtain permission from the local authority to do so, or else the building would be liable to removal without compensation if it conflicted with any planning scheme subsequently brought in. By 1st April 1939, 26,482,263 acres (more than half the country) were subject to interim development control.[2] But that was a purely negative situation, even more negative than the rest of statutory town planning had been since 1909, for it neither obliged nor assisted anybody to do anything.

By the outbreak of the Second World War, though town planning had been nominally absorbed in the wider function of town and country planning, and though new requirements and potentialities for it were being perceived, its actual practice had changed little. One new function had just been formally admitted. Under section 70 of the Civil Defence Act, 1939,[3] to render the whole or part of any area less vulnerable to air raids had been added to the list of purposes to be served by town-planning schemes. But that had hardly had time to produce any effect and there was little else new to record.

But there was an increased interest in town planning and there was widespread recognition among those directly concerned with it (as there had not been earlier) that statutory town planning as so far exercised had reached a dead end. The Barlow Commission did much to crystallize opinion about what town planning could or ought to do and what facilities it required. It was fortunately timed, for its report came quite close to the outbreak of war and the war changed profoundly both the conditions in which town planning had to function and the regard in which it was held by the public.

The report of the Barlow Commission was criticized in some quarters as an excessively mild document, but it expressed a far more

[1] *Royal Commission on Distribution of the Industrial Population, Report*, pp. 108–9.
[2] *Ibid.*, p. 108.
[3] 2 & 3 Geo. VI, c. 31.

comprehensive approach to town planning than any previous published official document and plainly indicated the need for great changes. It recognized that existing town-planning powers were inadequate and were not intended to deal with the problem which confronted the Commission.[1] So it tried to indicate what revisions of powers and machinery were required in order to deal with that fundamental problem. It pointed to the need for a new central authority with powers distinct from and beyond those of any existing government department. It stated that there should be national action to secure the continued redevelopment of congested urban areas, the decentralization or dispersal of industries and the industrial population from such areas, and the encouragement of a reasonable balance of industrial development throughout the various regions of Great Britain, with appropriate diversification of industry in each region. In particular, there should be immediate attention to the problem of the drift of industry and population to the Home Counties. Among the tasks deemed appropriate for the central authority were consideration of which congested urban areas it was desirable to subject to decentralization or dispersal; the decision as to the instances in which garden cities or garden suburbs, satellite towns, trading estates and the expansion of existing small towns should be encouraged; the inspection, if it so desired, of any existing or future town-planning scheme devised under current town and country planning legislation; and the study of the location of industry with a view to anticipating cases where depression was most likely to occur in future and encouraging other industries or public undertakings there before the crisis actually happened.[2] About the constitution of the new central authority opinion was divided. The majority recommended that it should be a board consisting of a chairman and three other members appointed by the President of the Board of Trade after consultation with the Ministers of Health, Labour, and Transport and the Secretary of State for Scotland. This board should have from the outset powers to regulate the establishment of additional industrial undertakings in London and the Home Counties, with provision for the extension of those powers by Order in Council to other areas. The board should also be obliged to state to the President of the Board of Trade what further powers it required in order to carry out its functions.[3] The minority, fearing

[1] *Royal Commission on Distribution of the Industrial Population, Report*, p. 106.
[2] *Ibid.*, pp. 195–203.   [3] *Ibid.*, pp. 204–7.

that such a board would be too subordinate in status to be an effective instrument, recommended instead that there should be a new government department, or one evolved from an existing department, to take over the town-planning powers of the Ministry of Health, some of the planning powers of the Ministry of Transport, the powers and functions of the Commissioners for Special Areas (which powers and functions would be extended to apply to the whole country), and possibly some of the housing functions of the Ministry of Health.[1]

This report was no mere spate of words, breathed on the air and dispersed by the winds. For one thing, the Commission perceived one of the root difficulties in making town planning effective. It understood that town planning was concerned with the allocation of land among various uses and that a great obstacle to its exercise had always been the high financial cost either of acquiring land or of diverting it to a use not chosen by its owner or lessee. It therefore suggested further expert investigation of this problem in an attempt to find a solution,[2] and this suggestion was acted on.[3] This willingness to go to the root of the matter, at least in discussion if not yet in action, was symptomatic of the growing importance attached to town planning.

It was, in fact, a function which was more in the public eye than it had been. For at the time when the Barlow Commission was concluding its labours some of the problems with which it had been confronted became much more acute. Evacuation at the outbreak of war was, of course, a temporary measure, but it was the first experiment in the re-location of a significant proportion of the population. The demands of war production led to the building of large numbers of new factories and involved not only the opportunity but the necessity for control over their location, with allowance both for safety from attack and for access to adequate supplies of labour. The positive achievement of these transfers of industry and population made it impossible to dismiss proposals for continuous control and stimulation of such movements as merely impracticable, which might otherwise have been the case. Moreover, these changes brought into prominence the social needs that had to be catered for whan a community was established in a new place. They thus helped

---

[1] *Ibid.*, pp. 218–23.   [2] *Ibid.*, p. 117.

[3] By the appointment of the Expert Committee on Compensation and Betterment (Uthwatt Committee).

to maintain and extend that internal shift in the content of town planning from emphasis primarily on architectural to emphasis on social considerations, which had been developing in the previous decade.[1]

The state of near-siege which war brought to an island normally dependent for its sustenance on foreign commerce naturally brought into relief also the precarious condition of home agriculture. The loss of food production from the indiscriminate transfer of agricultural land to other uses had long been on a large enough scale for it to be obvious to all. Now the obvious seemed to be important. The use that could or ought to be made of rural land was a matter deemed worthy of expert consideration.[2] The mutual relation of town and country was re-examined, and the economic and strategic weaknesses that had resulted from previous distribution of land among various uses provided a new argument for the exercise of some general supervision, initiatory as well as prohibitory, over that distribution in future, that is, for the exercise of the basic function of town and country planning.

But the greatest stimulus brought by war to town planning came through the shattering of cities by bombing, from the autumn of 1940 onwards. The ultimate rebuilding of large urban areas became a necessity for which it was prudent to take thought in advance. Since so much rebuilding was inescapable the most favourable opportunity was presented for planning the improvement of other city districts, which had long been shabby or inconvenient, though in most cases not positively unhealthy. It was, in fact, usually impracticable to treat the replanning of bombed districts in isolation; to study the relation of each area, each function, of the city to the whole was necessary unless great efforts were to produce only mean results. Most of the most-injured cities began to have plans prepared for their post-war reconstruction and invariably the need was stressed to use the opportunity created by war damage to make improvements comprehensive enough to remedy accumulated weaknesses of deeper origin. Of Plymouth, for instance, it was said:

[1] The architectural conception of town planning lingered long. Thus in 1937 the Hampstead Garden Suburb Trust (in *The Hampstead Garden Suburb. Its Achievements and Significance*) chose to reprint from *Country Life* an article by Mr. Christopher Hussey in which he classed the garden suburb as one of the three great English contributions to the art of architecture.

[2] It was considered by the Committee on Land Utilization in Rural Areas (Scott Committee), which reported in 1942.

'The immediate cause of the preparation of this comprehensive and positive plan for Plymouth is, without question, the destruction wrought by enemy action . . . Plymouth was no decayed or depressed area, no outworn town suffering from the aftermath of Victorian industrial prosperity and *laissez-faire*. . . . But like all old towns which have grown and prospered from small beginnings Plymouth was in need of a thorough overhaul—something more drastic than the preparation of a statutory planning scheme under existing planning powers which continually cramped the desires of the Corporation to bring their city up to date.'[1]

The replanners of London thought similarly of their subject. London, they declared, was ripe for reconstruction before the War: 'obsolescence, bad and unsuitable housing, inchoate communities, uncorrelated road systems, industrial congestion, a low level of urban design, inequality in distribution of open spaces, increasing congestion of dismal journeys to work—all these and more clamoured for improvement.'[2]

The scale of unavoidable reconstruction and the rediscovery that food production in the countryside was a matter of urgent national importance both strengthened the view that had been growing in the previous decade that town planning, to be effective, must be conceived in terms of larger units.[3] The result was seen in the preparation of a number of master-plans for various regions, into which more detailed individual town plans could subsequently be fitted. The preparation of regional plans was, of course, not new, but there was a considerable change in their nature. The latest regional plans were more than attempts to impose simultaneity and uniformity on town planning within a defined area; they were concerned to improve the contribution which each district could make to the region as a whole, they paid great attention to problems of the distribution of population and occupations throughout the region, even to the nature of the occupations and the relative level of employment to be sought among them. Fundamentally they studied some of the major needs which arose in the daily lives of

---

[1] J. P. Watson and P. Abercrombie, *A Plan for Plymouth*, p. 1.

[2] J. H. Forshaw and P. Abercrombie, *County of London Plan*, p. 20.

[3] It was sometimes suggested that a further influence in this respect was the introduction of administration through Regional Commissioners (e.g., W. A. Robson, *The War and the Planning Outlook*, p. 15), but it would be hard to substantiate this. It seems doubtful whether Regional Commissioners as significant instruments of Government ever made any serious impact on public consciousness.

whole communities, the extent to which they were met by existing conditions and, where there were deficiencies and weaknesses, the most effective way in which these could be remedied. A comparison of Sir Patrick Abercrombie's *Greater London Plan 1944* with the reports of the earlier Greater London Regional Planning Committee would show at once the great widening of scope that had taken place.

It was sometimes claimed that town planning was ceasing to be an art and becoming a science, though it must surely be always too imprecise a subject to merit the latter name. But it is true that planners, as they ceased to confine their efforts to the creation of a pleasing appearance, began to take account of the results of many branches of applied science and felt therefore able to make larger claims for their work. The new school of planners held that every plan should be based on a preliminary survey; that the plan should first set out what was on scientific grounds the most suitable use of each piece of land and then reconcile this with other existing interests.[1] The enormous range of data being considered in the preparation of plans may perhaps be most clearly and simply indicated by glancing at the chapter-headings of a contemporary textbook of the subject:[2] geology; the study of the soil; agriculture and forestry; land drainage, river and coastal works; water supply; sewerage; location, size and scale of towns; siting residential areas; industries and municipal services; ports; highways; railways; canals; airports.

Partly through the process of learning from its own frustrations, partly through the force of outside circumstances, town and country planning had come to concern itself with fundamental problems of social life. Whether or not it approached them in the most helpful way, it was no longer possible to dismiss the subject as decorative futility. Its organized exponents gained new confidence from their position and a new vigour in pursuing their aims. The Town and Country Planning Association adopted in 1941 a National Planning Basis, which was later approved in principle by the R.I.B.A., the National Council of Social Service, and the National Playing Fields Association.[3] Its main provisions were:

[1] L. B. Escritt, *Regional Planning. An outline of the scientific data relating to planning in Great Britain*, p. 55.

[2] *Ibid.*

[3] D. Tyerman (ed.), *Ways and Means of Rebuilding, being a report of the London Conference of the Town and Country Planning Association* 1943, p. 99.

(1) A Ministry (advised by a National Planning Council) should be set up to guide future development and redevelopment and the future grouping of industry and population.

(2) Distinction should be maintained between Town and Country in all development and sporadic building in rural areas discouraged.

(3) Good design and layout of buildings and roads should be an object of policy equally with sound construction, and outdoor advertising limited to approved situations.

(4) Residential density should be limited to provide adequate open space, and belts of country preserved round all towns.

(5) Any movements of population required should be directed to existing towns or to new towns carefully sited to meet the needs of industry, agriculture and social amenity. New and extending towns should be planned as compact units.

(6) The Planning Ministry should have power to prohibit or encourage the settlement of industrial undertakings in particular places.

(7) There should be new and improved legislation to deal with compensation and betterment.[1]

The Government was faced not only by the demands of organized bodies but also by the vague aspirations of the mass of the public. There was no specific promise of 'Homes for Heroes', but at a time when the general lot was one of austere exertion in the presence of physical destruction there was a need for something to look forward to, a condition that should be better not only than the ruin of the present but also than the condition of the immediate past. For the realization of such a hope a greatly increased attention to town and country planning was essential. 'There must be some plan of action ready to reward the valiant; works that can be put into immediate operation and will later fall into their ultimate place.'[2] Moreover, the extension of the practice of working to a previously prepared programme, of taking care to ensure that the conflicts between the demands of different economic programmes were removed, of by-passing the normal working of the market in the allocation of resources to various purposes, in fact of economic planning generally, which proved necessary for victory in war and which had large

[1] *Ibid.*, pp. 99–100.
[2] Forshaw and Abercrombie, *loc. cit.*

and evident successes, prompted a somewhat unreflecting public desire that similar processes should be continued in peace-time for different objects, in the hope that equally spectacular successes would be achieved. Town and country planning shared in the prestige acquired by planning generally.[1]

The Government, in the midst of its many other preoccupations, gradually allowed itself to recognize that town and country planning could play a significant part in the future and that immediate recognition of that future possibility had its own value. It began by taking away the main central responsibility for town and country planning from the Ministry of Health, which had shown so little appreciation of its functions, and placing it in a new Ministry of Works and Buildings, which soon became the Ministry of Works and Planning. Then in 1943 this department was divided and a separate Ministry of Town and Country Planning was at last created.[2]

An attempt was made immediately after this to ensure at least the absolute minimum of negative control over building in all districts: interim development control was extended to all areas where it had not already been obtained by the adoption of a resolution to prepare a planning scheme.[3] Provision was also made in 1944[4] for extended powers of compulsory acquisition of land for certain town-planning purposes, especially for reconstruction schemes. It is significant that the same act gave facilities in connexion with the rebuilding both of areas affected by bomb damage and those suffering from obsolescence and decay: there was a set of provisions for the acquisition of land in 'blitzed' areas and another for the same purpose in 'blighted' areas.

Nevertheless there was no fundamental remodelling of town planning law during the Second World War. At its conclusion the main operative acts were still the Town and Country Planning Acts of 1932, which had not been a conspicuous success up to 1939. Since then, the most important administrative change had been in the nature of central control. There had also been a very great increase of interest in town planning both among the public and among those

---

[1] The points mentioned in this paragraph were plainly expressed in 1941 in Robson, *op. cit.*, p. 7.

[2] Minister of Town and Country Planning Act, 1943 (6 & 7 Geo. VI, c. 5).

[3] Town and Country Planning (Interim Development) Act, 1943 (6 & 7 Geo. VI, c. 29). There was a separate act for Scotland (6 & 7 Geo. VI, c. 43).

[4] Town and Country Planning Act, 1944 (7 & 8 Geo. VI, c. 47). Provision was made for Scotland in a separate act in the following year (8 & 9 Geo. VI, c. 33).

more directly responsible for the exercise of town-planning powers. But in 1945, though the interest in town planning did not appear to be waning, it was uncertain how adequate an outlet would be given to it. Many difficulties remained. The administrative unit of town and country planning was still very small and there was no satisfactory means of implementing the policy of decentralization which was being widely demanded. The acquisition of land for planning purposes outside built-up areas was still difficult, and compensation charges as a result of planning schemes were apt to be heavy. True, the Expert Committee on Compensation and Betterment had reported and made drastic proposals,[1] but they had not been passed into law. Briefly, it had suggested that the compensation question should be settled once for all through the purchase by the State of the development rights of all undeveloped land;[2] and it had proposed to lessen the financial burden of improvements in built-up areas by imposing a periodic levy on annual increases in site value.[3] There were, however, private interests which expected injury from such arrangements and there were also many people to whom the proposals appeared to be too complicated to be practicable.

A real effort was made at the end of the war and in the first years of peace to ensure that legal and administrative obstacles to effective town and country planning, as it had come to be conceived, were lessened. The State accepted partial responsibility for the location of new industry and the decentralization of population. But it moved away from its recent effort to consolidate the administration of town and country planning, for of these two intimately related questions the former was placed under the Board of Trade and the latter under the Ministry of Town and Country Planning. A New Towns Committee had been appointed to consider the way in which a policy of decentralization of population might be carried out and, even before its final report was completed, the Government introduced legislation[4] to facilitate the policy. The location of new towns required the approval of the Minister of Town and Country Planning, and their creation was entrusted to public corporations specially established for the purpose. Preparations were soon in progress for the construction of several new towns under these powers.

Control over the location of industry was exercised mainly by

[1] These proposals are very clearly summarised, illustrated and discussed in G. M. Young (ed.), *Country and Town*.
[2] *E.C. on Compensation and Betterment, Report*, p. 27.   [3] *Ibid.*, p. 29.
[4] New Towns Act, 1946 (9 & 10 Geo. VI, c. 68).

requiring industrialists to obtain the approval of a Regional Distribution of Industry Panel before opening new or extended premises. This control began with the Distribution of Industry Act[1] in 1945. At first industrialists had only to report the location of any new factories which they occupied, but under the Town and Country Planning Act of 1947 the full procedure requiring prior approval for the location of new factories was introduced. The Regional Distribution of Industry Panel was an inter-departmental body on which the Board of Trade had the last word; the principles which governed its decisions, if there were any principles, were not revealed to the public. There appeared, in fact, to be three strands in the Government's location policy: a continuance of the earlier policy of encouraging new industries to settle in established centres of population which in the past had suffered depression; a removal of industry and population, on social grounds, from old centres (including some in the old 'depressed areas') to complete new towns; and an attempt to preserve the immediate economic advantages of existing regional specialization by approving manufacturers' own choice of sites as often as possible. No one made the attempt to explain the conditions in which these contradictory elements might be reconciled.

The general legal structure for town and country planning, at the local as well as the national level, was comprehensively changed by the Town and Country Planning Act, 1947,[2] and a companion measure for Scotland.[3] Planning became an obligatory function, to be treated on a larger scale: henceforward the county council became the local planning authority. The problem of the financial burden was tackled by the enactment of a modified version of the proposals of the Uthwatt Committee, their execution being entrusted to a Central Land Board. Private development of land was forbidden except with the consent of the planning authority, and all development rights in undeveloped land were transferred to the State, which set aside a sum of £300,000,000 from which to make *ex-gratia* payments in cases of hardship so caused. The Central Land Board was authorized to levy a betterment charge of indefinite and presumably variable amount in all cases where an owner was given permission to develop his land. Thus the anomalous situation was created in which, where a landowner's activities improved the value of his land, he was subject to a charge, but, where the value of his land increased

---

[1] 8 & 9 Geo. VI, c. 36.   [2] 10 & 11 Geo. VI, c. 51.
[3] 10 & 11 Geo. VI, c. 53.

because of outside influences or activities in which he had no share, he retained the whole of the increase. Other important provisions of the Act enabled town and country planning to be more comprehensive and more flexible. Planning authorities were given control over ribbon development, power to place a 'life' on existing buildings which, in the interest of good planning, required demolition, and power to control outdoor advertisements. They were given power to preserve woodlands, to protect buildings of historical or architectural interest (even if this involved compulsory purchase), and to require the proper maintenance of waste lands. There were also greatly increased powers of land purchase and the assurance of large grants from the Exchequer for this purpose; local authorities were empowered to buy compulsorily land needed for the exercise of any of their statutory functions up to ten years ahead. And the town plan thus made possible was no longer a once-for-all matter. It was susceptible of continuous adjustment and had to be reviewed every five years.

Thus the whole provision for town and country planning was changed. It is not the purpose of this book to discuss in detail the progress of town planning since 1947 nor to estimate its prospects in the near or distant future. It is enough to establish that in the last few years facilities have been created, and some use made of them, to plan and re-plan towns as a whole and in relation to their wider environment; that town planning has emerged from the obscurity of discussion and non-performance to the light of specific proposal and of practice, as a recognizable and distinct social function of government. That is new, though the name of statutory town planning is not new. For thirty years something was timidly and intermittently practised in that name, but it planned no towns nor ever proposed to do so. Yet the Planning Acts of 1947 were to a great extent responses to the same forces as led to the Act of 1909, although there were, of course, some immediate influences which affected only the former. If the whole process which has been the subject-matter of this book is regarded as one of genesis, perhaps the Act of 1909 may be considered to have been a still-birth, whereas in 1947 there was at least a living infant, though perhaps one somewhat slenderly equipped to face the wicked world.

It would be foolish to claim that a set of difficult problems received a false answer in 1909 and a correct one in 1947; some of the weaknesses of what was attempted in 1947 have already made themselves glaringly apparent. It would probably be nearer the mark to say that in the early days of statutory town planning its practitioners were to a great extent concerning themselves with irrelevant questions, whereas by the nineteen-forties they were asking some of the right questions though often providing the wrong answers. But in such matters there is no final truth, merely gradation of error. A key to the change that had come over town planning in the minds of some of its exponents may, however, be found in the phrase that it had become a distinct social function. Most of the town planning of the early twentieth century was not a distinct function; it was one way of housing, or it was one branch of architecture. Nor was it social; it was a way of ensuring that if one had not a pleasant countryside to look on, then one had a pretty avenue, not an ugly street. With what difficulty or ease the inhabitants of the avenues might find the means to pass their lives in a way that suited them and perhaps benefited their neighbours was seldom a matter for town plans. By the nineteen-forties that was changing. Town planning was becoming concerned with the way people lived as well as with the way buildings looked. And it was achieving distinctiveness because it began, at its occasional best, to concern itself with the nature and function of a town as a whole, which was a subject hitherto neglected; thus it had to consider the relation of different elements (both functions and districts) to one another; to consider also the way in which the town affected and was affected by what went on outside it. So town planning achieved an effective existence only by becoming merged in something larger, in town and country planning.

Town and country planning became a separate governmental function because it treated problems which were real and recognizable but otherwise untouched; in its early stages statutory town planning was obviously a failure because it did little more than pretend to do this: in actual fact it merely acted as a decorative appendage to the treatment of related but not identical problems by other means. When it abandoned the pretence and adhered to the reality the story of its genesis was over. Whether the story of its actual existence will be equally long will depend mainly on its success in remaining a distinct social function, so exercised as to satisfy the public that it improves the quality of daily life, rather than brings a new element of confusion into it. The problems with which it is concerned are not of the kind which when solved once are solved for ever; they are continuous and could be continuously treated. But people were not always convinced, and may not remain so, that town and country planning was the right and necessary way of dealing with those problems. Much of the difficulty of making town and country planning permanently acceptable to public opinion is administrative. To devise regulations and means of executing them which will remove abuses without creating new anomalies and hardships, and which will encourage vigorous action for desirable purposes without raising obstacles to the performance of other equally desirable activities, must be difficult even when aims are clearly seen and widely supported. But beyond that there are dangers in the common ambiguous conceptions of the subject.

On the one hand, the unique contribution of town and country planning may be overlooked by concentrating attention on 'planning' in general. There are some who would regard town and country planning simply as one element in a general system of regulation of social activity in which central economic planning must be a major element.[1] This is certainly not a case of imputing a relationship where none exists. The possible source of confusion is that the effectiveness of town and country planning may be assumed to depend on the continuance of economic planning on some particular lines or in some specific amount of detail. If the use of buildings and land is to be regulated effectively there must be clearly defined aims based on accurate knowledge and steadfastly maintained, there must be some system of licensing and in some cases powers of positive direction; but there is no presumption that this necessarily involves a state-conducted economy. Town and country planning does not, for its own purposes, require everything to be planned to the last detail. It may be desirable to lay down in a town plan that when a particular site is occupied it shall be used for industrial purposes, but, within wide limits, it is not necessary to say what kind of industry. The planning which says that there must be two extra factories for shoes and one for packing-cases and so on, because that is necessary for the achievement of a certain pattern of national economy suited to given needs, is of a different character. A town

---

[1] This is the view expressed, e.g., in D. V. Glass, *The Town and a Changing Civilization*, especially page 141, where it is indicated that town and country planning could be fully effective only in a Socialist state. But what is Professor Glass's definition of a Socialist state?

The relation between town and country planning and economic planning is also discussed in G. D. H. Cole, *Building and Planning*, especially pp. 43–4.

plan would have to lay down what sites were suitable for those additional factories; it would have to do the same if their erection were decided on by private manufacturers anticipating a profitable line of business.

A more pervasive danger comes from the fact that many town planners are apt to fashion their schemes in the image of too abstract or incomplete a picture of human society; and the danger is the greater because they remain unaware of the nature of this error. Most of them, for instance, are more skilled and, apparently, more interested in providing for transport or the enjoyment of leisure than in facilitating production. Many have written glibly of 'industrial balance' without any sign of recognition that it is useless to produce what the consumer is not prepared to buy, without any sign that they have ever pondered the nature of the advantages and disadvantages of regional industrial specialization. Many display great capacity for ignoring a multitude of economic facts. And in the non-economic aspects of town planning, proposals are also made which appear to be rooted in theories of social organization reached by intuition, but not adequately supported by observation or experience.

That a large subject, which until recently has had but little opportunity to test itself in practice, should suffer from some confusion both in aims and methods is, however, no necessary condemnation of its character. Town and country planning in its modern sense is very young, richer in error than in anything else, constantly in danger of being led astray. To bring it into being at all was a complex and difficult process, of which the fruition was long delayed, long uncertain. Whether that protracted process was worth while is a question whose answer is equally uncertain as yet and may well remain so through just as long a delay. The present has little to show but its aspirations. It is the performance that will be judged.

Select Bibliography

THE theme of this book is one which affects and is affected by most aspects of social life, however broadly that is defined. There can be little that has been written on the condition and activity of society in Great Britain in the last century and a half that does not contribute something to the development or understanding of that theme. Some of the material which has been most useful in the preparation of the book is listed below. This bibliography is primarily concerned with the central items of the subject: the physical and sanitary state of British towns, public health and housing policy, the growth of traffic problems, town and regional planning, and the growth of population; it also includes a selection of items bearing directly or indirectly on the main theme but reaching out into other fields. Some of the material is narrowly local in scope but has been included because it gives clear and particular illustration of important general points. Only a few localities are represented, none of them at all exhaustively, but they include most of the largest towns. Comparable material could be cited for many more towns and districts.

A. UNPUBLISHED MATERIAL

In the British Library of Political and Economic Science at the London School of Economics and Political Science:

BROSTER, E. J. *An Economic Study of the Growth of Travel in Great Britain, 1903–33.* Typescript.

OSBORN, F. J. *London, an Awful Warning to Glasgow.* Typescript.

Solly Collection. Miscellaneous manuscripts, letters, handbills and press-cuttings left by Rev. Henry Solly.

In the University of London Library:

PHILLIPS, R. H. S. *The Political Economy of Town Planning.* (University of London Ph.D. thesis.) Typescript.

238

B. OFFICIAL PUBLICATIONS

I. U.K. GOVERNMENT. (Note. B.P.P. = British Parliamentary Papers. The roman numerals after the letters B.P.P. and the date of the session refer to the number of the volume in the series as bound for the House of Commons.)

(*a*) *Population Returns*

Census of England and Wales. Decennially 1861–1931.

Census of Great Britain. Decennially 1801–51.

Census of Scotland. Decennially 1861–1931.

Crown Agent for Scotland. *Return relating to the population of Scotland.* B.P.P. 1883, LIV.

National Register. U.K. and Isle of Man. 1939.

(*b*) *Returns and Memoranda on other topics*

Local Government Board. *Report on back-to-back houses by Dr. L. W. Darra Muir.* B.P.P. 1910, XXXVIII.

Local Government Board. *Return showing the Rate in the Pound in the Municipal Boroughs of Liverpool, etc., in each of the Years ended Lady-day 1870, 1880 and 1890.* B.P.P. 1890–1, LXVIII.

Local Government Board. *Statistical Memoranda and Charts relating to Public Health and Social Conditions.* B.P.P. 1909, CIII.

Local Government Board. *Urban Water Supply, Return for every sanitary district in England and Wales.* B.P.P. 1878–9, LXI.

Local Taxation Returns (England and Wales) (now entitled *Local Government Financial Statistics.*) Annual from 1860–1. Returns for 1915–16 to 1918–19 and 1937–8 to 1940–1 inclusive were not published. B.P.P. until 1912–13.

Ministry of Health. *Memorandum on the Increase of Local Rates per Pound of Assessable Value.* B.P.P. 1920, XL.

Ministry of Health (previously Local Government Board). *Rates and Rateable Values in England and Wales* (previously entitled *Statement showing . . . the amount of the local rates,* etc.) Annual from 1913–14. Publication suspended 1940–3. B.P.P. 1913–14 to 1920–1.

Ministry of Labour. *Industrial Transference. Household Removal Scheme.* 1930.

(*c*) *Annual Reports*

Board of Trade. *London Traffic Branch.* 1908–15. B.P.P.

Board of Trade. *Survey of Industrial Development.* 1933–8.

Ministry of Health. *Annual Report.* From 1919–20. B.P.P. 1919–20, 1920–1 and 1939–41 onwards.

Ministry of Transport. *London and Home Counties Traffic Advisory Committee.* From 1925 (not published 1938–9 to 1945–6 inclusive).

(*d*) *Reports and Evidence from Commissions, Committees, etc.* (in chronological order) (Note.—D.C. = Departmental Committee; R.C. = Royal Commission; S.C. = Select Committee)

Report of the S.C. on Public Walks. B.P.P. 1833, XV.

First Report of the R.C. on Municipal Corporations of England and Wales. B.P.P. 1835, XXIII. *Appendix.* B.P.P. 1835, XXIII to XXVI.

Report of the S.C. on the Health of Towns. B.P.P. 1840, XI.

Poor Law Commissioners. *Report on an inquiry into the Sanitary Condition of the Labouring Population of Great Britain.* 1842.

Report on the Sanitary Condition of the Labouring Population of Great Britain: Supplementary Report on . . . the Practice of Interment in Towns, by Edwin Chadwick. B.P.P. 1843, XII.

First Report of the R.C. on the State of Large Towns and Populous Districts. B.P.P. 1844, XVII.

Second Report of ibid. B.P.P. 1845, XVIII.

Report of the Commissioners of Inquiry into the State of Education in Wales. Part I, Carmarthen, Glamorgan and Pembroke. B.P.P. 1847, XXVII.

First Report of the Royal Sanitary Commission. B.P.P. 1868–9, XXXII.

Second Report of ibid. B.P.P. 1871, XXXV, and 1874, XXXI.

Report of the R.C. on Municipal Corporations, Part I. B.P.P. 1880, XXXI.

Interim Report of the S.C. on Artizans' and Labourers' Dwellings Improvement. B.P.P. 1881, VII.

Final Report of ibid. B.P.P. 1882, VII.

Report of the R.C. on the Housing of the Working Classes. B.P.P. 1884–5, XXX and XXXI.

Report of the House of Lords S.C. on Town Improvements (Betterment). B.P.P. 1894, XV.

Final Report (England and Wales) of the R.C. on Local Taxation. B.P.P. 1901, XXIV. *Appendix to ibid.* B.P.P. 1902, XXXIX.

Select Bibliography

Report of the Joint S.C. of the House of Lords and House of Commons on Housing of the Working Classes. B.P.P. 1902, V.

Report of the Inter-Departmental Committee on Physical Deterioration. B.P.P. 1904, XXXII.

Report of the R.C. on London Traffic. B.P.P. 1905, XXX; 1906, XL–XLVI.

Report of the S.C. on the Housing of the Working Classes Acts Amendment Bill. B.P.P. 1906, IX.

Report of the R.C. on Housing in Scotland. B.P.P. 1917–18, XIV.

Local Government Board. *Report of the Committee on Building Construction in connection with the Provision of Dwellings for the Working Classes in England and Wales, and Scotland.* B.P.P. 1918, VII.

Ministry of Health. *Interim Report of the committee to consider and advise on the principles to be followed in dealing with unhealthy areas.* 1920.

First Report of the R.C. on Local Government. B.P.P. 1924–5, XIV.

Second Report of ibid. B.P.P. 1928–9, VIII.

Final Report of ibid. B.P.P. 1929–30, XV.

Final Report of the R.C. on Transport. B.P.P. 1930–1, XVII.

Ministry of Health. *Interim Report of the D.C. on Regional Development.* B.P.P. 1930–1, XVII.

Ministry of Health. *Report of the D.C. on Housing.* B.P.P. 1932–3, XIII.

Ministry of Health. *Report of the Committee on Local Expenditure (England and Wales).* B.P.P. 1932–3, XIV.

Scottish Office. *Report of the Committee on Local Expenditure (Scotland).* B.P.P. 1932–3, XIV.

Ministry of Health. *Report of the D.C. on Garden Cities and Satellite Towns.* 1935.

Report of the R.C. on the Distribution of the Industrial Population. B.P.P. 1939–40, IV.

Final Report of the Expert Committee on Compensation and Betterment. B.P.P. 1941–2, IV.

Ministry of Agriculture. *Report of the Committee on Land Utilisation in Rural Areas.* B.P.P. 1941–2, IV.

Ministry of Town and Country Planning. *Interim, Second Interim, and Final Reports of the New Towns Committee.* B.P.P. 1945–6, XIV.

Ministry of Town and Country Planning. *Report of the National Parks Committee (England and Wales).* B.P.P. 1946–7, XIII.

(*e*) *Parliamentary Debates*

Fourth and Fifth Series.

II. LOCAL AUTHORITIES

Birmingham, City of. *Report of the Housing Committee presented to the Council on the 3rd July,* 1906.

Edinburgh Commissioners of Police. *Papers relating to the Fetid Irrigations around the City of Edinburgh.* 1839.

London, Corporation of. Local Government and Taxation Committee. *Report on the City Day Census.* 1881.

London County Council. *London Statistics.* Annual from 1891.

Richmond, Surrey, Borough of. *Housing of the Working Classes. Memorandum.* 1892.

C. PERIODICALS AND ANNUALS

The Builder. From 1842.

Garden Cities and Town Planning. From 1908. (Published under the title *The Garden City,* 1904–8; now entitled *Town and Country Planning*).

Journal of the Town Planning Institute. From 1914.

Liverpool Health of Towns Advocate. 1845–6.

London Passenger Transport Board. *Annual Report and statement of accounts and statistics.* 1934–47.

National Housing and Town Planning Council (originally named the National Housing Reform Council). *Annual Report.* From 1901.

Sessional Proceedings of the National Association for the Promotion of Social Science. 1866–85.

Society for Promoting Industrial Villages. *Annual Reports.* 1885–8.

Town Planning Review. From 1910.

Transactions of the National Association for the Promotion of Social Science. 1857–84.

D. ARTICLES IN PERIODICALS

(Note.—Articles in the periodicals listed above are not cited separately in this section.)

BAKER, C. A. 'Population and Costs in Relation to City Management.' *Journal of the Royal Statistical Society,* vol. LXXIV. 1910–11.

BAKER, H. 'On the Growth of the Commercial Centre of Manchester.' *Transactions of the Manchester Statistical Society.* 1871–2.

Select Bibliography

COSTELLOE, B. F. C. 'The Housing Problem.' *Transactions of the Manchester Statistical Society.* 1898–9.

HONEYMAN, J., SPALDING, H., WALLIS, W. E., and FLEMING, O. 'Working-Class Dwellings.' *Journal of the R.I.B.A.,* 3rd series, vol. VII. 1900.

MARSHALL, A. 'The Housing of the London Poor. Where to house them.' *Contemporary Review,* vol. XLV. 1884.

MESS, H. A. 'The Growth and Decay of Towns.' *Political Quarterly,* vol. IX. 1938.

MULHALL, M. G. 'The Housing of the London Poor. Ways and Means.' *Contemporary Review,* vol. XLV. 1884.

PRICE WILLIAMS, R. 'On the Increase of Population in England and Wales.' *Journal of the Statistical Society,* vol. XLIII. 1880.

ROBINSON, G. T. 'On Town Dwellings for the Working Classes.' *Transactions of the Manchester Statistical Society.* 1871–2.

SYSON, E. J. 'On the Comparative Mortality in Large Towns.' *Transactions of the Manchester Statistical Society.* 1870–1.

TILLYARD, F. 'English Town Development in the Nineteenth Century.' *Economic Journal,* vol. XXIII. 1913.

TOWN PLANNING COMMITTEE, R.I.B.A. 'Suggestions to Promoters of Town Planning Schemes.' *Journal of the R.I.B.A.,* 3rd series, vol. XVIII. 1911.

VIVIAN, H., 'Garden Cities, Housing and Town Planning.' *Quarterly Review,* vol. CCXVI. 1912.

E. PAMPHLETS ON CONTEMPORARY ISSUES

ANON. *Growth of Cardiff from 1875 to 1880: with some particulars of Cardiff in the last century.* Cardiff, 1880.

ANON. *The Strangers' Guide through Birkenhead.* Birkenhead, 1847.

ANON. *The Visitors' Guide to Bournemouth and its Neighbourhood.* 3rd edn. London, 1850.

BLACKETT, B. *Speech on the Occasion of the Inauguration of the Welwyn (Garden City) Chamber of Commerce on July 6th, 1929.* n.p., n.d. [1929?].

BOOTH, C. *Improved Means of Locomotion as a First Step towards the Cure of the Housing Difficulties of London.* London, 1901.

BOURNVILLE VILLAGE TRUST. *Sixty Years of Planning. The Bournville Experiment.* n.p., n.d. [Bournville? 1943?].

BROWNING HALL CONFERENCE. *Report of Sub-Committee on Housing and Locomotion in London, 1902–7.* London, 1907.

CADBURY BROTHERS LTD. *Bournville Housing.* Bournville, 1922.

CONFERENCE OF DELEGATES ON QUESTIONS CONCERNING THE HOUSING OF THE PEOPLE. *Report of the 'Financial and Compensation Committee' of the Conference.* London, 1890.

'DAMON AND PYTHIAS'. *Guide to Garden City.* Hitchin, n.d. [1906?].

FABIAN SOCIETY. *The House Famine and How to Relieve it.* London, 1900.

FORSHAW, J. H. *Town Planning and Health.* London, 1943.

GARDEN CITY ASSOCIATION. *Garden Cities: Report of a public meeting at the Holborn Restaurant, June 2nd, 1902.* London, 1902.

GIBBS, E. M. *The Future Extension of the Suburbs of Sheffield. A Lecture delivered to The Sheffield Society of Architects and Surveyors, 9th March 1911.* Privately printed, n.d. [1911?].

HAMPSTEAD GARDEN SUBURB TRUST. *The Hampstead Garden Suburb: Its Achievements and Significance.* n.p., n.d. [Hampstead? 1937?].

HAMPSTEAD TENANTS LTD. *Cottages with Gardens for Londoners.* London, 1907.

HILL, O. *Letter to my Fellow-Workers.* Privately printed, 1904.

HORSFALL, T. C. *The Relation of Town-Planning to the National Life.* Wolverhampton, 1908.

INTERNATIONAL GARDEN CITIES AND TOWN PLANNING FEDERATION. *Report of Conference at Gothenburg, 1923.* London, n.d. [1923?].

J 47485. *One Hundred New Towns for Britain.* 3rd edn. London, 1934.

LABOUR PUBLICATIONS DEPARTMENT. *Up with the Houses! Down with the slums!* London, 1934.

LEWIS, G. *The State of St. David's Parish; with remarks on the moral and physical statistics of Dundee.* Dundee, 1841.

LONDON COUNCIL OF SOCIAL SERVICE AND MANSION HOUSE COUNCIL ON HEALTH AND HOUSING, JOINT HOUSING COMMITTEE. *Housing in Greater London.* London, 1928.

MADSEN, A. W. *House Famine and the Land Blockade.* London, n.d. [1920?]

MANCHESTER DIOCESAN CONFERENCE (1902). *Report of the Committee Appointed to Consider the Question of the Housing of the Poor.* Manchester, 1902.

MANCHESTER, SHEFFIELD AND LINCOLNSHIRE RAILWAY. *A Description of the New Docks at Great Grimsby.* Manchester, n.d. [1851?].

MOORE, H. E. *The Economic Aspect of the First Garden City. An Address to the Economic Section of the British Association, 1903.* Privately printed, n.d. [1903?].

NATIONAL DWELLINGS SOCIETY. *Homes of the London Working Classes: Philanthropy and five per cent.* London, 1887.

NATIONAL HOUSING AND TOWN PLANNING COUNCIL. *How to Town-Plan.* London, 1910.

NATIONAL HOUSING AND TOWN PLANNING COUNCIL. *1900–1910: A Record of Ten Years' Work for Housing and Town Planning Reform.* Leicester, n.d. [1910?].

NETTLEFOLD, J. S. *Slum Reform and Town Planning: The Garden City Idea applied to existing Cities and their suburbs.* Birmingham, n.d. [1910?].

O'LEARY, J. G. (ed.) *Public Services in Dagenham.* Dagenham, 1935.

OSBORN, F. J. *Transport, Town Development and Territorial Planning of Industry.* London, 1934.

OWEN, R. *A New View of Society, and other writings.* London (Everyman's Library), 1927.

[OWEN, R.] *A Statement regarding the New Lanark Establishment.* Edinburgh, 1812.

POWELL, J. H. *Powell's Popular Eastbourne Guide.* Eastbourne, 1863.

PRESBYTERY OF GLASGOW COMMISSION ON THE HOUSING OF THE POOR. *Report by William Smart on the Housing of the Poor in London.* Glasgow, n.d. [c. 1890?].

PUMPHREY, R., *Industry and Town Planning.* London, 1941.

RICHARDSON, B. W. *Hygeia, a City of Health.* London, 1876.

ROBSON, W. A. *The War and the Planning Outlook.* London, 1941.

ROYAL INSTITUTE OF PUBLIC HEALTH, BIRKENHEAD CONGRESS. *Inaugural Address by the President, W. H. Lever, Monday, July 18th, 1910.* With an appendix. Port Sunlight, n.d. [1910?].

S., J. *A Guide to Southport and the Surrounding Neighbourhood and Parish.* Liverpool, 1849.

SANDERSON FURNISS, A. D., and PHILLIPS, M. *The Working Woman's House.* London, n.d. [1920?].

SHAWCROSS, H. *The Cost of Land Development and House Building under Town Planning Schemes.* London, n.d. [1914?].

SOCIETY FOR THE ENCOURAGEMENT OF ARTS, MANUFACTURES AND COMMERCE. *Conference on the Health and Sewage of Towns, May, 1876.* London, 1876.

SOLLY, H. *Industrial Villages: a Remedy for Crowded Towns and Deserted Fields.* London, 1884.

THOMPSON, W. (ed.). *Town Planning in Practice. With an Account of the Ruislip (Middlesex) Town Planning Scheme.* London, 1911.

TOWN PLANNING INSTITUTE. *Town and Country Planning Compensation and Betterment. Report of Committee of the Institute, Approved by the Council of the Institute 31st May, 1940.* London, 1940.

UNWIN, R. *Nothing gained by overcrowding!* London, 1912.

VERINDER, F. *The Great Problem of Our Great Towns.* London, 1908.

VIVIAN, H. *Co-partnership in Housing in its Health Relationship.* London, 1908.

WELWYN ASSOCIATION. *Welwyn Garden City: Its Meaning and Methods.* n.p., n.d. [Welwyn? 1929?].

WELWYN GARDEN CITY LTD. *Welwyn Garden City: A New Town of National Importance.* n.p. [Welwyn?], 1921.

WILLIAMS, R. *The Face of the Poor or The Crowding of London's Labourers.* London, 1897.

WILLIAMS, R. *London Rookeries and Colliers' Slums.* London, 1893.

WILLIAMS, R. *The People the Nation's Wealth.* London, 1895.

F. BOOKS

ABERCROMBIE, P. *Greater London Plan, 1944.* London, 1945.

ABERCROMBIE, P. *Town and Country Planning.* London, 1933.

ABERCROMBIE, P., and ARCHIBALD, J. *East Kent Regional Planning Scheme. Preliminary Survey.* Liverpool, 1925. *Final Report.* Canterbury, 1928.

ABERCROMBIE, P., and BRUETON, B. F. *Bristol and Bath Regional Planning Scheme.* Liverpool, 1930.

ABERCROMBIE, P., and JOHNSON, T. H. *The Doncaster Regional Planning Scheme. The Report Prepared for the Joint Committee.* Liverpool, 1922.

ABERCROMBIE, P., and KELLY, S. A. *Cumbrian Regional Planning Scheme.* Liverpool, 1932.

ABERCROMBIE, P., KELLY, S. A., and JOHNSON, T. H. *Sheffield and District Regional Planning Scheme.* Liverpool, 1931.

ADAMS, T. *Recent Advances in Town Planning.* London, 1932.

ADAMS, THOMPSON and FRY. *North-East Kent Regional Planning Scheme.* London, 1930.

ADAMS, THOMPSON and FRY. *South-East Sussex Regional Planning Scheme.* London, 1931.

ADSHEAD, S. D. *The South Essex Regional Planning Scheme 1931.* London, 1931.

ALDERSON, J. W., and OGDEN, A. E. *The Halifax Equitable Benefit Building Society: Jubilee 1871–1921.* Halifax, 1921.

ALDRIDGE, H. R., *The Case for Town Planning.* London, 1915.

Select Bibliography

ANDERSON, J. *A History of Edinburgh from the earliest period to the completion of the half century 1850.* Edinburgh, 1856.

BAINES, T. *Liverpool in 1859.* London, 1859.

BALGARNIE, R. *Sir Titus Salt, Baronet: His Life and its Lessons.* London, 1877.

BARNETT, H. *The Story of the Growth of Hampstead Garden Suburb, 1907–1928.* n.p., n.d. [1928?].

BARON, S. (ed.) *Country Towns in the Future England.* London, 1944.

BARTON, M. *Tunbridge Wells.* London, 1937.

BELLMAN, H. *The Thrifty Three Millions. A Study of the Building Society Movement and the Story of the Abbey Road Society.* London, 1935.

BEVAN, G. P. *The Statistical Atlas of England, Scotland and Ireland.* Edinburgh, 1882.

BLOMFIELD, R. T. *Richard Norman Shaw, R.A. Architect, 1831–1912.* London, 1940.

BOARDMAN, P. *Patrick Geddes: Maker of the Future.* Chapel Hill, 1944.

BOSANQUET, C. B. P. *London: some account of its growth, charitable agencies and wants.* London, 1869.

BOWLEY, M. *Housing and the State, 1919–1944.* London, 1945.

BRITISH ASSOCIATION, *Britain in Recovery.* London, 1938.

BRUCE, J. C. *A Hand-Book to Newcastle-on-Tyne.* London, 1863.

BRUCE, R. *The North-East Lancashire Joint Town Planning Advisory Committee Regional Planning Report.* Manchester, 1929.

BUCKINGHAM, J. S. *National Evils and Practical Remedies.* London, 1849.

BURNLEY, J. *Sir Titus Salt, and George Moore.* London, 1885.

CADBURY, G., jun. *Town Planning with special reference to the Birmingham Schemes.* London, 1915.

CHALONER, W. H. *The Social and Economic Development of Crewe, 1780–1923.* Manchester, 1950.

CLARKE, J. J. *The Housing Problem: Its History, Growth, Legislation and Procedure.* London, 1920.

COCKBURN, LORD (ed. GRAY, W. F.) *Memorials of His Time.* Edinburgh, 1945.

COLE, G. D. H. *Building and Planning.* London, 1945.

COLE, G. D. H. and M. I. *Rents, Rings and Houses.* London, 1923.

CULPIN, E. G. *The Garden City Movement Up-to-Date.* London, 1914.

DALE, L. *Towards a Plan for Oxford City.* London, 1944.

DAVIDGE, W. R. *Cambridgeshire Regional Planning Report.* Cambridge, 1934.

DAVIDGE, W. R. *Planning for Swindon.* Swindon, 1945.

Select Bibliography

DAVIDGE, W. R. *Report on the Regional Planning of West Kent*. London, 1927.

DEWSNUP, E. R. *The Housing Problem in England: its Statistics, Legislation and Policy*. Manchester, 1907.

DOBSON, M. J. *Memoir of John Dobson, of Newcastle-on-Tyne*. London, 1885.

DUNDEE SOCIAL UNION. *Report on Housing and Industrial Conditions and Medical Inspection of School Children*. Dundee, 1905.

ESCRITT, L. B. *Regional Planning: An outline of the scientific data relating to planning in Great Britain*. London, 1943.

EVERSLEY, LORD. *English Commons and Forests: The Story of the battle during the last thirty years for public rights over the Commons and Forests of England and Wales*. London, 1894.

FARR, W. (ed. HUMPHREYS, N. A.). *Vital Statistics*. London, 1885.

FINER, S. E. *The Life and Times of Sir Edwin Chadwick*. London, 1952.

FORSHAW, J. H., and ABERCROMBIE, P. *County of London Plan*. London, 1943.

GEDDES, P. *Cities in Evolution. An introduction to the town planning movement and to the study of civics*. London, 1915.

GEDDES, P. *City Development. A study of parks, gardens and culture institutes*. Edinburgh, 1904.

GEORGE, W. L. *Labour and Housing at Port Sunlight*. London, 1909.

GILL, C., and BRIGGS, A. *History of Birmingham*. 2 vols. London, 1952.

GLASS, D. V. *The Town and a Changing Civilisation*. London, 1935.

GLASS, R. *The Social Background of a Plan: a study of Middlesbrough*. London, 1948.

GODWIN, G. *Town Swamps and Social Bridges*. London, 1859.

GRANVILLE, A. B. *The Spas of England and Principal Sea-Bathing Places*. 2 vols. London, 1841.

GREATER LONDON REGIONAL PLANNING COMMITTEE. *First Report*. London, 1929. *Second Report*. London, 1933.

GRINSELL, L. V., AND OTHERS. *Studies in the History of Swindon*. Swindon, 1950.

HAMMOND, J. L. and B. *The Bleak Age*. Revised edn. West Drayton, 1947.

HARRIS, G. M. *The Garden City Movement*. Hitchin, 1905.

[HEAD, F. B.]. *Stokers and Pokers*. New edn. London, 1861.

HILL, O. *Homes of the London Poor*. London, 1883.

HOBSON, O. *A Hundred Years of the Halifax. The History of the Halifax Building Society 1853–1953*. London, 1953.

HOLE, J. *The Homes of the Working Classes, with Suggestions for their Improvement.* London, 1866.

HOLFORD, W. G., and EDEN, W. A. *The Future of Merseyside: Town and Country Planning Schemes.* Liverpool, 1937.

HOLROYD, A. *Saltaire, and its Founder, Sir Titus Salt, Bart.* 2nd edn. Saltaire, 1871.

HORSFALL, T. C. *The Improvement of the Dwellings and Surroundings of the People: The Example of Germany.* Manchester, 1904.

HOSKING, W. *A Guide to the Proper Regulation of Buildings in Towns, as a means of promoting and securing the Health, Comfort and Safety of the Inhabitants.* London, 1848.

HOWARD, E. (ed. OSBORN, F. J.). *Garden Cities of Tomorrow.* London, 1946.

HOWARTH, E. G., and WILSON, M. (eds.). *West Ham: a study in social and industrial problems, being the report of the Outer London Inquiry Committee.* London, 1907.

JENNINGS, H. *Brynmawr: A Study of a Distressed Area.* London, 1934.

JENNINGS, W. I. (ed. ROBERTS, J. R. H.). *The Law Relating to Town and Country Planning.* 2nd edn. London, 1946.

JEPHSON, H. *The Sanitary Evolution of London.* London, 1907.

LAING, S., jun. *National Distress; its causes and remedies.* London, 1844.

'LE CORBUSIER'. *Urbanisme.* Paris, 1925.

LEICESTERSHIRE REGIONAL TOWN PLANNING JOINT ADVISORY COMMITTEE. *Regional Planning Report.* London, 1932.

LEVERHULME, SECOND VISCOUNT. *Viscount Leverhulme by his Son.* London, 1927.

LEWIS, R. A. *Edwin Chadwick and the Public Health Movement 1832–1854.* London, 1952.

LIBERAL LAND COMMITTEE. *Towns and the Land.* London, 1925.

LIEPMANN, K. K. *The Journey to Work.* London, 1944.

MCALLISTER, G. and E. *Town and Country Planning.* London, 1941.

MCALLISTER, G. and E. (eds.) *Homes, Towns and Countryside.* London, 1945.

MCCALLUM, I. R. M. (ed.). *Physical Planning: The groundwork of a new technique.* London, 1945.

MACFADYEN, D. *Sir Ebenezer Howard and the Town Planning Movement.* Manchester, 1933.

MASTERMAN, C. F. G. *The Condition of England.* London, 1909.

MATE, C., and RIDDLE, C. H., *Bournemouth: 1810–1910.* Bournemouth, 1910.

MAYO, EARL OF, ADSHEAD, S. D., and ABERCROMBIE, P. *Regional Planning Report on Oxfordshire*. Oxford, 1931.

MEAKIN, B. *Model Factories and Villages: Ideal Conditions of Labour and Housing*. London, 1905.

MILLER, A. *The Rise and Progress of Coatbridge and Surrounding Neighbourhood*. Glasgow, 1864.

MORGAN, J. M. *The Christian Commonwealth*. London, 1850.

MORGAN, J. M. *Letters to a Clergyman on Institutions for Ameliorating the Condition of the People: chiefly from Paris, in the autumn of 1845*. London, 1849.

MORRIS, M. *William Morris, Artist, Writer, Socialist*. 2 vols. Oxford, 1936.

MORRIS, W. *Architecture, Industry and Wealth*. London, 1902.

MUMFORD, L. *City Development*. London, 1946.

MUMFORD, L. *The Culture of Cities*. London, 1938.

'NASEWEIS, SEBALDUS'. *Edinburgh and its Society in 1838*. Edinburgh, 1838.

NETTLEFOLD, J. S. *Practical Town Planning*. London, 1914.

OSBORN, F. J. *Green-belt Cities: The British Contribution*. London, 1946.

OSBORN, F. J. *New Towns after the War*. 2nd edn. London, 1942.

P.E.P. *Report on the Location of Industry in Great Britain*. London, 1939.

P.E.P. INDUSTRIES GROUP. *Housing England*. London, 1934.

PERRY, C. A. *Housing for the Machine Age*. New York, 1939.

PICTON, J. A. *City of Liverpool: Municipal Archives and Records from A.D. 1700 to the passing of the Municipal Reform Act, 1835*. Liverpool, 1886.

PURDOM, C. B. *The Building of Satellite Towns*. London, 1925.

PURDOM, C. B. (ed.). *Town Theory and Practice*. London, 1921.

RAISTRICK, A. *Two Centuries of Industrial Welfare: The London (Quaker) Lead Company, 1692–1905*. London, 1938.

RASMUSSEN, S. E. *London: The Unique City*. London, 1937.

REDFORD, A., and RUSSELL, I. S. *The History of Local Government in Manchester*. 3 vols. London, 1939.

RICHARDSON, B. W. *The Health of Nations. A Review of the Works of Edwin Chadwick*. 2 vols. London, 1887.

ROWNTREE, A. (ed.). *The History of Scarborough*. London, 1931.

ROWNTREE, B. S. *Poverty: A Study of Town Life*. 2nd edn. London, 1902.

ROWNTREE, B. S., and PIGOU, A. C. *Lectures on Housing*. Manchester, 1914.

Select Bibliography

SENNETT, A. R. *Garden Cities in Theory and Practice.* 2 vols. London, 1905.

SHARP, T. *Town and Countryside: Some Aspects of Urban and Rural Development.* Oxford, 1932.

SHARP, T. *Town Planning.* Harmondsworth, 1940.

SIMON, A. P. *Manchester Made Over.* London, 1936.

SIMON, E. D. *Rebuilding Britain—a Twenty Year Plan.* London, 1945.

SIMON, E. D., and INMAN, J. *The Rebuilding of Manchester.* London, 1935.

SIMON, J. *English Sanitary Institutions.* London, 1890.

SIMON, J. (ed. SEATON, E.). *Public Health Reports.* 2 vols. London, 1887.

SMITH, D. H. *The Industries of Greater London, being a survey of the recent industrialisation of the northern and western sectors of Greater London.* London, 1933.

SOUTH-WEST LANCASHIRE JOINT TOWN PLANNING ADVISORY COMMITTEE. *The Future Development of South-West Lancashire.* Liverpool, 1930.

STONEHOUSE, J. *The Streets of Liverpool.* Liverpool, n.d. [1870?].

SUMMERSON, J. *Georgian London.* London, 1945.

TAYLOR, W. COOKE. *The Natural History of Society.* 2 vols. London, 1840.

TAYLOR, W. COOKE. *Notes of a tour in the Manufacturing Districts of Lancashire; in a series of letters to His Grace the Archbishop of Dublin.* 2nd edn. London, 1842.

THOMPSON, W. H. *Somerset Regional Report.* London, 1934.

THOMSON, J., and MACLAREN, J. *The History of Dundee.* Dundee, 1874.

TOUZEAU, J., *The Rise and Progress of Liverpool from 1551 to 1835.* Liverpool, 1910.

TRIPP, H. A. *Town Planning and Road Traffic.* London, 1942.

TYERMAN, D. (ed.). *Ways and Means of Rebuilding, being a report of the London Conference of the Town and Country Planning Association 1943.* London, 1944.

UNWIN, G., AND OTHERS. *Samuel Oldknow and the Arkwrights.* Manchester, 1924.

UNWIN, R. *Town Planning in Practice.* 2nd edn. London, 1911.

VAUGHAN, R. *The Age of Great Cities.* 2nd edn. London, 1843.

WALMSLEY, H. M. *The Life of Sir Joshua Walmsley.* London, 1879.

WARREN, H., and DAVIDGE, W. R. (eds.). *Decentralisation of Population and Industry: A New Principle in Town Planning.* London, 1930.

WATERHOUSE, P., and UNWIN, R. *Old Towns and New Needs: also The Town Extension Plan: being the Warburton Lectures for 1912.* Manchester, 1912.

WATSON, J. P., and ABERCROMBIE, P. *A Plan for Plymouth.* Plymouth, 1943.

WEBER, A. F. *The Growth of Cities in the Nineteenth Century.* New York, 1899.

WELLS, H. G. *Anticipations of the reaction of mechanical and scientific progress upon human life and thought.* Revised edn. London, 1914.

WHITE, J. T. *The History of Torquay.* Torquay, 1878.

WILKINS, C. *The History of Merthyr Tydfil.* Merthyr Tydfil, 1908.

WILLIAMS-ELLIS, C. *England and the Octopus.* London, 1928.

WOLFE, L. *The Reilly Plan, a new way of life.* London, 1945.

WOLTON, D. G. (ed.). *Trading Estates: The Growth and Development of the Modern Factory Unit.* London, n.d. [1938?].

YOUNG, G. M. (ed.). *Country and Town.* Harmondsworth, 1942.

YOUNG, T. *Becontree and Dagenham.* London, 1934.

Index of Place-Names

Index of Place-Names

Index of Persons and Subjects

257

259

The International Library of

Sociology

and Social Reconstruction

Edited by W. J. H. SPROTT

Founded by KARL MANNHEIM

ROUTLEDGE & KEGAN PAUL

BROADWAY HOUSE, CARTER LANE, LONDON, E.C.4

CONTENTS

PRINTED IN GREAT BRITAIN BY HEADLEY BROTHERS LTD
109 KINGSWAY LONDON WC2 AND ASHFORD KENT

GENERAL SOCIOLOGY

Brown, Robert. Explanation in Social Science. *208 pp. 1963. (2nd Impression 1964.) 25s.*

Gibson, Quentin. The Logic of Social Enquiry. *240 pp. 1960. (3rd Impression 1968.) 24s.*

Homans, George C. Sentiments and Activities: Essays in Social Science. *336 pp. 1962. 32s.*

Isajiw, Wsevelod W. Causation and Functionalism in Sociology. *165 pp. 1968. 25s.*

Johnson, Harry M. Sociology: a Systematic Introduction. *Foreword by Robert K. Merton. 710 pp. 1961. (5th Impression 1968.) 42s.*

Mannheim, Karl. Essays on Sociology and Social Psychology. *Edited by Paul Keckskemeti. With Editorial Note by Adolph Lowe. 344 pp. 1953. (2nd Impression 1966.) 32s.*

Systematic Sociology: An Introduction to the Study of Society. *Edited by J. S. Erös and Professor W. A. C. Stewart. 220 pp. 1957. (3rd Impression 1967.) 24s.*

Martindale, Don. The Nature and Types of Sociological Theory. *292 pp. 1961. (3rd Impression 1967.) 35s.*

Maus, Heinz. A Short History of Sociology. *234 pp. 1962. (2nd Impression 1965.) 28s.*

Myrdal, Gunnar. Value in Social Theory: A Collection of Essays on Methodology. *Edited by Paul Streeten. 332 pp. 1958. (3rd Impression 1968.) 35s.*

Ogburn, William F., and **Nimkoff, Meyer F.** A Handbook of Sociology. *Preface by Karl Mannheim. 656 pp. 46 figures. 35 tables. 5th edition (revised) 1964. 45s.*

Parsons, Talcott, and **Smelser, Neil J.** Economy and Society: A Study in the Integration of Economic and Social Theory. *362 pp. 1956. (4th Impression 1967.) 35s.*

Rex, John. Key Problems of Sociological Theory. *220 pp. 1961. (4th Impression 1968.) 25s.*

Stark, Werner. The Fundamental Forms of Social Thought. *280 pp. 1962. 32s.*

FOREIGN CLASSICS OF SOCIOLOGY

Durkheim, Emile. Suicide. A Study in Sociology. *Edited and with an Introduction by George Simpson. 404 pp. 1952. (4th Impression 1968.) 35s.*

Professional Ethics and Civic Morals. *Translated by Cornelia Brookfield. 288 pp. 1957. 30s.*

Gerth, H. H., and **Mills, C. Wright.** From Max Weber: Essays in Sociology. *502 pp. 1948. (6th Impression 1967.) 35s.*

Tönnies, Ferdinand. Community and Association. *(Gemeinschaft und Gesellschaft.) Translated and Supplemented by Charles P. Loomis. Foreword by Pitirim A. Sorokin. 334 pp. 1955. 28s.*

SOCIAL STRUCTURE

Andreski, Stanislav. Military Organization and Society. *Foreword by Professor A. R. Radcliffe-Brown. 226 pp. 1 folder. 1954. Revised Edition 1968. 35s.*

Cole, G. D. H. Studies in Class Structure. *220 pp. 1955. (3rd Impression 1964.) 21s. Paper 10s. 6d.*

Coontz, Sydney H. Population Theories and the Economic Interpretation. *202 pp. 1957. (3rd Impression 1968.) 28s.*

Coser, Lewis. The Functions of Social Conflict. *204 pp. 1956. (3rd Impression 1968.) 25s.*

Dickie-Clark, H. F. Marginal Situation: A Sociological Study of a Coloured Group. *240 pp. 11 tables. 1966. 40s.*

Glass, D. V. (Ed.). Social Mobility in Britain. *Contributions by J. Berent, T. Bottomore, R. C. Chambers, J. Floud, D. V. Glass, J. R. Hall, H. T. Himmelweit, R. K. Kelsall, F. M. Martin, C. A. Moser, R. Mukherjee, and W. Ziegel. 420 pp. 1954. (4th Impression 1967.) 45s.*

Jones, Garth N. Planned Organizational Change: An Exploratory Study Using an Empirical Approach. *About 268 pp. 1969. 40s.*

Kelsall, R. K. Higher Civil Servants in Britain: From 1870 to the Present Day. *268 pp. 31 tables. 1955. (2nd Impression 1966.) 25s.*

König, René. The Community. *232 pp. Illustrated. 1968. 35s.*

Lawton, Denis. Social Class, Language and Education. *192 pp. 1968. (2nd Impression 1968.) 25s.*

McLeish, John. The Theory of Social Change: Four Views Considered. *About 128 pp. 1969. 21s.*

Marsh, David C. The Changing Social Structure in England and Wales, 1871-1961. *1958. 272 pp. 2nd edition (revised) 1966. (2nd Impression 1967.) 35s.*

Mouzelis, Nicos. Organization and Bureaucracy. An Analysis of Modern Theories. *240 pp. 1967. (2nd Impression 1968.) 28s.*

Ossowski, Stanislaw. Class Structure in the Social Consciousness. *210 pp. 1963. (2nd Impression 1967.) 25s.*

SOCIOLOGY AND POLITICS

Barbu, Zevedei. Democracy and Dictatorship: Their Psychology and Patterns of Life. *300 pp. 1956. 28s.*

Crick, Bernard. The American Science of Politics: Its Origins and Conditions. *284 pp. 1959. 32s.*

Hertz, Frederick. Nationality in History and Politics: A Psychology and Sociology of National Sentiment and Nationalism. *432 pp. 1944. (5th Impression 1966.) 42s.*

Kornhauser, William. The Politics of Mass Society. *272 pp. 20 tables. 1960. (3rd Impression 1968.) 28s.*

Laidler, Harry W. History of Socialism. Social-Economic Movements: An Historical and Comparative Survey of Socialism, Communism, Co-operation, Utopianism; and other Systems of Reform and Reconstruction. *New edition. 992 pp. 1968. 90s.*

Lasswell, Harold D. Analysis of Political Behaviour. An Empirical Approach. *324 pp. 1947. (4th Impression 1966.) 35s.*

Mannheim, Karl. Freedom, Power and Democratic Planning. *Edited by Hans Gerth and Ernest K. Bramstedt. 424 pp. 1951. (3rd Impression 1968.) 42s.*

Mansur, Fatma. Process of Independence. *Foreword by A. H. Hanson. 208 pp. 1962. 25s.*

Martin, David A. Pacificism: an Historical and Sociological Study. *262 pp. 1965. 30s.*

Myrdal, Gunnar. The Political Element in the Development of Economic Theory. *Translated from the German by Paul Streeten. 282 pp. 1953. (4th Impression 1965.) 25s.*

Polanyi, Michael. F.R.S. The Logic of Liberty: Reflections and Rejoinders. *228 pp. 1951. 18s.*

Verney, Douglas V. The Analysis of Political Systems. *264 pp. 1959. (3rd Impression 1966.) 28s.*

Wootton, Graham. The Politics of Influence: British Ex-Servicemen, Cabinet Decisions and Cultural Changes, 1917 to 1957. *316 pp. 1963. 30s.*
Workers, Unions and the State. *188 pp. 1966. (2nd Impression 1967.) 25s.*

FOREIGN AFFAIRS: THEIR SOCIAL, POLITICAL AND ECONOMIC FOUNDATIONS

Baer, Gabriel. Population and Society in the Arab East. *Translated by Hanna Szöke. 288 pp. 10 maps. 1964. 40s.*

Bonné, Alfred. State and Economics in the Middle East: A Society in Transition. *482 pp. 2nd (revised) edition 1955. (2nd Impression 1960.) 40s.*
Studies in Economic Development: with special reference to Conditions in the Under-developed Areas of Western Asia and India. *322 pp. 84 tables. 2nd edition 1960. 32s.*

Mayer, J. P. Political Thought in France from the Revolution to the Fifth Republic. *164 pp. 3rd edition (revised) 1961. 16s.*

CRIMINOLOGY

Ancel, Marc. Social Defence: A Modern Approach to Criminal Problems. *Foreword by Leon Radzinowicz. 240 pp. 1965. 32s.*

Cloward, Richard A., and **Ohlin, Lloyd E.** Delinquency and Opportunity: A Theory of Delinquent Gangs. *248 pp. 1961. 25s.*

Downes, David M. The Delinquent Solution. A Study in Subcultural Theory. *296 pp. 1966. 42s.*

Dunlop, A. B., and **McCabe, S.** Young Men in Detention Centres. *192 pp. 1965. 28s.*

Friedländer, Kate. The Psycho-Analytical Approach to Juvenile Delinquency: Theory, Case Studies, Treatment. *320 pp. 1947. (6th Impression 1967). 40s.*

Glueck, Sheldon and **Eleanor.** Family Environment and Delinquency. *With the statistical assistance of Rose W. Kneznek. 340 pp. 1962. (2nd Impression 1966.) 40s.*

Mannheim, Hermann. Comparative Criminology: a Text Book. *Two volumes. 442 pp. and 380 pp. 1965. (2nd Impression with corrections 1966.) 42s. a volume.*

Morris, Terence. The Criminal Area: A Study in Social Ecology. *Foreword by Hermann Mannheim. 232 pp. 25 tables. 4 maps. 1957. (2nd Impression 1966.) 28s.*

Morris, Terence and **Pauline,** assisted by **Barbara Barer.** Pentonville: A Sociological Study of an English Prison. *416 pp. 16 plates. 1963. 50s.*

Spencer, John C. Crime and the Services. *Foreword by Hermann Mannheim. 336 pp. 1954. 28s.*

Trasler, Gordon. The Explanation of Criminality. *144 pp. 1962. (2nd Impression 1967.) 20s.*

SOCIAL PSYCHOLOGY

Barbu, Zevedei. Problems of Historical Psychology. *248 pp. 1960. 25s.*

Blackburn, Julian. Psychology and the Social Pattern. *184 pp. 1945. (7th Impression 1964.) 16s.*

Fleming, C. M. Adolescence: Its Social Psychology: With an Introduction to recent findings from the fields of Anthropology, Physiology, Medicine, Psychometrics and Sociometry. *288 pp. 2nd edition (revised) 1963. (3rd Impression 1967.) 25s. Paper 12s. 6d.*
The Social Psychology of Education: An Introduction and Guide to Its Study. *136 pp. 2nd edition (revised) 1959. (4th Impression 1967.) 14s. Paper 7s. 6d.*

Homans, George C. The Human Group. *Foreword by Bernard DeVoto. Introduction by Robert K. Merton. 526 pp. 1951. (7th Impression 1968.) 35s.*
Social Behaviour: its Elementary Forms. *416 pp. 1961. (3rd Impression 1968.) 35s.*

Klein, Josephine. The Study of Groups. *226 pp. 31 figures. 5 tables. 1956. (5th Impression 1967.) 21s. Paper 9s. 6d.*

Linton, Ralph. The Cultural Background of Personality. *132 pp. 1947. (7th Impression 1968.) 18s.*

Mayo, Elton. The Social Problems of an Industrial Civilization. With an appendix on the Political Problem. *180 pp. 1949. (5th Impression 1966.) 25s.*

Ottaway, A. K. C. Learning Through Group Experience. *176 pp. 1966. (2nd Impression 1968.) 25s.*

Ridder, J. C. de. The Personality of the Urban African in South Africa. A Thematic Apperception Test Study. *196 pp. 12 plates. 1961. 25s.*

Rose, Arnold M. (Ed.). Human Behaviour and Social Processes: an Interactionist Approach. *Contributions by Arnold M. Rose, Ralph H. Turner, Anselm Strauss, Everett C. Hughes, E. Franklin Frazier, Howard S. Becker, et al. 696 pp. 1962. (2nd Impression 1968.) 70s.*

Smelser, Neil J. Theory of Collective Behaviour. *448 pp. 1962. (2nd Impression 1967.) 45s.*

Stephenson, Geoffrey M. The Development of Conscience. *128 pp. 1966. 25s.*

Young, Kimball. Handbook of Social Psychology. *658 pp. 16 figures. 10 tables. 2nd edition (revised) 1957. (3rd Impression 1963.) 40s.*

SOCIOLOGY OF THE FAMILY

Banks, J. A. Prosperity and Parenthood: A study of Family Planning among The Victorian Middle Classes. *262 pp. 1954. (3rd Impression 1968.) 28s.*

Bell, Colin R. Middle Class Families: Social and Geographical Mobility. *224 pp. 1969. 35s.*

Burton, Lindy. Vulnerable Children. *272 pp. 1968. 35s.*

Gavron, Hannah. The Captive Wife: Conflicts of Housebound Mothers. *190 pp. 1966. (2nd Impression 1966.) 25s.*

Klein, Josephine. Samples from English Cultures. *1965. (2nd Impression 1967.)*
1. Three Preliminary Studies and Aspects of Adult Life in England. *447 pp. 50s.*
2. Child-Rearing Practices and Index. *247 pp. 35s.*

Klein, Viola. Britain's Married Women Workers. *180 pp. 1965. (2nd Impression 1968.) 28s.*

McWhinnie, Alexina M. Adopted Children. How They Grow Up. *304 pp. 1967. (2nd Impression 1968.) 42s.*

Myrdal, Alva and Klein, Viola. Women's Two Roles: Home and Work. *238 pp. 27 tables. 1956. Revised Edition 1967. 30s. Paper 15s.*

Parsons, Talcott and Bales, Robert F. Family: Socialization and Interaction Process. *In collaboration with James Olds, Morris Zelditch and Philip E. Slater. 456 pp. 50 figures and tables. 1956. (3rd Impression 1968.) 45s.*

Schücking, L. L. The Puritan Family. *Translated from the German by Brian Battershaw. 212 pp. 1969. About 42s.*

7

THE SOCIAL SERVICES

Forder, R. A. (Ed.). Penelope Hall's Social Services of Modern England. *288 pp. 1969. 35s.*

George, Victor. Social Security: Beveridge and After. *258 pp. 1968. 35s.*

Goetschius, George W. Working with Community Groups. *256 pp. 1969. 35s.*

Goetschius, George W. and **Tash, Joan.** Working with Unattached Youth. *416 pp. 1967. (2nd Impression 1968.) 40s.*

Hall, M. P., and **Howes, I. V.** The Church in Social Work. A Study of Moral Welfare Work undertaken by the Church of England. *320 pp. 1965. 35s.*

Heywood, Jean S. Children in Care: the Development of the Service for the Deprived Child. *264 pp. 2nd edition (revised) 1965. (2nd Impression 1966.) 32s.*

An Introduction to Teaching Casework Skills. *190 pp. 1964. 28s.*

Jones, Kathleen. Lunacy, Law and Conscience, 1744-1845: the Social History of the Care of the Insane. *268 pp. 1955. 25s.*

Mental Health and Social Policy, 1845-1959. *264 pp. 1960. (2nd Impression 1967.) 32s.*

Jones, Kathleen and **Sidebotham, Roy.** Mental Hospitals at Work. *220 pp. 1962. 30s.*

Kastell, Jean. Casework in Child Care. *Foreword by M. Brooke Willis. 320 pp. 1962. 35s.*

Morris, Pauline. Put Away: A Sociological Study of Institutions for the Mentally Retarded. *Approx. 288 pp. 1969. About 50s.*

Nokes, P. L. The Professional Task in Welfare Practice. *152 pp. 1967. 28s.*

Rooff, Madeline. Voluntary Societies and Social Policy. *350 pp. 15 tables. 1957. 35s.*

Timms, Noel. Psychiatric Social Work in Great Britain (1939-1962). *280 pp. 1964. 32s.*

Social Casework: Principles and Practice. *256 pp. 1964. (2nd Impression 1966.) 25s. Paper 15s.*

Trasler, Gordon. In Place of Parents: A Study in Foster Care. *272 pp. 1960. (2nd Impression 1966.) 30s.*

Young, A. F., and **Ashton, E. T.** British Social Work in the Nineteenth Century. *288 pp. 1956. (2nd Impression 1963.) 28s.*

Young, A. F. Social Services in British Industry. *272 pp. 1968. 40s.*

SOCIOLOGY OF EDUCATION

Banks, Olive. Parity and Prestige in English Secondary Education: a Study in Educational Sociology. *272 pp. 1955. (2nd Impression 1963.) 32s.*

Bentwich, Joseph. Education in Israel. *224 pp. 8 pp. plates. 1965. 24s.*

Blyth, W. A. L. English Primary Education. A Sociological Description. *1965. Revised edition 1967.*

1. Schools. *232 pp. 30s. Paper 12s. 6d.*
2. Background. *168 pp. 25s. Paper 10s. 6d.*

Collier, K. G. The Social Purposes of Education: Personal and Social Values in Education. *268 pp. 1959. (3rd Impression 1965.) 21s.*

Dale, R. R., and Griffith, S. Down Stream: Failure in the Grammar School. *108 pp. 1965. 20s.*

Dore, R. P. Education in Tokugawa Japan. *356 pp. 9 pp. plates. 1965. 35s.*

Edmonds, E. L. The School Inspector. *Foreword by Sir William Alexander. 214 pp. 1962. 28s.*

Evans, K. M. Sociometry and Education. *158 pp. 1962. (2nd Impression 1966.) 18s.*

Foster, P. J. Education and Social Change in Ghana. *336 pp. 3 maps. 1965. (2nd Impression 1967.) 36s.*

Fraser, W. R. Education and Society in Modern France. *150 pp. 1963. (2nd Impression 1968.) 25s.*

Hans, Nicholas. New Trends in Education in the Eighteenth Century. *278 pp. 19 tables. 1951. (2nd Impression 1966.) 30s.*
Comparative Education: A Study of Educational Factors and Traditions. *360 pp. 3rd (revised) edition 1958. (4th Impression 1967.) 25s. Paper 12s. 6d.*

Hargreaves, David. Social Relations in a Secondary School. *240 pp. 1967. (2nd Impression 1968.) 32s.*

Holmes, Brian. Problems in Education. A Comparative Approach. *336 pp. 1965. (2nd Impression 1967.) 32s.*

Mannheim, Karl and Stewart, W. A. C. An Introduction to the Sociology of Education. *206 pp. 1962. (2nd Impression 1965.) 21s.*

Morris, Raymond N. The Sixth Form and College Entrance. *231 pp. 1969. 40s.*

Musgrove, F. Youth and the Social Order. *176 pp. 1964. (2nd Impression 1968.) 25s. Paper 12s.*

Ortega y Gasset, José. Mission of the University. *Translated with an Introduction by Howard Lee Nostrand. 86 pp. 1946. (3rd Impression 1963.) 15s.*

Ottaway, A. K. C. Education and Society: An Introduction to the Sociology of Education. *With an Introduction by W. O. Lester Smith. 212 pp. Second edition (revised). 1962. (5th Impression 1968.) 18s. Paper 10s. 6d.*

Peers, Robert. Adult Education: A Comparative Study. *398 pp. 2nd edition 1959. (2nd Impression 1966.) 42s.*

Pritchard, D. G. Education and the Handicapped: 1760 to 1960. *258 pp. 1963. (2nd Impression 1966.) 35s.*

Richardson, Helen. Adolescent Girls in Approved Schools. *Approx. 360 pp. 1969. About 42s.*

Simon, Brian and Joan (Eds.). Educational Psychology in the U.S.S.R. *Introduction by Brian and Joan Simon. Translation by Joan Simon. Papers by D. N. Bogoiavlenski and N. A. Menchinskaia, D. B. Elkonin, E. A. Fleshner, Z. I. Kalmykova, G. S. Kostiuk, V. A. Krutetski, A. N. Leontiev, A. R. Luria, E. A. Milerian, R. G. Natadze, B. M. Teplov, L. S. Vygotski, L. V. Zankov. 296 pp. 1963. 40s.*

SOCIOLOGY OF CULTURE

Eppel, E. M., and **M.** Adolescents and Morality: A Study of some Moral Values and Dilemmas of Working Adolescents in the Context of a changing Climate of Opinion. *Foreword by W. J. H. Sprott. 268 pp. 39 tables. 1966. 30s.*

Fromm, Erich. The Fear of Freedom. *286 pp. 1942. (8th Impression 1960.) 25s. Paper 10s.*
The Sane Society. *400 pp. 1956. (4th Impression 1968.) 28s. Paper 14s.*

Mannheim, Karl. Diagnosis of Our Time: Wartime Essays of a Sociologist. *208 pp. 1943. (8th Impression 1966.) 21s.*
Essays on the Sociology of Culture. *Edited by Ernst Mannheim in co-operation with Paul Kecskemeti. Editorial Note by Adolph Lowe. 280 pp. 1956. (3rd Impression 1967.) 28s.*

Weber, Alfred. Farewell to European History: or The Conquest of Nihilism. *Translated from the German by R. F. C. Hull. 224 pp. 1947. 18s.*

SOCIOLOGY OF RELIGION

Argyle, Michael. Religious Behaviour. *224 pp. 8 figures. 41 tables. 1958. (4th Impression 1968.) 25s.*

Nelson, G. K. Spiritualism and Society. *313 pp. 1969. 42s.*

Stark, Werner. The Sociology of Religion. A Study of Christendom.
Volume I. Established Religion. *248 pp. 1966. 35s.*
Volume II. Sectarian Religion. *368 pp. 1967. 40s.*
Volume III. The Universal Church. *464 pp. 1967. 45s.*

Watt, W. Montgomery. Islam and the Integration of Society. *320 pp. 1961. (3rd Impression 1966.) 35s.*

SOCIOLOGY OF ART AND LITERATURE

Beljame, Alexandre. Men of Letters and the English Public in the Eighteenth Century: 1660-1744, Dryden, Addison, Pope. *Edited with an Introduction and Notes by Bonamy Dobrée. Translated by E. O. Lorimer. 532 pp. 1948. 32s.*

Misch, Georg. A History of Autobiography in Antiquity. *Translated by E. W. Dickes. 2 Volumes. Vol. 1, 364 pp., Vol. 2, 372 pp. 1950. 45s. the set.*

Schücking, L. L. The Sociology of Literary Taste. *112 pp. 2nd (revised) edition 1966. 18s.*

Silbermann, Alphons. The Sociology of Music. *Translated from the German by Corbet Stewart. 222 pp. 1963. 32s.*

SOCIOLOGY OF KNOWLEDGE

Mannheim, Karl. Essays on the Sociology of Knowledge. *Edited by Paul Kecskemeti. Editorial note by Adolph Lowe. 352 pp. 1952. (4th Impression 1967.) 35s.*

Stark, W. America: Ideal and Reality. The United States of 1776 in Contemporary Philosophy. *136 pp. 1947. 12s.*

The Sociology of Knowledge: An Essay in Aid of a Deeper Understanding of the History of Ideas. *384 pp. 1958. (3rd Impression 1967.) 36s.*

Montesquieu: Pioneer of the Sociology of Knowledge. *244 pp. 1960. 25s.*

URBAN SOCIOLOGY

Anderson, Nels. The Urban Community: A World Perspective. *532 pp. 1960. 35s.*

Ashworth, William. The Genesis of Modern British Town Planning: A Study in Economic and Social History of the Nineteenth and Twentieth Centuries. *288 pp. 1954. (3rd Impression 1968.) 32s.*

Bracey, Howard. Neighbours: On New Estates and Subdivisions in England and U.S.A. *220 pp. 1964. 28s.*

Cullingworth, J. B. Housing Needs and Planning Policy: A Restatement of the Problems of Housing Need and "Overspill" in England and Wales. *232 pp. 44 tables. 8 maps. 1960. (2nd Impression 1966.) 28s.*

Dickinson, Robert E. City and Region: A Geographical Interpretation. *608 pp. 125 figures. 1964. (5th Impression 1967.) 60s.*

The West European City: A Geographical Interpretation. *600 pp. 129 maps. 29 plates. 2nd edition 1962. (3rd Impression 1968.) 55s.*

The City Region in Western Europe. *320 pp. Maps. 1967. 30s. Paper 14s.*

Jackson, Brian. Working Class Community: Some General Notions raised by a Series of Studies in Northern England. *192 pp. 1968. (2nd Impression 1968.) 25s.*

Jennings, Hilda. Societies in the Making: a Study of Development and Redevelopment within a County Borough. *Foreword by D. A. Clark. 286 pp. 1962. (2nd Impression 1967.) 32s.*

Kerr, Madeline. The People of Ship Street. *240 pp. 1958. 28s.*

Mann, P. H. An Approach to Urban Sociology. *240 pp. 1965. (2nd Impression 1968.) 30s.*

Morris, R. N., and **Mogey, J.** The Sociology of Housing. Studies at Berinsfield. *232 pp. 4 pp. plates. 1965. 42s.*

Rosser, C., and **Harris, C.** The Family and Social Change. A Study of Family and Kinship in a South Wales Town. *352 pp. 8 maps. 1965. (2nd Impression 1968.) 45s.*

RURAL SOCIOLOGY

Chambers, R. J. H. Settlement Schemes in Africa: A Selective Study. *Approx. 268 pp. 1969. About 50s.*

Haswell, M. R. The Economics of Development in Village India. *120 pp. 1967. 21s.*

Littlejohn, James. Westrigg: the Sociology of a Cheviot Parish. *172 pp. 5 figures. 1963. 25s.*

Williams, W. M. The Country Craftsman: A Study of Some Rural Crafts and the Rural Industries Organization in England. *248 pp. 9 figures. 1958. 25s. (Dartington Hall Studies in Rural Sociology.)*
The Sociology of an English Village: Gosforth. *272 pp. 12 figures. 13 tables. 1956. (3rd Impression 1964.) 25s.*

SOCIOLOGY OF MIGRATION

Humphreys, Alexander J. New Dubliners: Urbanization and the Irish Family. *Foreword by George C. Homans. 304 pp. 1966. 40s.*

SOCIOLOGY OF INDUSTRY AND DISTRIBUTION

Anderson, Nels. Work and Leisure. *280 pp. 1961. 28s.*

Blau, Peter M., and Scott, W. Richard. Formal Organizations: a Comparative approach. *Introduction and Additional Bibliography by J. H. Smith. 326 pp. 1963. (4th Impression 1969.) 35s. Paper 15s.*

Eldridge, J. E. T. Industrial Disputes. Essays in the Sociology of Industrial Relations. *288 pp. 1968. 40s.*

Hollowell, Peter G. The Lorry Driver. *272 pp. 1968. 42s.*

Jefferys, Margot, with the assistance of Winifred Moss. Mobility in the Labour Market: Employment Changes in Battersea and Dagenham. *Preface by Barbara Wootton. 186 pp. 51 tables. 1954. 15s.*

Levy, A. B. Private Corporations and Their Control. *Two Volumes. Vol. 1, 464 pp., Vol. 2, 432 pp. 1950. 80s. the set.*

Liepmann, Kate. Apprenticeship: An Enquiry into its Adequacy under Modern Conditions. *Foreword by H. D. Dickinson. 232 pp. 6 tables. 1960. (2nd Impression 1960.) 23s.*

Millerson, Geoffrey. The Qualifying Associations: a Study in Professionalization. *320 pp. 1964. 42s.*

Smelser, Neil J. Social Change in the Industrial Revolution: An Application of Theory to the Lancashire Cotton Industry, 1770-1840. *468 pp. 12 figures. 14 tables. 1959. (2nd Impression 1960.) 50s.*

Williams, Gertrude. Recruitment to Skilled Trades. *240 pp. 1957. 23s.*

Young, A. F. Industrial Injuries Insurance: an Examination of British Policy. *192 pp. 1964. 30s.*

ANTHROPOLOGY

Ammar, Hamed. Growing up in an Egyptian Village: Silwa, Province of Aswan. *336 pp. 1954. (2nd Impression 1966.) 35s.*

Crook, David and Isabel. Revolution in a Chinese Village: Ten Mile Inn. *230 pp. 8 plates. 1 map. 1959. (2nd Impression 1968.) 21s.*
The First Years of Yangyi Commune. *302 pp. 12 plates. 1966. 42s.*

Dickie-Clark, H. F. The Marginal Situation. A Sociological Study of a Coloured Group. *236 pp. 1966. 40s.*

Dube, S. C. Indian Village. *Foreword by Morris Edward Opler. 276 pp. 4 plates. 1955. (5th Impression 1965.) 25s.*
India's Changing Villages: Human Factors in Community Development. *260 pp. 8 plates. 1 map. 1958. (3rd Impression 1963.) 25s.*

Firth, Raymond. Malay Fishermen. Their Peasant Economy. *420 pp. 17 pp. plates. 2nd edition revised and enlarged 1966. (2nd Impression 1968.) 55s.*

Gulliver, P. H. The Family Herds. A Study of two Pastoral Tribes in East Africa, The Jie and Turkana. *304 pp. 4 plates. 19 figures. 1955. (2nd Impression with new preface and bibliography 1966.) 35s.*
Social Control in an African Society: a Study of the Arusha, Agricultural Masai of Northern Tanganyika. *320 pp. 8 plates. 10 figures. 1963. (2nd Impression 1968.) 42s.*

Ishwaran, K. Shivapur. A South Indian Village. *216 pp. 1968. 35s.*
Tradition and Economy in Village India: An Interactionist Approach. *Foreword by Conrad Arensburg. 176 pp. 1966. (2nd Impression 1968.) 25s.*

Jarvie, Ian C. The Revolution in Anthropology. *268 pp. 1964. (2nd Impression 1967.) 40s.*

Jarvie, Ian C. and **Agassi, Joseph.** Hong Kong. A Society in Transition. *396 pp. Illustrated with plates and maps. 1968. 56s.*

Little, Kenneth L. Mende of Sierra Leone. *308 pp. and folder. 1951. Revised edition 1967. 63s.*

Lowie, Professor Robert H. Social Organization. *494 pp. 1950. (4th Impression 1966.) 50s.*

Mayer, Adrian C. Caste and Kinship in Central India: A Village and its Region. *328 pp. 16 plates. 15 figures. 16 tables. 1960. (2nd Impression 1965.) 35s.*
Peasants in the Pacific: A Study of Fiji Indian Rural Society. *232 pp. 16 plates. 10 figures. 14 tables. 1961. 35s.*

Smith, Raymond T. The Negro Family in British Guiana: Family Structure and Social Status in the Villages. *With a Foreword by Meyer Fortes. 314 pp. 8 plates. 1 figure. 4 maps. 1956. (2nd Impression 1965.) 35s.*

DOCUMENTARY

Meek, Dorothea L. (Ed.). Soviet Youth: Some Achievements and Problems. *Excerpts from the Soviet Press, translated by the editor. 280 pp. 1957. 28s.*

Schlesinger, Rudolf (Ed.). Changing Attitudes in Soviet Russia.

2. The Nationalities Problem and Soviet Administration. Selected Readings on the Development of Soviet Nationalities Policies. *Introduced by the editor. Translated by W. W. Gottlieb. 324 pp. 1956. 30s.*

Reports of the Institute
of Community Studies

(*Demy 8vo.*)

Cartwright, Ann. Human Relations and Hospital Care. *272 pp. 1964. 30s.*
Patients and their Doctors. A Study of General Practice. *304 pp. 1967. 40s.*

Jackson, Brian. Streaming: an Education System in Miniature. *168 pp. 1964. (2nd Impression 1966.) 21s. Paper 10s.*

Jackson, Brian and **Marsden, Dennis.** Education and the Working Class: Some General Themes raised by a Study of 88 Working-class Children in a Northern Industrial City. *268 pp. 2 folders. 1962. (4th Impression 1968.) 32s.*

Marris, Peter. Widows and their Families. *Foreword by Dr. John Bowlby. 184 pp. 18 tables. Statistical Summary. 1958. 18s.*
Family and Social Change in an African City. A Study of Rehousing in Lagos. *196 pp. 1 map. 4 plates. 53 tables. 1961. (2nd Impression 1966.) 30s.*
The Experience of Higher Education. *232 pp. 27 tables. 1964. 25s.*

Marris, Peter and **Rein, Martin.** Dilemmas of Social Reform. Poverty and Community Action in the United States. *256 pp. 1967. 35s.*

Mills, Enid. Living with Mental Illness: a Study in East London. *Foreword by Morris Carstairs. 196 pp. 1962. 28s.*

Runciman, W. G. Relative Deprivation and Social Justice. A Study of Attitudes to Social Inequality in Twentieth Century England. *352 pp. 1966. (2nd Impression 1967.) 40s.*

Townsend, Peter. The Family Life of Old People: An Inquiry in East London. *Foreword by J. H. Sheldon. 300 pp. 3 figures. 63 tables. 1957. (3rd Impression 1967.) 30s.*

Willmott, Peter. Adolescent Boys in East London. *230 pp. 1966. 30s.*
The Evolution of a Community: a study of Dagenham after forty years. *168 pp. 2 maps. 1963. 21s.*

Willmott, Peter and **Young, Michael.** Family and Class in a London Suburb. *202 pp. 47 tables. 1960. (4th Impression 1968.) 25s.*

Young, Michael. Innovation and Research in Education. *192 pp. 1965. 25s. Paper 12s. 6d.*

Young, Michael and **McGeeney, Patrick.** Learning Begins at Home. A Study of a Junior School and its Parents. *About 128 pp. 1968. 21s. Paper 14s.*

Young, Michael and **Willmott, Peter.** Family and Kinship in East London. *Foreword by Richard M. Titmuss. 252 pp. 39 tables. 1957. (3rd Impression 1965.) 28s.*

14

The British Journal of Sociology. *Edited by Terence P. Morris. Vol. 1, No. 1, March 1950 and Quarterly. Roy. 8vo., £3 annually, 15s. a number, post free. (Vols. 1-18, £8 each. Individual parts £2 10s.*

All prices are net and subject to alteration without notice

1268 H.B.